W9-DJL-094

A HARD DAY'S NIGHT

THE BEATLES

IN RICHARD LESTER'S

A HARD DAY'S NIGHT

A COMPLETE PICTORIAL RECORD OF THE MOVIE

EDITOR

J. PHILIP DI FRANCO

INTRODUCTION

ANDREW SARRIS

CHELSEA HOUSE PUBLISHERS
NEW YORK, LONDON
1977

FOR DYLAN AND JESSE

Project Editor: Karyn Gullen Browne
Art Director: Susan Lusk
Design: Don Longabucco
Jacket Design: Peter McKenzie
Managing Editor: Laurie Likoff
Associate Editor: Stephanie Saia

Library of Congress Cataloging in Publication Data
Main entry under title:
The Beatles in Richard Lester's A hard day's night.
1. Hard day's night. [Motion picture]
I. Lester, Richard. II. The Beatles
PN1997.H2593B4 791.43'7 77-22792
ISBN 0-87754-012-8

CHELSEA HOUSE PUBLISHERS

Harold Steinberg, Chairman, Publisher Andrew E. Norman, President
A Division of Chelsea House Educational Communications, Inc.
70 West 40 Street, New York 10018

CONTENTS

NOTE TO THE READER

The text in brackets — [ ] — or — ▌ — indicates material deleted from the original script and not in the finished film.

Italicized text in parentheses indicates material *added* to the original script and thus included in the finished film.

ABBREVIATIONS FOR SHOT DESCRIPTIONS

SIZE

XCU	Extreme close-up (i.e., an eye)
CU	Close-up (i.e., a head)
MCU	Medium close-up (i.e., head and shoulders)
MS	Medium shot (i.e., from the waist up)
3/4S	3/4 shot (i.e., from the knees up)
FS	Full shot (i.e., from the feet up)
LS	Long shot (i,e., a full setting)
XLS	Extreme long shot (i.e., a far setting)

LIGHTING

HK	High key
MK	Medium key
DK	Dark key

ANGLE

LA	Low angle (i.e., camera below eye level, usually shooting up)
NA	Normal angle (i.e., camera at eye level, usually shooting straight on)
HA	High angle (i.e., camera above eye level, usually shooting down)

CAMERA MOTION

PANNING (camera pivots on a fixed point):

PL	Pan left
PR	Pan right
PU	Pan up
PD	Pan down

TRAVELING (camera actually moves, as on a dolly):

TL	Travel left
TR	Travel right
TU	Travel up
TD	Travel down
TI	Travel in
TO	Travel out

ZOOMING (with a zoom lens):

ZI	Zoom in
ZO	Zoom out

MOTION

Normal Motion — Action appears as we normally see it.
Accelerated motion — Action appears faster than normal.
Slow motion — Action appears slower than usual.

NOTE:

If a shot was simple, only one photo enlargement was made and therefore only one number denoted for the shot.

If a shot was complex (i.e., a pan from one person to another), two (or more) photo enlargements were made and therefore the denotations "A," "B," "C," etc. were attached to each component of the shot.

Richard Lester

FOREWORD

This book's purpose is simple enough, but its technique and scope are both complex and almost completely unprecedented. Our purpose was to relate the original shooting script of a classic film, The Beatles' "A Hard Day's Night," to the final finished film. We wanted to recreate the film as a "book" of the movie by presenting every "shot" together with the sound track and the complete screenplay. We wanted to show the total artistic evolution from script to finished film — as it was shot and edited.

We also wanted to show how Richard Lester made "A Hard Day's Night" into a great film about a great rock group. It is great *because* of its content (The Beatles), its technique, its charisma, its exuberant joy and its ability to capture the wonderful feeling of a day in the life of The Beatles. Lester had the genius to create a breakthrough in style, a fabulous marriage of form and content; "A Hard Day's Night" is indeed the "Citizen Kane of Juke Box Movies" as Andrew Sarris described it. The film has spawned many imitations.

Artistically speaking, the movie proceeds in *visual* flow rather than being linked to a strong narrative line. Thus the choice and sequence of photographs was all-important. In order to capture the content, style and spirit of this film, we used special technical equipment to achieve the best possible reproductions. Remember that we are representing a highly fluid, dynamic medium (the film) as the basis for a static production (the book). Great care and much time was spent choosing the precise representative photographs.

For those who love the movie and The Beatles in it, for film students and the general public this "book" of the movie is the best permanent record available. There are more than 1200 photographic reproductions of some 900 shots from "A Hard Day's Night." The breakthrough we hope to be making with this book is to present a visual record toward the analysis of a masterpiece.

As Richard Lester says, " 'A Hard Day's Night' is about communication without words." This book seeks to show how it works — from the script through the directorial process to shot film and then to the final edited and dubbed version. Lester's sense of visual style and humor elevate the "verbal" script to a great cinematic experience. Here is how he worked and included in the book are the complete shooting script, dialogue, action, screen direction and director's notes.

J. Philip di Franco
Los Angeles
1977

ACKNOWLEDGEMENTS

I am indebted to Harold Steinberg, Jeffrey Steinberg, Robert Hector and Andy Norman for believing in the concept of "A Hard Day's Night" and venturing into the project with confidence and trust. I am also indebted to Stephanie Saia whose knowledge of the film made this book possible and whose aid and assistance was invaluable. For their grueling hours spent under hot lights taking photographs, I must thank Deborah and Peter Altschuler and Mike Robinson. For her acute sense of hearing and driving enthusiasm while transcribing the interview tapes, I thank Kathe Nack. For her incredible sense of editorial design and for keeping it all together, I thank Karyn Browne. For the major work of layout and design, I thank Don Longabucco, Susan Lusk and Peter McKenzie. For inspiration, I thank George Amberg, Robert Gessner and especially Elaine Church.

J. Philip di Franco

ANDREW SARRIS
Village Voice *Aug. 27, 1964*

As to what the Beatles "mean," I hesitate to speculate. The trouble with sociological analysis is that it is unconcerned with aesthetic values. *A Hard Day's Night* could have been a complete stinker of a movie and still be reasonably "meaningful." I like the Beatles at this moment in film history not merely because they mean something, but rather because they express effectively a great many aspects of modernity which have converged inspiredly in their personalities. When I speak affectionately of their depravity, I am not commenting on their private lives about which I know less than nothing. The wedding ring on Ringo's finger startles a great many people as a subtle Pirandellian switch from a character like Dopey of the Seven Dwarfs to a performer who chooses to project an ambiguous identity. It hardly matters. When we are fourteen, we learn to our dismay that all celebrities are depraved, and that the he-man actor we so admired would rather date a mongoose than a girl. Then at fifteen we learn that all humanity is depraved in one way or another, and that Albert Schweitzer gets his kicks by not squashing flies. Then at sixteen we realize that it doesn't matter how depraved we all are; all that matters is the mask we put on our depravity, the image we choose to project to the world once we have lost our innocence irrevocably. There is too much of a tendency to tear away the masks so as to probe for the truth beneath. But why stop with the masks? Why not tear away the flesh as well and gaze upon the grinning skeletons lurking in all of us?

Consequently, what interests us about the Beatles is not what they are, but what they choose to express. Their "Arthur" hairdos, for example, serve two functions. They become unique as a group, and interchangeable as individuals. Except for Ringo, the favorite of the fans, the other three Beatles tend to get lost in the shuffle, and yet each is a distinctly personable individual behind their collective facade of androgynous soleness, a facade appropriate incidentally, to the undifferentiated sexuality of their sub-adolescent fans? The Beatles are not merely objects, however. A frequent refrain of their middle-aged admirers is that the Beatles don't take themselves too seriously. They take themselves seriously enough all right, it is their middle-aged admirers and directors they don't take too seriously. The Beatles are a sly bunch of anti-establishment anarchists, but they are too slick to tip their hat to the authorities. People who have watched them handle their fans and the press tell me that they make Sinatra and his Clan look like a bunch of rubes at a country fair. Of course, they have been shrewdly promoted, and a lot of hysteria surrounding them has been rigged with classic fakery and exaggeration. They may not be worth a paragraph in six months, but right now their entertaining message seems to be that everyone is "people." And that includes Beatles and squealing sub-adolescents as much as Negroes and women and so-called senior citizens. The fact is that however much alike "people" may look in a group or a mass or a stereotype, there is in each soul a unique and irreducible individuality.

INTRODUCTION ● ANDREW SARRIS

Could there ever have been a time when the Beatles were not taken seriously by their elders? Such a period of unbelievable unenlightenment actually preceded the opening of *A Hard Day's Night* in the summer of 1964. After that cataclysmic cultural event, however, nothing would ever be the same again. Popular commercial art could never again be dismissed out of hand as *kitsch.* An era had ended, for better or worse, and another had begun.

My own reaction at the time as film critic of *The Village Voice* was one of pleasant surprise but with no special discernment. I had no idea then and have little more now as to the identity of the prime mover and creator. Was it director Richard Lester, screen writer Alun Owen, or the Messrs. Lennon, McCartney, Harrison and Starr?

To some extent *A Hard Day's Night* was a happy accident, but one which has not been repeated. Its sequel—*Help!*—contains some exquisite songs, particularly the title number, and a few irreverent moments, but does not approach the sustained wit and frolicsome energy of *A Hard's Day's Night.*

But back in 1964 I was not prepared to embrace the Beatles. Aging satirists like Al Capp, with their ancient liberal credentials, were still relatively influential with people who should have known better, and the Beatles were put down as an aberration of infantile tastes and shrewdly commercial promotion. It was not generally known, for example, that McCartney and Lennon wrote their own songs. Indeed, the score for *A Hard Day's Night* surpasses in emotional lucidity and melodic invention every other musical show of the sixties from every medium.

However, the success of the film is attributable not only to the Beatles and their music, but to a genuinely modern style of film making. Even at the time I was aware that *A Hard Day's Night* would turn out to be the *Citizen Kane* of jukebox musicals, a brilliant crystallization of such diverse cultural particles as the pop movie, rock 'n' roll, *cinema-verité,* the *nouvelle vague,* free cinema, the affectedly hand-held camera, frenzied cutting, the cult of the sexless sub-adolescent, the semi-documentary, and studied spontaneity.

So help me, I resisted the Beatles as long as I could. As a cab-driver acquaintance of that epoch observed, "So what's new about the Beatles. Didn't you ever hear of Ish Kabibble?" Alas, I had. I kept looking for openings to put down the Beatles. Some of their sly crows' humor at the expense of a Colonel Blimp character in a train compartment is a bit too deliberate. "I fought the war for your sort," sez he. "Bet you're sorry you won," sez they. "Old Osborne ooze," said I. But previously, the fruitiest looking of the four predators (the lewd Lennon, of course) looks up enticingly at the bug-eyed Blamp, and simpers, "Give us a kiss." Depravity of such honest frankness, I wrote, is worth a hundred pseudo-literary exercises like *Becket.* And why did I refer over and over again to depravity in discussing the Beatles? I suppose because, like all the over-30's, I felt directly menaced by the unnatural sophistication of these striplings. It was only much later that I diagnosed their strangeness (vis-à-vis the Marx Brothers) by reworking an old Priestly passage to the effect that whereas the Marx Brothers tried to be mad in a sane world, the Beatles try to be sane in a mad world.

Stylistically, *A Hard Day's Night* was everything Tony Richardson's frenetic version of *Tom Jones* tried to be and wasn't. Thematically, it was everything Peter Brook's version of *Lord of the Flies* tried to be and wasn't. Fielding's satiric gusto was coupled here with Golding's primordial evil, and the strain showed. At the time, I could have done with a bit less of a false saber-tooth, rattling-wreck of an old man tagged with sickeningly repetitious irony as a "clean" old man. Also, the pop movie mannerism of the inane running joke about one of the boy's managers being sensitively shorter than the other might have been dispensed with at no great loss.

The foregoing were trifling reservations, however. about a movie that seemed to work on every level for every kind of audience. (Well, perhaps not every audience; the hard-core action movie buffs in the Times Square flea pits seemed befuddled by all the *brio.*) The open-field helicopter-shot sequence of the Beatles on a spree was one of the most exhilarating expressions of high spirits I had ever seen on the screen. The razor-slashing wit of the dialogue had to be heard to be believed and appreciated. One as horribly addicted to alliteration as this otherwise sensible scribe could hardly resist a line like: "his (Ringo's) drums loom large in his legend."

Even today when the words in the Beatles songs are more clearly understood and more perceptively appreciated for their heterosexual generosity, the words serve also to emphasize the poundingly ritualistic meaning of the beat. It is in the beat that passion and togetherness is most movingly expressed, and it was in the beat that the kids in the audience picked up back then, shrieking and drowning out words they had already heard a thousand times. To watch the Beatles in action with their audience was to watch the kind of direct theater that went out with Aristophanes or perhaps even the Australian bushman.

Toward the end of *A Hard Day's Night* I began to understand the mystique of the Beatles. Lester's crane shot facing the audience from behind the Beatles established the emotional unity of the performers and their audience. It is a beautifully Bazinian deep-focus shot of hysteria to a slow beat punctuated by the kind of exhaustive zoom shots I have always deplored in theory, but here had to admire in practice. Quite frankly, my critical theories and preconceptions were all shook up, and I was profoundly grateful to Lester and the Beatles for softening my hardening aesthetic arteries.

Nowadays we know more about both Lester and the Beatles, and we can place *A Hard Day's Night* in a more precise historical and creative perspective. Richard Lester's involvement with Peter Sellers and other *Goon Show* types in the eternally rediscovered comedy short *The Running, Jumping and Standing Still Film* undoubtedly influenced his fragmentary, absurd editing and timing of visual gags, not only in *A Hard Day's Night* but also in *The Knack . . . And How to Get It, Help!, A Funny Thing Happened on the Way to the Forum, How I won the War* and *The Bed Sitting Room.* Lester's work on television commercials constituted marvelous technical training for polishing his emotionally manipulative effects on the Moviola. Curiously, of all his films, only *A Hard Day's Night* and the generally underrated *Petulia* produced warm feelings.

It is probable also that the synchronized tracks of Resnais in *Hiroshima, Mon Amour,* the delirious tracks of Truffaut in *The 400 Blows,* and the striking jump cuts of Godard in *Breathless* created the proper stylistic climate for Lester's audacious technique in *A Hard Day's Night.* Certainly new films of the sixties seem as generally symptomatic of the decade as does *A Hard Day's Night* and fewer films still seem as worthy of serious, detailed study.

HOW IT CAME TOGETHER ● WALTER SHENSON, PRODUCER

In 1963 when Bud Orenstein, the head of United Artists in England, called and said "We want to make a picture with the Beatles," I said. "Why?" I was not a Beatles fan—I was 45 years old—and I had children who were driving me crazy playing Beatle records. Bud said, "Look, we want a low budget comedy; you do those things very well. Do us a favor. Go back to London and make a film for us with the Beatles." The reason they wanted this picture was that their music people—UA records—would get the sound track album. I said "Okay. I'll go to London and see what I can do."

During the negotiations that ensued, Dick Lester called me for lunch. When I mentioned the Beatles' movie idea, Dick jumped on the chair in the Hilton Coffee Shop and said, "My God, can I direct it?" And I said, "I'd love you to direct it. I think you'd be perfect for it. Leave it up to me. Let me see what I can do; let's get them signed—let's get this thing going."

Next I met with Brian Epstein, the Beatles' manager. He said, "The boys want to make the film; can we come to your office?" We made a date for him to bring the Beatles to my office. At the agreed upon time Brian showed up without the Beatles. I had an English secretary who was a nervous wreck waiting for the boys to show up. She had the tea and Cokes ready, but they didn't come. I suggested we try to find them at home, so Brian and I jumped into a taxi and instructed the driver to stop by their flat in Mayfair which was very near my office. They came down just as we pulled up and piled into the taxi with Brian and me. London cabs are small—they only seat four people—it was like being in the middle of a Marx Brothers movie. Every time we came to a "Stop" sign one of them jumped out and bought a newspaper which had Beatle headlines. The taxi driver asked for their autographs for his granddaughter. It was an incredible thing.

So I called back Dick Lester and said "I think we got our foot in the door. Meet me and we'll go see the boys." They were concerned about a script, and I said "Well, so are we, but leave it up to me. We'll get a good script." One of the Beatles, I think it was Paul McCartney, suggested Alun Owen, a Welsh writer, living in London, who had done some very fine television plays. The key to Alun was that *he was from Liverpool* and would know the idiom for the script, if not the story. So, Alun came in and the first thing he questioned was the type of script he was to do. I answered the obvious—"an exaggerated day in the life of the Beatles." He said, "What's a day like in the life of the Beatles?" I said, "They're in Dublin this weekend; you fly to Dublin and I'll arrange for you to move into the hotel with them."

Alun flew to Dublin, came back after the weekend and said "I've got it—they are prisoners of their success. They go from the airport to the hotel to the theater or stadium or concert hall back to the hotel back to the airport. In any city it's always the same. They literally travel in a cocoon of Liverpool. There's the manager, the road manager, a publicity man, the car driver, the guy that carries the equipment. That's all they see, because they'd be mobbed if they got out of the car or out of the hotel room or away from the concert hall. I see the story as them being prisoners of their success. And now I've got an idea about one of them having a grandfather...it'll give me some plot things. I also see a scene where they break out from backstage and they just sorta walk about." Well, that's a classic scene in our movie. It is true that Dick did a brilliant job of interpreting the scene and adding music to it and all that. But that scene was in essence written by Alun Owen.

But, as well as the filming progressed, there was still no title to the picture. It was called "Beatles No. 1" or something like that. We were constantly asked by United Artists for a title so they could publicize the movie. The shooting almost drew to a close before we actually came up with a title. During a lunch break conversation, John Lennon mentioned to me that Ringo misused the English language. When I asked for an example, he said Ringo calls an all-night recording session "a hard day's night." John laughed, but I said, "My God, that would make a marvelous title." I mentioned it to Dick Lester and the other Beatles and they said, "Great, that's it." When I phoned UA with the title, it was received blandly, but I said we weren't going to improve on it—it's very provocative. It means nothing. Has nothing to do with the story. But it sounds like a Beatles title.

Well, it dawned on me very soon after that there was no song in our movie called A HARD DAY'S NIGHT. I remember one evening, while directing John Lennon in the looping session, I mentioned to him that we really should have a song called A HARD DAY'S NIGHT. "We've already recorded all the music and where would you fit it in?" he questioned. I said,

"Obviously over the titles." John asked if the lyrics of such a song should reflect the story of this movie. And I said no because none of the other songs had anything to do with the story but were put in as background or on camera when the boys were rehearsing for television shows. I said that it must be an up tempo sort of song, something like "Twist and Shout."

About 8:30 the next morning, the assistant director called me and said that John Lennon wanted to see me in his dressing room. I had no idea what it was, but I went in to see John. He was standing there with Paul McCartney, guitars in their hands. John took out an ordinary matchbook cover and put it up on the dressing room table, opened it up, and they played the song A HARD DAY'S NIGHT from the lyrics John had scribbled the night before.

London, 1970

When this book was first conceived, our plan was to look back on the making of the film with the director — through the "eyes of history." Thus, I traveled to Twickenham Film Studios to meet with Richard Lester for a full day of interviews.

The experience with Lester was fantastic, as he remembered the making of "A Hard Day's Night" many years after. His memory of the film increased as he saw the photos before him (and as we drank more and more cognac). He then became totally involved with his memory of the film *and* the time it was made, the events of history in the 1960's and the cultural milieu in which the incredible Beatle phenomenon occurred.

Though Richard Lester went off on tangents, we have not edited these out: they are part of his own artistic nature as a person and they reflect the times.

Thus, in London in 1970, we had Richard Lester, a master filmmaker, looking back at one of his finest films about the most exciting popular music group of the century. This book and the interview represent a kind of "freezing" of time and experience. Simply stated, there could never be another "A Hard Day's Night," there could never be another Beatles phenomenon, and Richard Lester could never be like he was in 1964.

The world is different now. This book preserves the memory of a time gone by.

AN INTERVIEW WITH RICHARD LESTER

LESTER: It fascinates me to see the direction and how, in essence, in something like *The Knack,* we started in the reverse way by taking the stage version and just destroying it totally in the first screenplay. And taking a wild abstract fantasy, not with four people but with three, which could never have been filmed, but just allowing one's wildest dreams about the project—trains going over the fourth bridge filled with women, which comes up in the middle of Hyde Park and then explodes into . . . And then slowly cut back away, then slowly work back towards the original project, saying what do we absolutely need, what can we not leave out in terms of visual fantasy, what scene is necessary to put back in? And that's the way I am trying to work. In some cases, like *How I Won The War,* we started with a complete fantasy version of the book, and the book never came back in because as we got into it, we disliked the book so enormously and what it stood for that it was eventually destroyed. And so the only thing that is left is that the name of the book and the film are the same and the names of about four characters and one joke. And *Petulia* was a case of working again. I was given a first draft screenplay and I said, I don't believe any of this. It seems horribly untrue and unreal. Let's sit down and think given a scene like this, what to do to make it seem more correct. And so that becomes the vague exercise in saying I don't believe *you* and I don't believe *you,* but put the two of you in a scene, how can you do things that I believe in? Well, unfortunately, *Hard Day's Night* was, first of all, a very fast job. And remember Alun's first screenplay, and I don't think it was ever mimeographed or ever run off. We just looked at it. And I remember some frightening things. This screenplay which I have here is the screenplay from which we shot.

What happens with me is that I start working with a particular screenplay like this and then I lose it. I leave it on a bus or something. And so I use someone else's for about three weeks and then someone finds it. So there are long bits in this that I can see I never got to. But there are bits of ideas for rewrites and things of that sort in there and some were shot and scenes were taken out. I put a list of the crew and that is that.

This is the script which I went out with every day. The difficulty is that only in a few scenes did I ever work from it day by day. Because I know that I always lose them. It is some classic thing with me. I lose a script and a coat roughly every day.

DiFRANCO: Well, what we are trying to get at is your style of filmmaking. How and why do you cut, cross cut, jump cut or shoot a particular scene this way or that. What theory do you use to make films?

LESTER: Well, I think all those things are valid, but you lose the kind of cutting that normally exists. The focus puller has lost focus because he has gone the wrong way with the handle, or the opening and the end of the shot are excellent, and the middle is blurred, so you lose it, and you have to piece it where you couldn't see who is in it.

That is the first kind of editing for me. If you want to go into it, I will show you shot by shot, list by list, of where you are saving a catastrophe by editing. For example, in *A Funny Thing Happened On The Way To The Forum,* Buster Keaton was picked for a role in which he has to do what he usually does, which is be physical. He arrived dying, in the last stages of an incurable disease and we find that he can walk, but certainly not run. Therefore we have to find a double for Buster Keaton. When you have a shot where he is supposed to be coming along, he does a bit of action, bumps into a tree and falls down, you end up using eight cuts because Buster can't run that distance. So you have to have a shot to establish that it is Buster, then the long shot for the double, then another shot to remind everybody that it is Buster, then another long shot, etc. . . . a close-up for him when he says his lines. All that is totally wrong in terms of one's principles, one's hopes, one's feelings towards the scene, but that is what you do. That is number two. I am afraid that I must stick everything that you said down at the end at number three.

DiFRANCO: All of this analysis is post-production. Perhaps it is not possible to relate this theoretical analysis to what the filmmaker actually does. So let's say that we rule out the whole theoretical approach. What I am after here is exactly this discrepancy between theoretical stances and actual filmmaking. We want to investigate the two basic evolutionary processes through which a film goes—the directorial process of creating shot film from the script and the editorial process of creating a work of art from this shot film.

LESTER: There are things put in the script by me which are therefore directorial, and there are things as yet untouched by me. I know which they were—or at least I think I can tell you, because one's memory goes in one direction. You take credit for all the things which you would like to see in the film. But I think it shouldn't be too difficult because primarily the screen writers that I have worked with are verbal writers. Alun is certainly a non-visual writer, and Charles Wood is a non-visual writer. So any sequence that seems to be based on a visual idea would have been mine.

DiFRANCO: That is very important.

LESTER: So I want to go through it and see if I know what came in between the first and second draft, and what went out after shooting. For example, there is a scene with Paul and a girl, Carol, which seemed to be important which was rewritten, but was completely removed from the picture.

First of all, I must say I have not seen the film in five and a half years.

DiFRANCO: I wonder what your reaction to it will be after five and a half years.

LESTER: I saw *Help* last week.

DiFRANCO: Oh you did? What did you think?

LESTER: I loved *Help.* I, for very complex reasons, prefer *Help* to *Hard Day's Night.* But I am not to be judged in that respect.

DiFRANCO: By the way, did you know that there is a shot in *Hard Day's Night* which you are in?

LESTER: Oh, yes.

DiFRANCO: Just one, though. Are there more?

LESTER: Just one. I'm wearing a black corduroy suit, walking across the stage.

DiFRANCO: Right.

LESTER: I am in, actually, a lot of films but it is not through a wish to be in them, but either because there is nobody to do the part, or it is absurd to get out of the way when, in that case, I could just keep going.

DiFRANCO:: These are the shots in the original picture that we'll use in the book. These are photostats of everything. I had visions of losing the whole thing over the Atlantic so I left the originals home and brought the photostats.

LESTER: My how the Beatles have all changed. It brings back such memories . . . that last sequence . . .

DiFRANCO: You mean the end. You must have gone crazy.

LESTER: In one day—we shot seventeen minutes of cut film.

DiFRANCO: How long did it take to shoot the whole film?

LESTER: Six and one half weeks . . . It's too bad we don't have the continuity sheets, but I cannot imagine anyone would have kept that. It's only me. I keep things like that for sentiment. Then I throw them out because, you know, sentiment runs out. It drips through the drawer and you find a dry drawer after the years.

What would have been fascinating would have been to get an interview before the film starts, and one just after the film is finished, and then now. Because I would really do my best to be honest, but I know I would lie. I can't help it. I know I would say things based on contemporary opinions and attitudes about filmmaking. Undoubtedly I'd elbow a lot of useful people out of the way talking about it. How can I help it? Somebody has been doing a television program here by taking interviews with people and putting them in a vault, and bringing them back in five or ten years' time. Asking them what they they want to do, what they think is important, and then bringing them back live and making them watch what they said and then comment on it. Which I think is a very interesting idea. I have done one of them and it was stuck away in the vault.

DiFRANCO: When did you make the tape?

LESTER: Last year. They ask very boring questions. I don't think I would have asked those questions.

DiFRANCO: Well, do you want to start?

LESTER: The way we really worked was to make it as light as possible. So that you are not really aware that there was anything serious or important going on. Just keep it on a terribly easy level.

DiFRANCO: Yes, that is what I was wondering. Everyone talks about the Lester style, the Lester approach to filmmaking. It seems that there is not a conscious effort at a particular style. You just use form to suit your content–the Beatles. You just use the Beatles. You shoot them as they are.

LESTER: There is something about the Beatles. Before we started we knew that it would be unlikely that they could: A. learn, B. remember, or C. deliver with any accuracy a long speech. So the structure of the script had to be a series of one-liners. This enabled me, in many of the scenes, to turn a camera on them and say a line to them and they would say it back to me. If it didn't turn out terribly well I would say it again in another way and they would say it back in another way.

DiFRANCO: There was that give and take with the lines?

LESTER: Oh, yes. Or I would say a fake line and they would say a fake line back, and then I would say a joke and they would say a joke back. And that was all. Certainly that interview with the reporters, especially the press conference, which we weren't planning to shoot. If you look in the script, there are no questions, no answers written. Or if there were, we certainly didn't use them.

DiFRANCO: All that was improvised?

LESTER: Right. We were on the streets, a crowd gathered so much and so rapidly, that the police threw us off the streets. And they said you must not shoot on the streets. You are causing too much of an obstruction. We were building one of the television booths inside the La Scala theatre, which you know is dead–so we had the right to use it. So we went upstairs and I said to the assistant, get me as many people as you can find. Get these reporters who are waiting to see the Beatles. Get anyone you can find, and we will all go up to this room and in two hours' time we will start shooting. And in two hours' time we had sixty or seventy people. Some were real reporters, some were real photographers, some were extras. One was the wife of a journalist. I wrote down a series of questions and they started giving answers. Sometimes they would give a joke and then I would give that as a question to someone else, and then cut the answers of one person to the wrong question and then I made the scene out of that.

DiFRANCO: Do all these people have to be paid if you take them off the streets?

LESTER: Yes, I think they do or they have to sign a release form.

DiFRANCO: Right. That's what I was wondering. Because in New York for a director to do that . . . my God!

LESTER: Yes, I remember in *Petulia* it was much more difficult. They said, You can't go out and film those people walking down the streets. I said why not? And in fact, legally there is no reason why you can't.

DiFRANCO: Well, legally . . .

LESTER: Well, you see, the battle was always illegal. They could sue you if they didn't want to be in the picture. But you are not putting a line over it saying 83% of the people in the U.S. have gonorrhea, which is an implication which is libelous. But if you are just showing a street scene in which George Scott gets out of a car and people are walking down San Francisco streets, those people are walking down San Francisco streets. It is not our responsibility to find out if they were with their mistress when they should have been with their wife. We are not libelously responsible. I checked on that and it is true.

DiFRANCO: That's good to know.

LESTER: So I just went out and shot it. You know, they always say that it is because of libel action, but it cannot be if you are implying that they are in no way anything but what they are, or what you see them to be. In *The Knack* I took lots of shots of people and put fascist dialogue over them in the streets. Incidentally, by accident we shot one of the dubbing editor's aunties out of the window. When he started work on the film he said, What did you do with me auntie? I said who? And he said, That woman who you gave that terrible line to. Look, for God's sake give her another line, so we gave her another line.

DiFRANCO: That's great! Well this probably seems like an awesome task.

LESTER: I'm sure it is an awesome task. Then we'll just begin. They don't seem to be in order.

DiFRANCO: Right. Because on a contact sheet this is the first shot.

LESTER: Shouldn't you have had a Japanese director? He would have understood this much better.

DiFRANCO: Let me explain the numbering. Every number is a shot. Now 1A would be this and then you have a closer view; then the title comes on to 1B, 1C, closer and the next title comes on.... Do you get it?

LESTER: Do you mind if I don't? You see, I never think in shots. I think in sequences.

DiFRANCO: Oh, you do? That would be fine.

LESTER: I think in a total image of the scene and then I go in normally to do the scene in probably one shot. And find that it is not possible and then do it in another one—not thinking about cutting them in any order, not thinking about montage in the scene, but thinking about a series of shots which are useful. Having done two or three of those, I then think, if I have to use them all, what is the best way to put the mortar in and use those inserts? How can I point up little pieces that will be useful so that eventually if I have to put all those shots together I can have a flowing sequence? But I do not pre-plan that. I don't pre-plan anything. If we went into shooting this scene I would think, "Well, I know that I got a master"—well, I will not say a master because that is not normally done that way and I certainly don't start thinking, "Well, I will have a wide shot and then I will come in." I think there is this room and what is interesting is that we are all huddled up in one corner. The first thing I would do is accentuate that and play the whole thing, letting the actors feel their way through. And shoot as early as possible, just making sure that everyone knows the lines and we all agree that they are roughly the lines that should go into the scene. By the third rehearsal I will either be telling the actors that I am shooting the scene or not telling the actors that I am shooting them. Having done that, I get the feeling of how it is going. I would not plan it the night before because I wouldn't know that it is going to be raining and that I might put this light on. Or I didn't know that you would be wearing these clothes or I could have planned this scene for a sixty year old man with gray hair and a business suit. You just don't know. And having done that, little bits will become interesting. They may be your coat hanging out... but there will not be any orderly path.

DiFRANCO: There won't be. So you start with a concept of the scene...

LESTER: I think the classic example of this is the boys playing in the field. It says in the script, "Ringo . . . fire escape . . . space." All that. It doesn't say there is going to be a musical number. It doesn't say what they are going to be doing. On that first day that I met the Beatles they had just gotten back from Sweden and I asked John, "Did you like Sweden?" And he said, "Yes, very much. It was a room and a car and a car and a room and a concert and we had cheese sandwiches sent up to the hotel room." So that feeling of claustrophobia was how we tried to think of the whole first sequence, the whole first third of the film. In closed spaces: prisoners in space, prisoners of fans, prisoners by car, train, small hotel rooms—do this, do that, sign this. And that moment of saying no, that was the bit. So we knew that we wanted it to come at that place . . . we didn't know how.

DiFRANCO: You said the first third?

LESTER: Roughly. I may be right and I may be wrong. I seem to remember talking to Alun and saying about one third of the way through . . .

DiFRANCO: So you saw the film in terms of sections?

LESTER: Yes. . . . As it turns out, it looks like a little more than halfway through.

DiFRANCO: Yes. About halfway. We can tell by the pictures where it happens.

LESTER: Shot 437. Yes, except all those musical numbers must have made the end much longer. The end is very long.

The general aim of the film was to present what was apparently becoming a social phenomenon in this country. Anarchy is too strong a word, but the quality of confidence that the boys exuded! Confidence that they could dress as they liked, speak as they liked, talk to the Queen as they liked, talk to people on the train who "fought the war for them" as they liked. You must accept that this is a film based on a class society. It is difficult for someone coming from America, where there is a society based on money, to realize the strength, in 1963, despite Osborne, despite Colin Wilson and all that . . . I mean a society that was still based on privilege—privilege by schooling, privilege by birth, privilege by accent, privilege by speech. They were the first people to attack this—not just to the effete theatrical crowd, but right down to the factory floor grass roots. They said if you want to do something, do it. You can do it. Forget all this talk about talent or ability or money or speech. Just do it. And this has been their great strength.

In *Help,* we sent them on that sequence in the snow, and said go across and teach yourselves how to bloody ski. And don't come back until you have. We put two zoom lenses—two Arriflexes—and I was on one and the operator on the other and we just shot them doing it. And that became that number. What I am saying is that by the end of six or seven hours, three out of the four of them could ski—with no planning, no instruction. They said that they wanted to learn how to ski. They knew it was useful for me but primarily they didn't want to be beaten by these great lumps of wood on the ends of their feet and they did it. They attacked that bloody snowy mountain until they could stand up. John especially just attacked it. And it was that confidence and determination that spread through England. And was only killed by *Time* magazine's swinging London articles, which said isn't it great! Which immediately made everybody say, oh . . . and they went to look for something else.

DiFRANCO: Yes, it became so self-conscious.

LESTER: But it was there and that was the primary aim for me in the film. If there was a kernel, it was to somehow try and capture that. There are many reasons why I was chosen, which I am sure are in all the interviews. The Beatles had seen me in interviews and I was musical and they liked that, and we spent a weekend in Paris and I at least could play the piano with them. But the final one was my having accepted that the style, the format, seemed to automatically be that one created a surrounding similar to the way they actually lived, so that they could demonstrate that behavior. Not in a fantasy way or a story way, but in a way that they could show their relationship to the rest of England, to their fans, to authority, to established places. All right, the next thing to examine was whether they had already become prisoners of that behavior and therefore that claustrophobia and that breaking out. But that's how they managed to survive when others didn't. Finally, we tried to produce an element of irritation, an irritant, which was the grandfather, which I think is the least successful part of the film. Originally there was a lot more and we cut it out, cut it down. But you can see the intent to produce within their own environment, their group, a tension because the two managers were just kindly extensions—because they were based on the people who were their road managers.

The other thing, which comes later, was to try to produce a time check, so the audience felt that although this is a meandering film there is some problem which has to be resolved within a certain time. That was as spurious as possible, because to take it seriously that Ringo was going to leave the group or commit suicide—anything like that would be out of character. So it had to be a tiny spurious thing—unimportant, but important in terms of the story. Appearing for one of their concerts is important. And therefore, if they are not going to show up—where is he? And beyond that, at the end, we have to give the audience what it expected, which is a great daub of uninhibited singing, so that would have to be the climax of the picture, no matter what story you told.

DiFRANCO: One of the things that comes off with Victor Spinetti, the TV director, is that he kind of represents, and the whole studio represents, the establishment which is using the Beatles. And the whole way they are exuberant contrasts with the studio, which is absolutely on time—they have to be there and they have to do certain things.

LESTER: Also the Kenneth Hague character. He was a man who was with George in a scene. He was a kind of executive accountant type. He was talking about marketing and was doing a television program about trends and hip images and all that.

DiFRANCO: Oh, you mean he went into his office by accident?

LESTER: This was a quite specific case of the middle-aged man in mod clothing, the man who is capitalizing, the middle-aged shirt manufacturer who sells Beatle shirts, trendy, you know.

DiFRANCO: The other question I would ask you about the structure is that you build to a chase, and climax.

LESTER: Yes, of course.

DiFRANCO: The chase is particularly slapstick and cinematic. You deliberately worked towards the escape of Ringo or the leaving of Ringo, the desertion, winding up with the general chase. The chase is a kind of climax before you go into the real climax, which is arriving at the studio—the real end.

LESTER: Yes, the real meat of the piece. Well, I think the only answer to that is, think what that would be like if you had the scene reversed—in other words, if you had a correct structure. If there had been a concert in the middle of the escape, or the chase begins and then the film finishes. I cannot see that working.

DiFRANCO: Yes, that is exactly what I felt. But I wanted to know if it was deliberate.

LESTER: I think it was deliberate only in the sense that I don't think we had an alternative to it.

DiFRANCO: Because it is a grand climax—the fast shots at the end as we see them—fabulous.

LESTER: There is very little more structure that was planned except that we knew that we had to punctuate the film with a certain number of songs. We didn't decide before we started shooting how many musical numbers there would be.

DiFRANCO: Was some of that done afterwards? The decisions to put in musical numbers, or when you were shooting the various scenes?

LESTER: Yes. By the time we shot a number we knew what that number was going to be. The numbers were written not too long before we started shooting. But there are no indications of musical numbers in the script. They were left to us.

DiFRANCO: Walter Shenson talked about how you met the Beatles before and in some of your interviews you mentioned how Walter Shenson tapped you for the job. How did that come about?

LESTER: It came about because Walter Shenson was a producer who had made about two films before. His first film was *The Mouse That Roared,* and then he made *A Matter Of Who* with Terry Thomas, which I don't think was released. Then he made *Mouse On The Moon,* which was my second film. I was suggested for *Mouse On The Moon* by Peter Sellers, because he was in *The Mouse That Roared,* and wasn't in the next one. And he thought I should do it because I had worked with Sellers for years.

DiFRANCO: In New York, I'm not sure how *The Mouse that Roared* was received. It was a strange film.

LESTER: I think it did well. I don't know, not being involved with the thing. All I know is that certainly one should never make sequels! Everything was done. The costumes had to be the same as before, the cast was the same, gags that had to be related . . . and I felt, What am I here for? What am I doing here?

DiFRANCO: Who directed the first?

LESTER: Jack Arnold, I think. So I had heard of the Beatles again by accident.

DiFRANCO: Did you like the Beatles?

LESTER: Very much. My first film had a group in it called the Temperance Seven, which were . . . how to describe them? You don't know the group?

DiFRANCO: I know their name, but I have never seen them.

LESTER: They played music of the twenties and dressed the part and they had a surrealist quality about them. And they would also have three or four extra members who were articulate dummies that played with them, stuffed full-size camels with Union Jacks on the back. They were almost all art directors and doing this. They became full-time and then went back. One of them was an art director for ABC in Manchester, which is across the river from Liverpool. I was a friend of his from that and we both worked at ABC television years back. So he had parties and he would bring back the first records from Liverpool because he used to go see the Beatles, the Undertakers, Jerry and the Pacemakers, and all that before they were nationally known. I don't say that in any way I was responsible for any of their success; but at least I had heard of them. So when Walter Shenson said he had been asked by the music company to make a film with the Beatles, and had I heard of them?, at least I could say yes. Which is more than he could, and at that point we went to meet them and we seemed all to get on so well. In terms of the freedom to make this, actually to be able to make the kind of film I felt we had to make, there was no difficulty or conflict with them at all.

DiFRANCO: What kind of difficulty do you mean?

LESTER: Dollars—pounds, 180,000 pounds, which in those days would have been 2.8 of that. The idea was suggested by the United Artist Music Company as an exploitation film. And their principle was to make it as quickly as possible and get it out before their popularity faded. It was to be made as a local picture for the English market, because at that point they had not gone on American tour. It was made really for the English . . .

DiFRANCO: You had no idea that this would be a classic film, one which is now studied in schools?

LESTER: No, I still don't, and I think it a bit silly.

DiFRANCO: I don't know if you know Andrew Sarris' review of the movie—he loved it. He called it the *Citizen Kane* of juke box movies. But it does represent, at least in terms of the kind of filmmaking going on, a certain milestone. It has been imitated by so many people, which is unfortunate in a way—they can't do their own thing.

LESTER: Yes, that's why I said it was silly. Because I know how we approached making it. We were totally sincere about making it, making a useful picture. But the style and the way it was shot were purely subservient to the content and how was I to do it. The making of it was down to the simple economics of getting it done. For example, we shot on a train—how can we get a train? There is only one station in England that allows you to shoot on Sunday, so we can only allow for a certain amount of time, so that is what that sequence is going to be. Then the train goes back and forth under escort down to the West Country and back every day. So you go there shooting on one side this way because all the trees have to be going in one direction, and you come back shooting on the other side. So in the morning you have to shoot this kind of thing and in the afternoon you have to shoot that. The danger is that in examining it one finds other meanings and other reasons, but that purely and simply is that, if you don't want the trees to appear to be going in the wrong direction or the train going backwards or something of that sort. You know that these shots have to be done in the morning and these shots in the afternoon, and that is all there is. And you do the press conference because you were kicked off the streets by the police.

DiFRANCO: Well, that is exactly what I am after: that very thing where plans break down. The spontaneous moment—what the director decides to do then and there as he is filming.

LESTER: I just looked at the first of these frame enlargements and I remember the second time I saw the film with an audience. All this opening music had been written for it, which we wrote after the film, which they recorded. Well, once we got the title *Hard Day's Night,* as opposed to *The Beatles* . . .

DiFRANCO: Oh, it was originally titled *The Beatles?*

LESTER: We waited for Ringo to get drunk. He said things like that never knowing what he said. He said "hard day's night," not quite knowing the meaning. He said things like "tomorrow never knows," which is another one of his favorite ones. Oh, and then there was the great "he who laughs last, last laughs laughs last last..."

DiFRANCO: Is he a skid thinker then?

LESTER: Absolutely.

DiFRANCO: What I am after is that if you take a script by Hitchcock, every shot is not only mapped out specifically but probably has the storyboard—and that would be one kind of approach for the book to have, too. *Vertigo*—to have it down exactly. Whereas here it is exactly the opposite. Instead of one equals one, one equals anything—twenty, thirty maybe.

LESTER: Yes, no planning at all.

In terms of the opening, while we were shooting we had this terminal for two days which is the Marylebone station. Each Sunday we could use it because there are no trains coming in on Sunday. Which meant that all the things that have to do with the train station had to be done on those two Sundays.

DiFRANCO: This raises a question: essentially, the entire film was staged. I mean, there were no real events you decided to cover?

LESTER: Some things were—vaguely. For example, when we did the scene with Ringo down by the river, a boat went through, and I grabbed a camera and shot it. And by accident the boat turned over and then I thought well, I will find a place for it in the sequence somewhere.

DiFRANCO: I see, the event in the television studio—the final numbers were all staged for the film?

LESTER: Yes.

DiFRANCO: What I am getting at is that there is a documentary quality in the film but it is all staged.

LESTER: All these people in the film are extras, hired for the day.

DiFRANCO: They were?

LESTER: Some might have been grabbed off the streets and we said look, please help. There is one shot at the end of the titles—the last shot of the opening sequence, where you see people on the station, and the shot goes to black—is that right?

DiFRANCO: I believe so.

LESTER: We shot from the train as they get in and the train slowly closes in. Now that was the first day of shooting of the whole film. At eight o'clock in the morning we were on the train, and the crew was on, and the Beatles. By this time there was an enormous number of press and fans and everybody around because they had heard the Beatles were there. And the Beatles had to be brought in under police escort, hidden, and they made a dash for the train. So when I saw them coming, I grabbed a camera and plugged it in, and I was standing there shooting as they arrived. And they ran onto the train. They went through, and George went through, and he was furious with me because they were all rather terrified. And I remember him shaking his fist into the camera, and he meant it, he was actually livid.

DiFRANCO: Why?

LESTER: Because they thought, "At least we are going to be able to make a film for God's sake," and they thought that somehow our security had slipped up.

LESTER: These were actually people that had gathered somehow. They saw film people about to get on a train and nobody went to work that was on that platform—it was just a mass of people. And the Beatles thought poor security—if we are going to have this kind of behavior, trying to fight our way through the crowd just to start shooting, we will never get through the picture. And this was their attitude. So I shot it. I don't know whether if you take it frame by frame, you can see any of the Beatles in that particular shot, but they are not wearing the same clothing.

DiFRANCO: I don't think it's noticeable.

LESTER: I have a feeling that I caught it just as their heads went past, and the bobbies and everybody closed in, and the train started off. The continuity girl wrote down in her notes that she sent to the editor, "First shot taken while I was in the ladies' toilet. I have no idea who was in it. I think they were the Beatles, but they were wearing clothing that they came in, and not what was supposed to be worn. It was photographed by the director. I trust this is not the way we intend to go on. God help me." That was the first report.

DiFRANCO: Was that an indication of things to come?

LESTER: Yes, it was.

DiFRANCO: I am not sure how clear the shot was, and whether they are visible or not. I don't think they are. It is so difficult to tell from the photographs.

LESTER: You see them from the outside going in. That was a staged shot. This was from the inside—that hand waving—you will find that is one of the Beatles in there. Certainly wearing the wrong clothing. It closed down until almost completely black, then you cut again to a staged shot of them moving down a corridor to go into the compartment.

DiFRANCO: Then the whole running toward the camera...

LESTER: Well we had this building for two days, and I wanted to get as much of that opening sequence as we could.

DiFRANCO: This number in the script is essentially a scene number?

LESTER: A location number. If you have to change the location—in other words, streets outside. Because theoretically you could shoot that on another day if you have an architectural link with the next scene, so if you didn't get it that day, you could fix it up some place else.

DiFRANCO: Then the terminal platform. I'm not sure that we can make a direct correspondence . . .

LESTER: I just ad-libbed. "They grabbed instruments . . ." We just threw that out.

DiFRANCO: "This stopped the girls in their tracks . . ."—that's all out—that's really critical.

LESTER: The reason why it is all out is really between the Beatles and myself. It is really because it is the last thing they would ever do. . . .

DiFRANCO: You mean grab their instruments to stop the onrush of girls? Of course it has a certain Freudian quality to it.

LESTER: It has also that early Elvis Presley feeling . . . you know—we will give the fans what they want.

DiFRANCO: Then we cut to the reserved compartment.

LESTER: Yes, they are on the train—up to Shot 40.

DiFRANCO: So much of this seems to be hand-held.

LESTER: The whole train sequence was hand-held.

DiFRANCO: Really!

LESTER: I have a picture.

DiFRANCO: Right, I saw it. You were holding the bloody Arriflex the whole time?

LESTER: Yes, and it is an Arriflex with a base plate on it.

DiFRANCO: It has no handle.

LESTER: And also no blimp, which meant we post-synched the whole thing.

DiFRANCO: It is a very good job of synching. It doesn't look at all post-synched.

LESTER: The entire train is post-synched all the way through and was done on a hand-held Arriflex, rather than a wild one. That is why the base plate—it is coming off synch pulse.

DiFRANCO: What do you use, a Nagra or a Stellovox?

LESTER: In those days it was pre-Nagra, so it would have been the big Westrex system.

DiFRANCO: Oh my God.

LESTER: It was in the luggage compartment of the train. So you had to yell down the train, "Turn over sound, Turn over sound, Turn over sound, ready on sound—ready on sound—ready on sound. . . .

DiFRANCO: How many cars away was he?

LESTER: Three.

DiFRANCO: How many on the crew?

LESTER: Full union crew . . . Anyway, this—was an alleyway we found nearby. The difficulty in shooting with the Beatles is that you almost always have to create a diversion. And that if you are on the streets you take a certain number of extras and put them a couple of streets further away and imply that is where you are going to be shooting, so that all the hangers-on and all the fans and all the people will go there. And then you really race through to do it. This was shot once. Almost every exterior shot in the film where you are on an actual street was one take. And that is good luck to you. Because by the end of the first take you just couldn't shoot. I remember at one point we were shooting a sequence—I don't think it is still in—I think we went back and re-used the same location for *The Knack*, and I am sure it isn't in. They went into a pub and came back out the other side. Have you seen *The Knack?*

DiFRANCO: Yes.

LESTER: They were bringing the bed around, and as they went around a building someone went into the pub and came out with sandwiches and jumped onto the bed. Well, I had a similar thing for the Beatles with that same pub because I liked the look of those two streets. I went to shoot it, and by the time we were set up the Beatles car arrived, and there was a police estimate of two and a half thousand people in that one street. And we couldn't physically get the car through into it. So we had to scrub it.

DiFRANCO: Was that in the script?

LESTER: No, it wouldn't be, because it was a location that I just thought of something for. Anyway, the biggest memory of this I have is the second time I saw the film with an audience, because it had a live organist playing in the London Pavillion, and he didn't finish in time. Instead of getting rid of him they put these opening scenes on and had the sound off, and he was playing a medley of Beatles hits on the Hammond organ, and he finished after forty-four seconds—I timed him. Forty-four seconds after the film had started, he was still going. He smiled at the audience and down he went and they slowly faded the sound back on. So much for the plans of the magic opening. I guess that I will never forget that, and that was the last time I saw the film. Anyway —this—was all in a zoom. And I think that you will find that John fell—that was an accident that we just kept in. It was not long in shooting—and the delight on their part that they would not have to do it again, that no one would mind that they had fallen. Then this—was just for Victoriana. And these—are pick-ups—girls—extras. I just told them, You are chasing the Beatles, and they did. That is on Shots 4 and 5. I have a feeling that there is a shot here where they must have been confused and not known where the Beatles had gone, or they were lost. I don't remember. I think that was the intent.

DiFRANCO: The telephone would be Shots 6 A, B, C. It is a cut, and I believe that it is panning. You pan quickly from A to B to C. Pan left—well, it depends on who is here . . .

LESTER: That's John.

DiFRANCO: The planning would be in the notes?

LESTER: Yes.

DiFRANCO: Rather than a cutting method? I mean instead of cutting close-ups you swish pan. What do you call it here when you quick pan?

LESTER: Whip pan.

DiFRANCO: Whip pan. We call it swish pan.

LESTER: Yes, I seem to remember. Nowadays it doesn't make any sense to me because they should have had the doors closed. If you had the doors closed, you couldn't have seen them.

DiFRANCO: The doors weren't closed?

LESTER: They were using it as a means of hiding from the fans—which they are not.

DiFRANCO: Right.

LESTER: It seemed to be a gag—a set gag. Well, it was the intention I think . . . they look a bit confused here—. They have been on the train, riding around, and then you find them absolutely static, set inside this thing and talking to each other. . . . A gag repeated in *Help*. This was just because I find these milk cartons hysterical because they absolutely are impossible. If you buy them, there are these little instructions on how to drink milk—but you can't. If you go into these stations and try to drink one, they go all over you. I went to the station that we had for two days, and while everyone is lining up, or trying to get the crowd or having lunch, you just wander around and try to find the absurdities of the place, and use as much as you can. This—is a buffet —a luncheon buffet, isn't it? I remember that. They went down a dead alley. But this—looks like a dissolve, and I don't think there would have been a dissolve in the early sequence. There was a long shot there (Shot 11), of them coming out of a lunch counter and going down that street. Then you cut to a girl seeing them and screaming and then you force them into a position where, I believe, he had to jump up. Is that right?

DiFRANCO: Yes. They climbed up. They come out into the alleyway on Shot 11 and then on 12 they dash around the corner. They dash this way, and then they dash that way. Then in 12C, they climb over.

LESTER: When they come down they find themselves in motion—on the platform. They climb in 15 . . . let's see . . .

DiFRANCO: They climb over in 13 . . . they are on the platform in 14.

LESTER: Which is a series of newspapers being moved—just an old visual gag—you jump down and find yourself in motion. This—is a continuation of that. This is more to get them back to the train.

DiFRANCO: On 20 you have the station and then pan slightly on 21A.

LESTER: Right. Pan onto Paul and Grandfather reading, with all that madness going on behind them.

DiFRANCO: On 21C you zoomed in on moustache and beard.

LESTER: As you can see, I do get involved in this. There is a whole sequence in *The Knack* based on this—which in fact I remember thinking of when we were doing this. The idea of going in and stripping off. . . . Rita Tushingham watches this dirty old man bring a girl in to take erotic photographs—because she sees her leg-knickers open. I am still very fond of that. But I remember thinking of it at that time because it didn't fit. In fact, nor did this. But it was, in other words, just a place to hide. But not resolved as a gag if you remember.

DiFRANCO: Shot 22B . . .

LESTER: They have been hiding and then pop out. But obviously there should have been a pay off-gag in there and having to do with photographs. But obviously there wasn't. Because the other gag I thought of was stripping, which was pointless. That—is shot from inside the booth. That—is outside the booth—they run out of it and then you cut from the inside as they run out.

DiFRANCO: They must have moved in somehow, because that is the same shot—22C.

LESTER: All these close-up things— . . . I remember they were done at the end of the day, and at the last gasp we just grabbed girls that seemed could do things and staged a series of close-ups. There are a lot of them through here to indicate change of direction. Because beforehand I would just put the Beatles in a shot and say get them to the girls, and they would just run, with no card saying keep behind them or keep up with them, do anything. I just said to the Beatles, "Bloody well keep out of their way. Go as fast as you can from there to there." I wouldn't tell the extras where they were going. I would just say, "OK turn over," and I would follow the Beatles and away they would go.

DiFRANCO: You don't have any problems with unions just grabbing the camera like that? And shooting yourself and all . . . ?

LESTER: No, not at all—nor did I in America. My whole first day I didn't let the operator touch the camera—because I wanted them to know how I intended to go on.

This—shows the progression towards the train, the chase, getting on the train, and getting the beards off. This—I remember, was a series of shots of feet, things which were intercut very much in the tempo of the numbers. They started off in four-bar cuts and then two-bar cuts.

DiFRANCO: And you matched exactly to the bars?

LESTER: Yes—not in the shooting, but in the editing.

DiFRANCO: You matched the shots to the exact rhythms?

LESTER: It's terribly easy actually, because you know you start on a foot shot anyway. I remember working this—gradually cutting in half the deceleration pattern of the number. The danger in the early stages was in getting carried away with the rhythm and tempo, which was so powerful earlier on that one overcut the middle section of it—the free-form part of it—leaving oneself with nothing left. So one made each one of the shots a little longer than they normally would have been in the earlier time. So this part, just before they get on the train, was cut down to be shot at that tempo.

DiFRANCO: I felt that you had done that.

LESTER: That—is the final famous bit on the train. That's slate one.

DiFRANCO: That's Shot 41B—no, A.

LESTER: Then we go into that—which was the first shot. This—was slate two, which was the first day's shooting—the first time they were in their proper clothing. That—was the first thing we did. Again, the plan was as much as possible to include practicals—in other words, all the natural light sources that we could in the film. You know, having settled on this social reality then the obligation of everyone working on the film was to produce as close to a documentary effect as possible. Thus the hand-holding, thus the trying to light the film with the practical light that was in it. When we didn't or when we couldn't, to boost the practicals that were there, or to put light to imply that the light source came from natural light only. And to allow the background to burn out. Don't try to match it. Don't put neutral densities on the windows, don't wrap gell on the windows. Let it go.

DiFRANCO: What kind of film were you shooting with?

LESTER: Double X.

DiFRANCO: What's the lens on the Arriflex?

LESTER: Almost all the shots in the train were shot with a 14mm. lens. The 9mm. hadn't been invented in those days. *Help* was one of the first films to use the 9—or misuse it. So we were using the 14 which, as you know, is not one of the best lenses to use in terms of keystoning and distortion. Also there is a 3.5, almost a 4.0 lens. The 18 is faster, and the 9 is faster. The 14 is the pig of the three lenses—the wide angles. But it was the only lens we had in those days. And the only way, by standing in the corridor, to get a wide shot was with your head pressed against the other wall of the train.

DiFRANCO: You were back on the other side of the train?

LESTER: Yes, these are corridor trains. There would be the interior and that would be the width you have. The sequence was covered in a conventional way. Everything was covered in one close-up on each boy. Three shots on either side. The master...

DiFRANCO: Some of the gags in here—were their own doing? It comes a little later, I think. The part with the bottle...

LESTER: Those are all mine. They're not gag writers. They are marvelously free, but they don't create things. If you give them the barest glimmer, they can build on it. But they won't create, won't suggest. It wasn't in their nature to suggest. In this, nor in *Help*. They did as we asked them to do. Ringo having a camera was based purely on the fact that he was learning photography and he was keen on it at the time. So it seemed like a good thing to do. But a lot of the gags by the river were ad-libbed at the time, which meant we weren't planning to save it. I don't think that at this time we had worked out any of the gags with the camera. We just knew that he had them and it would be useful to have a prop for him to play with.

DiFRANCO: Yes, it works very well. This—is the military man. He is referred to in one of the listings.

LESTER: City Englishman, and then he is called Johnson.

DiFRANCO: He is a perfect counterpoint to the four of them.

LESTER: Well, he is all part of this—why the film was made. I mean this is the most obvious reference to it. It's quite specific early on in the film. There you are about eight minutes into the film and you see quite clearly their behavior and people's attitudes toward them and the way they are being treated and so on.

DiFRANCO: I was wondering about that—shot 127, where you have them running outside, which is the first break.

LESTER: I put it in. We were at the station and it was at the part when the train comes around, turns around, and comes back while we were shooting it. Because we went down to the West Country and wherever the hell it was and we came to Trotten I think it was. Since we had some time—it was either just before or just after lunch—I put this in. I didn't know whether it would work, but somewhere I knew that before they did the first musical number there had to be something to prepare the audience for the surrealism of the number where they are sitting and suddenly they had instruments and were playing—which was essentially the way the musical numbers in the film would be constructed, the way they would work. It was a break in the reality, if you were dealing with absolute documentary reality. I felt that it would take so long to get used to it in that baggage number that there should be some indication, some warning that you can play about with things like that. And this seemed to be not the best because it was a bit fast. But it seemed to be the only place that one could insert it, so we did. I had no guarantee in the shooting that it would work, but it seemed to, so we left it in.

DiFRANCO: And the lines in this—...

LESTER: I think you will find they are exactly as is. There was a lot more in this dining room scene, I believe. Stuff like that. Is that still in the film?

DiFRANCO: Oh, yes, that's all in there. He is with the middle-aged woman that the grandfather is after a little later.

LESTER: That might be cut. Just as an historical note, George met his wife on this day's shooting.

DiFRANCO: Oh, he met her then?

LESTER: I had used her in some advertisement films. I put her in the film. And they met on that day.

DiFRANCO: In the dining car?

LESTER: Yes.

DiFRANCO: This was all planned.

LESTER: Yes. She was there. I think you will find that in the script. Here is the woman—. That—was the scene with the champagne—we cut almost all that out and put something else in and I think it was done in post-synch. Oh, I remember, I re-shot that in a corner of the studio.

DiFRANCO: Re-shot 173?

LESTER: Because I could tell that is not a real train. That—was shot in a studio. Whatever was said there was to replace that and to get into the baggage compartment.

DiFRANCO: The other thing is to get back to the woman, shot 168, in this whole dialogue that happens with Ringo—this is fairly surreal action too. I mean all of a sudden there is this girl there, waving him on. There is this great line about playing havoc with me drumskins.

LESTER: I am wondering where it was in the script. Probably in a different place.

DiFRANCO: This word surreal pops up quite often in interviews and articles.

LESTER: Well, it is a terribly useful word, but I don't think any of us know exactly what it means.

DiFRANCO: Right—and therefore useful.

LESTER: I know in my own mind what surrealism means to me—but it very rarely is what it means to most people. Mine is just a personal vision of it.

DiFRANCO: Do you want to go into that?

LESTER: Sure, it's in most of the interviews—this point at which two concentric circles of reality meet. Visually, let's say if you had a spiral staircase, there would have been chorus girls and a U boat commander coming down—both correct in each of their own realities, because that is common to both worlds. But if they come down together, or one after the other, the point where they meet is surrealism, the point is the staircase. Or in the dialogue—Captain, what's your course? Prunes and custard. The word course means different things—that is the point at which they meet. That's the area I like. I think the finest single image will always be for me Magritte's reversed mermaid, where the top part is fish and the bottom part is woman. It is the most staggering thing, it's not just a straight painting—he reversed the two—this fish with a woman starting at the pubic hair. Not only is it disturbing, but it is erotic. And unbearable. Marvelous.

DiFRANCO: There is a marvelous transition from them playing cards, could we go over that? There is the part where they start playing cards and I think they lay the cards down on the barrel and then it starts....

LESTER: The music has started.

DiFRANCO: The music has started before they actually play.

LESTER: Right. They are still doing cards and it cuts as if to background music.

DiFRANCO: Did the camera when he clicks it really go into the water by accident?

LESTER: No, that was planned, that was a gag. No, we got a body of an Arriflex and took the lens off before we shot—put a fake lens on. We returned the body to the people we had rented it from. We did ask the prop man to make a fake lens. I'm very proud of that.

DiFRANCO: And there is a transition to them with instruments—.

LESTER: What I did was shoot the number twice. Once with playing cards all the way through and once with instruments all the way through.

DiFRANCO: Then you just cut in?

LESTER: Just cut in when I wanted to—just put the two pieces together.

DiFRANCO: What is your opinion of *Hard Day's Night?* You say that *Help* is your favorite?

LESTER: Of the two I prefer *Help.* However, my personal taste is suspect. I think *How I Won The War* is my best film. Of all the people I know, Stanley Kauffmann is the only person who agrees with me. I was very interested in the reviews of *How I Won The War,* because it was a film that produced such interesting opinions....

DiFRANCO: I think *How I Won The War* is probably the most important in terms of content, at least for my own taste, although I also liked *Petulia.*

LESTER: I despised the book. It was just total lunacy—just middle-aged dentistry. The fact that the word kook is in the title sums up the whole book.

DiFRANCO: Have you seen *I Am Curious Yellow?* I understand that they dub the sex —there is no real "penetration," as they say in the law courts.

LESTER: You mean like getting in a hands artist for making a commercial?

DiFRANCO: Yes, it is really strange. The term I use is dubbing the sex, but there are certain parts where the actress refuses to be part of the . . . so they get someone else's breast.

LESTER: It's very much in the tradition of seventeenth-century painting, where you get your friend, because he's very good at flowers, to come in and paint the vase of flowers on the table. All those masterpieces, the main chap that was doing it did the main part and you fill in the rest. You bring in the grapes man. . . .

DiFRANCO: Now let's look at the studio shots of the various song numbers.

LESTER: What I would normally do is to get two or maybe three cameras for each time they did the number and cover it straight through each time, and I would always operate one of the cameras, I always have. Therefore, within reason, all we would do—they would have to do a number two, or at the most three times, and that was enough, because I had nine set-ups to play with, each of them being given a series of things to go for in the number. So you end up with enough angles to cut it. And it takes you a quarter of a day.

DiFRANCO: Your editing situation is very critical. You work very closely, then, with the editor.

LESTER: Yes.

DiFRANCO: Who was the editor on this?

LESTER: John Jimson. He will be in the list.

DiFRANCO: You worked very closely with him. In a sense then, you cut your own film.

LESTER: Certainly, in parts—it's difficult to say. We did them together. I liked *Help* in many ways, as I became a sort of assistant editor while we were in the cutting room. Because he has fantastic physical dexterity, which I don't, and so I am the one that's getting out the shots and offering him the trims and putting things away and getting those little pieces that are missing—you know, just working as an assistant, which seems the best way. But with this one had to have twenty or thirty possible shots, so then you could use them at whatever rhythm the Beatles seemed to dictate. One starts with the structure of it and breaks it down.

DiFRANCO: Presumably, that's done on all of the musical numbers.

LESTER: Yes.

DiFRANCO: Do you have a background in music at all?

LESTER: I play—not more than I taught myself to play, not more than I taught myself to compose. But I am not trained. I mean I read very badly. I write much better than I can read.

DiFRANCO: Let me ask you this. You know there are all these allusions to what film relates to best in the other arts—theater, literature, etc. My own feeling is that it relates better to music than most anything—or painting.

LESTER: Mine would be line drawing—line cartoons, social cartoons, James Thurber, or that. . . . I see things as a drawing—a non-moving gag.

DiFRANCO: You see an image, essentially, of what you want to say. You think visually —which I think is apparent in your films. Do you have story plots at all? Or do you just see it and shoot it? I'm wondering whether it would be true to say that if you are doing a film that has structure, whether you see a master idea of the whole thing.

LESTER: Yes, you do try to look. Because when you reach say a first draft stage, you start thinking, because that is the way films are made. Who shall I get to photograph it? And then you chose a person who would be in tune with the subject matter. Now he's going to come in and say, "I would love to work with you or phone me again or whatever." And from that time on, which is very early in the concept of the film, he would likely say, "What kind of film do you see?" And from that time on you have to begin to say, "What I would like to have is a film that is like such and such—a film that is like those tests for optical illusions, you know, where the four sides of the square keep going out." So at that stage you are already trying to find a simple visual explanation of whatever the complexity of the thought is. And one chose Gil Taylor for this because I knew he could do this kind of lighting. I had worked with him before on this kind of work. And soon—the art director and everything else was geared to making this kind of film. So very early on, one knows what one wants it to look like.

DiFRANCO: You see it. Is it possible, then, that the structure of your films proceeds on exactly that kind of cartoon where the image proceeds, and you have at certain points very definitive ideas. . . .

LESTER: It does, but that implies less of a contribution by the script writer, which isn't true, because you will suddenly find that an absolutely marvelous scene will be written, which has no visual equipment. One can just put a little button tag on the end of it which is visual. Just to keep the visual style going—which is unsatisfactory, but I find that I quite do it a lot. But sometimes scenes have to be verbal, they have to be structured by verbal images.

DiFRANCO: This reminds me of something that you said, which is in Robert Gessner's *The Moving Image*. You said that *Hard Day's Night* is about communication without speech and *The Knack* is about speech without communication. Did you say that in an interview?

LESTER: Yes, I did. Somewhere.

DiFRANCO: Did you see the article in *Time* magazine?

LESTER: Yes, I did. A cheap writer. I also read one in *Holiday* which was absolutely vicious. Incredibly vicious. Totally untrue. Untrue, I mean, in that making points that I know I never said and silly things like, "The best way to tell what he is like is how he got into his car and put a double safety strap on to drive three miles." Just in the simple technique of it—I mean there is a law in British cars, you are not allowed not to do that, and it went on and on and on like that. It said I was the most destructive thing in filmmaking in the last twenty years.

DiFRANCO: This particular piece just left me and my assistants aghast. "When you leave him sitting in his bare monkish office, you feel like a retreating camera, for he is a demanding man, and one on whom you must focus; he attracts your attention and deserves it. He is cool, he is intelligent, he is very sexy. One other thing about him is certain: he is very bald." Absurd.

LESTER: Here is an interesting thing: "In *The Knack,* the line 'I swear on my mother's life' is followed by a cut of a casket being lowered into a grave." First of all, that isn't the line in *The Knack*—I had nothing to do with that, and there is nothing like that in it... nothing at all. Actually I know what it is, it's from *Shoot the Pianist,* the Truffaut thing . . . It's ". . . made my mother drop dead. . . ."

DiFRANCO: You know I thought of that when I read it.

LESTER: Well, it's not in the screenplay of *The Knack*. It's lovely to keep them. Because I met her (the reviewer) and had a great argument about *How I Won The War*.

* Irma Kurtz, "Richard Lester," in *Eye magazine*.

She spent all her time saying how marvelous *The Knack* was. *Time* magazine's thing on *Bed Sitting Room* said how great *Petulia* was and then I found *Time* magazine's review of *Petulia,* and they hated it. These can get very depressing.... Well, we left the train coming into the station, with the camera stuck out the side—... The taxi—was in the original script and was just shot.

DiFRANCO: How many cameras do you need for something like this?

LESTER: Two. Myself and the actual operator. Again, trying to use as much natural light as possible.

DiFRANCO: So far as lighting is concerned, it's mostly the use of natural lighting.

LESTER: Well, things were artificially lit for filler . . .

DiFRANCO: Do you use little filler lights?

LESTER: Well, I don't think they were around in 1964. You mean the little quartz lights? I think they came out about three years later. I have a feeling that this sequence —and that—...

DiFRANCO: Right—in the car as they run out...

LESTER: That was not staged. I know that the car leaving—236 and 237—was a real event. They were leaving the place where we were shooting, I mean it was the last shot of the day. I got into the car with a camera, with them—and I think you will find, again, that they are in the wrong clothing. I told them they could change because they were going home, and I just thought well, we might be able to grab something . . . There they were in a station, the train station. And that's—an old record cover—George Shearing, I think you will find.

DiFRANCO: I was wondering. That whole thing with the waiter coming out, was that in the original script?

LESTER: Yes, it was. And then leads to them enjoying themselves.

DiFRANCO: Which pub was that—?

LESTER: It was underneath a restaurant in Hyde Park. We just used it. It's intercut, isn't it? Yes it's intercut. That—was shot upstairs. Yes, that was shot, actually, in two places. That was shot—well that's the gambling part, which was shot in a club—and this—is a discotheque.

DiFRANCO: Yes, they are separate in the film.

LESTER: And this—is just two numbers that I wrote—no dialogue. All this—dancing. We have some old gags—the getting more money . . .

DiFRANCO: I meant to ask you about that—that's a Chaplin routine I've seen. You didn't know it, though?

LESTER: No, obviously I didn't know, but it's logical that you would use it in a place that needs a line, especially in terms of chips, because you know you pay in chips, and then he uses them to gamble again. But I didn't know. Bouncing . . . Then this—is all done silently and then brought back.

DiFRANCO: When you shot the dancing, that was all improvised—just quickly in one shot?

LESTER: Yes. And then we cut all this—out, didn't we?

DiFRANCO: Yes. That "bingo" thing was nice. No, the bingo was in—some of the rest was out. And this with the coat—, that was marvelous.

LESTER: That was Alun's idea. I remember quite specifically wanting to do that. Especially after the cutting of this sequence. It seemed to be funnier cut to go back—then the camera itself is sort of doing takes. You see each person went in and saw him and ignored him.

DiFRANCO: It seems that you are assaulted in the dancing scene—in many, many shots—with the grandfather. And then you have this long shot—with a pan back and forth—it does something there is a kind of break there. And I found, going through the shots, that what you do is quick cutting.

LESTER: Yes. You are always trying to do it. What's nice is if you can do it without much thinking about it. Sometimes it goes all to pieces because the whole sequence doesn't work. I am often obliged to cut a scene to a certain rhythm, out of its own rhythm, to help cut it in a way that it will be in comparison to the next scene, when its own metabolism demands another type. And that, I think, is where so much of it goes wrong.

DiFRANCO: That part about Shake at the end trying to get in—he gets stopped and the Beatles get through. They are stopped and Norm gestures to look who they are, and the man at the door says, "Oh of course," but he stops Shake and Shake says, "I'm Ringo's sister." That's not in the screenplay....

LESTER: No, that was obviously done on that day. And the next scene, which is the bath—, I know we cut.

DiFRANCO: That's the beginning of the second reel.

LESTER: Yes, you see that scene has been taken out.

DiFRANCO: Which one is that? Oh, you mean after they leave the gambling . . .

LESTER: They were at the studio—that was in. We shot this—. Jumping out and attacking a Rolls Royce . . . that's out. I didn't shoot it. And in its place, because we put that in after the script was written.

DiFRANCO: So the whole part about John in the bathroom— . . .

LESTER: Was an addition. I remember how pleased we were when we did it. It was nearly the last day shooting, and we built this tiny tiny piece, it was only two walls that size in here. I remember the producer seeing it and saying, "But I can see John's bathing trunks, you have got to re-shoot it." And I said, "Oh Christ—so he takes a bath with bathing trunks. I'm not re-shooting it."

DiFRANCO: Can you see them? Yes, you can, right there—.

LESTER: He got terribly upset, Walter, because you could see his bathing trunks.

DiFRANCO: But the finale is when Norm sees the bathtub's empty and John isn't in it.

LESTER: That was ad-libbed. We tried it with three different endings not knowing which would work best. I can't remember what the others were. But I remember there was one other that was quite funny as well. We didn't know how to finish the scene. There is probably nothing in here to indicate how it finishes. Here. He pulls the plug and waits to see if the bath is empty. Cut from bath to Norm, and then John's head comes into frame. "I wonder how I did it?" So we worked that far. Now at the moment he has just left, hasn't he? Now this is the remains, I should think, of that whole car scene. Oh, yes, John does come back in. And says something like, What are you standing about? So I should think that this set-up is the only remains of that car thing. This—was this ad-libbed restaurant. Fortunately, we found somebody from *Life* magazine who had one of those motor cameras, because it is a difficult thing to find, one of these cameras with a motor on it. We had no time to order any of these things. But there it was. This—was done in a whole series of dissolves, wasn't it?

DiFRANCO: Yes, exactly. They are all dissolves. And that—was preconceived and was done in the editing room . . . ?

LESTER: No, we shot it straight, and then we put it together. Again it seemed not to have a series of fast cuts in this—and would have been of more use in other scenes.... She—is the wife of a journalist... those—are Beatle stand-ins, we were really recruiting everybody we could. Somewhere in there I think you will find that you can see the cameraman—the actual cameraman that we used. We had the whole crew—everyone—because where are we going to get these people? And this—is the La Scala Theatre on which we had built the T.V. studio.

DiFRANCO: You couldn't get a regular T.V. studio?

LESTER: No, because they are always in use. We had it for four days. This was the first day we had it. The show was the final thing—the last day.

DiFRANCO: Was all the dialogue with Victor Spinetti in the script? It's marvelous when he comes in with the grandfather.

LESTER: He's based on a real television director that both Alun and I have worked with. When Alun wrote plays for television, he directed them. He once did something of mine, and I have known him for many years. In fact he just made a couple of films. I won't tell you his name . . . but he had more of the same kind of thing. And I told Victor, do you know Philip? Well, do him and all the things around his neck and the cigar and that terrible mohair sweater. And this—is a famous comedian's son, Ted Gray, and this—is Robin Gray.

DiFRANCO: That's a great little thing they do at the end—touching the cymbals. . . .

LESTER: That's in. The press conference had been written. That's what Alun had written. The drum duel . . . did that happen? We knew that Paul was a very accomplished drummer and one of the ideas was to show somewhere what a really good drummer he was. That's where we sort of got to, but we never bothered doing it. We had him just setting up the kit, and it was all part of this gradual build-up in terms of plot point—Ringo sulking and feeling put upon.

DiFRANCO: Is Ringo really like that in any way—or was he just arbitrarily chosen?

LESTER: He was just chosen—even in *Help,* in which it became more specific that Paul was the sexy one, John was clever and sarcastic, Ringo was lovable, and George was mean. It was really simple. We set out to produce the same gag that can be dealt with over and over, like Jack Benny—you know, he has three characteristics that he has been using for thirty years. We were trying to separate their characters officially, because they were—especially at this time—more like each other than was safe. And so we were desperately trying to give them separate characteristics. Especially in *Help* —you know everything that George says in *Help* had to do with meanness or money. That was a device to try and produce separate characters. I remember meeting Groucho Marx, who had just been told that the Beatles were very much like the Marx Brothers. He went to see *Hard Day's Night,* and hated it. He came over here to do a commercial that I had directed and was absolutely vicious. He said "We were real people, we each were different. You could tell the difference between Harpo and Zeppo. I couldn't even tell *them* apart." And he was right. The Beatles are enormously alike—or at least they were in those days. They all had all these characteristics, and they just used to take turns being on. In parties afterwards or during *Help,* you could see that some would rest one night and just be the laughers, and it would be Ringo's turn to be the entertainer, and he would be marvelous—and the next night he would be passive and calm and George would be on.

DiFRANCO: Do you still see them?

LESTER: Not much, no. I see Ringo a bit . . . This—is one of my gags that I have always liked.

DiFRANCO: You like the doves?

LESTER: Oh, I loved the doves. It has nothing to do with the film . . .

DiFRANCO: Someone was saying that that is the one part that is surreal . . .

LESTER: This full scene—was shot at three different times and places. The shooting of the fire escape was last.

DiFRANCO: The field was a different place ...

LESTER: The field was shot where we shot the end, with the helicopter taking off—it had to be a place where a helicopter could take off—and that's—a helicopter launch pad. We have to have a helicopter to do the end sequence, and since we had the time it seemed a good thing for the other half of the day—to do other shots, top shots of the field sequence, because it had all that marvelous exuberence, in fact it isn't indicated here . . . So from 436 that was the first part of the day. I went up in the helicopter myself—I had an operator with me—and I said do any of the three or four things that you feel like doing and do them in any order that you like and I will find you—just mess about. I suggested three or four things and they were free to do anything else. We did only stuff up from the helicopter that day. Then two weeks later, after having seen the helicopter stuff, all these top shots, I came down and did that.

DiFRANCO: What number is that?

LESTER: Shot 437—and all those close-ups there—. Now the reason why I did that as it stands, a lot of it, was that Paul was terribly sick and didn't show up—he was hung over. You will see in those photographs that Paul isn't there. Those are my feet—. I wore dark trousers and the same kind of shoes and I became the fourth person and a lot of it became subjective—because you will notice that in a good deal of that sequence there is no Paul.

In all this stuff round there—, it is simply because he didn't arrive. And then there was a bit where John had to go off to a literary luncheon, so he wasn't there. So we had to do a great deal of the things that were shot separately. All the stuff on the ground . . . this—you see is a fake launching pad which we built.

DiFRANCO: And all that leaping into the air?

LESTER: That was the second day.

DiFRANCO: What did they jump off of—a trampoline?

LESTER: No, just one of the ladders that one of the electricians had.

LESTER: It was all ad-libbed.

DiFRANCO: Because there is a part where they seem to go up and down.

LESTER: I think I reversed one of the shots. A la Leni Riefenstahl—.

DiFRANCO: Olympia diving sequence . . . right. I wondered how you did this. I pictured this trampoline going up and down....

LESTER: No, it's just reversed. And it was totally ad-libbed. Including all this in the lines.

DiFRANCO: The end of the line too?

LESTER: I think you will find it, there is a line like it ... right. And this—I think was a new scene. That was done in one shot, if I remember ... The tailor was waiting for them. Then they come back and John meets Anna Quayle—.

DiFRANCO: How did this come about, this woman ... —?

LESTER: Again, that was just to capture some of the terrible things that people used to say to them, like "It's not for me, it's for my niece." These are things that happen to everyone, it's just a classic thing.

DiFRANCO: The ending ... "I don't know you at all" ... it's a great progression.

LESTER: Now I think we changed the positions of these scenes around. Because that scene is earlier. That's Shot 415. Oh, that's Norm and Victor Spinetti waiting for them . . . you see, the order is changed because we have put in George's scene with *him* and also this production number between John's scene with Millie.

DiFRANCO: Between the end of Millie . . . in other words, that's between Shots 48 and 49.

LESTER: And those scenes actually took place. Well, they are miles away . . . here they are. They came after Ringo's walk with the boy in the script. With George and Simon. And I remember we cut it in there originally and it seemed to ruin whatever mood that thing with Ringo had. So we moved it up here.

DiFRANCO: I'll check that. And this was all planned?

LESTER: Well, this line was mine.

DiFRANCO: Which line?

LESTER: "Well, you don't see many of these nowadays."

DiFRANCO: Oh, with the work of art . . . was that any particular work of art?

LESTER: I told them to get me the typical set and it arrived and it seemed so ridiculous. This was again done in a day. And this is Stanley Holloway's son—that's 473. But this time was just the beginning of pop art and pop posters and these semi-mobile semi-paintings—1964-65.

DiFRANCO: Simon Marshal . . .

LESTER: He was exhausted. I remember he was playing Caligula at the time . . .

DiFRANCO: He must have made a good Caligula.

LESTER: He's a marvelous actor. He's now playing Napoleon in a film that is being shot with Gielgud. Everybody is making a film on Napoleon now—Kubrick is making one, Brian Forbes is now not making his—and this thing is being made with Ken Hague playing Napoleon. I think it is about his life on Saint Helena, just that part of it. Anyway there is this—I don't even remember the gag. With the singing . . . We got an operatic society to bring in their costumes. I think these people—must have been the people from the operatic society. I know this must have been planned because—see, there is your backstage, people standing about in costume, one is knitting a loose sweater, three spaced white plates. Grandfather enters eating a plate of spaghetti. The girl who is knitting the sweater measures the sweater against him. He puts his plate of food on the table between plates two and three. And the juggler's assistant comes in, takes one of the plates without looking—oh, that's right. There was one of those jugglers who balance tall poles and I wanted to do a gag that was like that, where you never knew what went wrong—except it was just off there, you saw the result of it. And that's how we shot it.

DiFRANCO: And that is in the script?

LESTER: *That* is in the script, and that—was mine—I'll take credit for that. This whole set—well, the first film I did was called *It's Trad Dad,* and we had so little money, so we built a set out of these multiple blocks, that could be turned upside down and become one color and fit to become a jigsaw for something else, so we did something like twelve different numbers just with the one piece of scenery. Sometimes you had them up and sometimes you laid them down, Now this scene was just a repeat of that. I asked for a whole series of these things to be built so that whatever I wanted to do, I could keep changing it around. This we built—the whole control room as built. We asked EMI to put stuff in. EMI—Electrical Musical Institute, who had the cameras and got them fairly reasonably, fortunately. But what is interesting is that you get a by-line in your television. You know the difference in terms of synch, if you photograph television tubes, unless you shoot on twenty-five frames instead of twenty-four, which is what we did. So this entire stuff in the La Scala is done on twenty-five frame synch motors. Fortunately in England the current is fifty cycles—in America it's sixty cycles—so if you shoot twenty-five you are exactly half, and you can produce, you can get in synch with the shutter. In those days we had Arriflexes and a little dental mirror that's used to open the blimp—with the little dental mirror you look through to see if the line is in the center of the picture. It will not be visible when the film is projected. There is a little spinning wheel on the outside of the Arriflex, and we all had gloves on, and you would stick your finger on that and it would slow up or speed it up until you found that in the center of each of these images on the television there was a bar which then meant the thing was OK. We had to do that for every shot.

DiFRANCO: Did you have a T.V. man come in?

LESTER: No, I did it myself, because I was a T.V. man and I started in television in the days when you used to punch your own shows. So I knew how to do that—in fact that is probably me. I did all the punching of the faders and all this with the camera behind me.

DiFRANCO: They don't do live shows anymore, do they?

LESTER: No, not any more. They are all tape now.

DiFRANCO: I read one thing about a dog sleeping, with two people, one in the seventeenth century costume and the other . . .

LESTER: No, one in sixteenth century and the other in nineteenth century out on a park bench. Each thought that he was dreaming and that the other was the figment of his dream. And it turned out they were all in the dog's dream. Because the dog got up and he was tied to the scenery. And he pulled it down and walked off. And these smart-assed reviewers the next day. . .

John's interest in beards was developed in *Help* in that scene where they disguise themselves—it is extraordinary how much they look like themselves today if you notice it. Get a picture of it if you can. John looks exactly like himself today, with the round glasses and the beard. George is identical to today. In *Petulia* the father was played by Joe Cotten—exactly twenty-five years after *Citizen Kane,* when in *Kane* he had to age twenty-five years. To watch *Kane* and to see how an actor was, to see what he would be like in twenty-five years—fascinating.

DiFRANCO: How did you decide to shoot *Petulia* in San Francisco?

LESTER: I felt that I would be much too fascinated by Los Angeles, because it is so bizarre and does have so many visual elements that are too easy, as it were, and I was afraid that I would end up making a documentary about Los Angeles, and I wanted something that was much cooler, much more sinister.

DiFRANCO: Have you read Wolfe's *Candy Colored Tangerine Flake Streamlined Baby?* Because that's about L.A. too. San Francisco is a beautiful city.

LESTER: *It's* much more insidious.

DiFRANCO: Yes, much more—and that motel going up—was that true?

LESTER: It was from another hotel, but it was true. Everything is true. Renting the television set in the hospital—we went to look for locations and I saw these dummy sets. I ad-libbed that scene when we actually did it, but it's actually true. Everything in *Petulia* was true. All the most bizarre lines of dialogue and everything were lines in bars that I had heard—and I heard some of the most extraordinary lines. There is a line that is right at the back of a *Petulia* sequence—"So Chiang Kai Shek says, 'come now, how can I make a nickel'? It costs 2½ cents to put the average Chinese up the soap boiler and it's costing us $30,000 to put a V.C. underground, and that seems to be the basic flaw in the democratic society, don't you think, Ed?" And I heard this at a bar . . . ! I gave it to somebody—the boys in the Committee, you know. On the plane going from Los Angeles to San Francisco to start shooting I heard a business man ask a soldier, Where are you going? And the soldier said, We are going to Viet Nam. And he said, You must be very concerned. And he said, No, no. And he said, But surely it's not all that fun over there? And he said, Well actually I am in the Quartermaster Corps, and actually I cannot wait to see the Bob Hope Christmas Show. Incredible. And I thought well, I will put that in the film . . . but if I do nobody will believe it and people will just say gratuitously bad taste joke—and it is absolutely true. Another thing which I had in and took out which was so beautiful that it didn't fit—we were out in Muir Woods, which is a redwood park which we shot in, and it says Keep to the road, don't do this, stay over here . . . and in the middle of it, as we were looking for locations, came a wasp short-trousered guide with a hat, taking around a party of twenty-five young American Indians. As they went past, the little boy turned to his guide and said what happens next? They looked slightly confused and said Spring, and then they walked off. It was such a knockout, and I shot it and I am pretty sure I cut it out of the film.

DiFRANCO: No, that is not in the film. But the part I was thinking of in *Petulia* was when they were in this park sitting and this guard has this megaphone . . .

LESTER: That was also true. I hired an actor to do it and wrote it for him. He had never acted much before. I think he was a piano player . . .

DiFRANCO: In articles and interviews on you, I find a lack of understanding—like in *How I Won The War,* I found this interview with Tynan, the whole question of how to treat comedy reaches a point where a man slips on a banana peel and if he doesn't get hurt it's funny and if he does it's not and the point you make about *How I Won The War,* about it being an anti-war-film film. I find that people seem to miss the reality as grotesquery. They seem not to believe that reality can be more grotesque than any grotesquery.

LESTER: It's like the review of *Petulia* in *Newsweek,* which hated the film and said that this is a dirty, dishonest big atrocious picture. Surely there must be more redeeming qualities—in other words, saying this is much too black a picture of America. It happened to appear in the issue that also had the death of Robert Kennedy. And every page in the whole magazine was one atrocity after another. And there is this reviewer who had written it two weeks weeks before to meet the deadline, saying Surely things are better than this—and the magazine itself, it's as though it were dripping with blood. I'm not going to fight criticism because if I do it seeps over into what we are doing now in that it contributes to it. One must accept the fact that it does.

DiFRANCO: You also said something about the Moratorium, about Viet Nam, when the Americans went into Germany and instead of finding "six million dead Jews," finding families, women and children dead.

LESTER: That's why there is this feeling with Viet Nam and why there was not this feeling in Germany. It all goes back to that sequence in *War.* "You are a very lucky man young man. You are going to Germany soon and when you get there take your boots off, take your mark of being an officer off. Because you are fighting a war that may well turn out to be a crusade, if I know the Hun—a good soldier but a bit frightful—and with any luck, he has been up to some pretty revolting things behind barbed wire. But if he isn't, take your boots off. Because your men would put a bullet through your back for what you made them do so far. But don't worry, I don't think Jerry is going to disappoint us." And that is absolutely my feeling. That line at the end is the whole thing—you haven't a very big part in this, and this Viet Nam thing—still the money is good . . .

DiFRANCO: By the way, do you know if the men got to the moon?

LESTER: I think the next ones are going to go there and come back. They will be the first astronauts who didn't actually get an audience with the President. He was too busy. He sent the Chairman of the House or something. How would you like to be the first astronaut who didn't actually meet the President because he didn't have the time? It's really coming to that. Nobody gives a shit about it. The children don't even care about this. What are they going to do, pick up one rock? They don't care. They do it once and that is enough. Orson Welles was like that. When you do *Citizen Kane* in your early twenties, what do you do for the rest of your life?

DiFRANCO: I understand he's doing a commercial—or did a commercial.

LESTER: He's done a lot of voices for commercials. He's done one for me. He's a marvelous fellow. He's so literate. So articulate—Christ, he makes us all look sick.

DiFRANCO: Mike Nichols says that Welles can tell when he is in focus.

LESTER: Oh, he can, he can smell it. I'm sure.

DiFRANCO: What did he do with you, though—a commercial?

LESTER: No, he did a voice-over for a commercial that I did. I did a commercial with Groucho Marx which I thought was very interesting and very funny.

DiFRANCO: I heard you had a problem with him though—how did you approach Groucho?

LESTER: Oh, you heard the joke? He came in the wrong way, missed his lines, forgot to take the cigar out of his mouth, missed his gag, and then went off—it was supposed to be done in one shot. I said "Cut" and the whole studio went dead—I mean what was I going to say to this genius? And I couldn't say anything and I opened my mouth and he came loping back round and he said, I suppose you're going to tamper with perfection, kid? It was super.

LESTER: Now— . . . it's a series of sight gags, wasn't it? Things in the back of the frame . . .

DiFRANCO: Is this Shot 580 in the part where they are dancing on the set and John comes out? That was planned, wasn't it?

LESTER: Oh my God, yes. We spent half a day trying to do a stop-frame sequence with Paul and all the Beatles in single frame. I got a Morrograph, an old American camera which is a single-frame hand-cranked camera, and set it up and got someone to work it all out. It was one of those things where they do all the dancing like that—they just held the position. Single frame—shoot frame by frame, you know shoot one frame and then move them two inches and then shoot another frame, and everybody in the background has to stand absolutely still and rigid. Well, we got the idea for it much too late—typically me—and we got the Beatles to do it and we started shooting this bloody thing and all this dancing is what's left of it. You know, we did something in case it didn't work . . .

DiFRANCO: And it didn't work?

LESTER: My Christ, it didn't work. What happened was you really have to lock the people in the background—rigid—it was grueling. It took two hours of standing in the same position and moving Paul while the others stood stock still. And we measured everything out, and we worked it out frame by frame and at the end I said, OK, that's it, and I think it was George who said, "I can't wait for take two."

DiFRANCO: Do you have the outs on that?

LESTER: No, they will have been destroyed by now. They are destroyed after about a year and a half because of space in the studios. In fact, I'm starting to destroy *Bed Sitting Room* now.

DiFRANCO: You really have to destroy them?

LESTER: There is just no storage space.

DiFRANCO: Legally can you give them away?

LESTER: No, I don't think so.

DiFRANCO: Because the studios destroy things that for the history of film are so fantastic—the outs from all those films would be fabulous to have.

LESTER: This—is Lionel Blair dancing. This—looks like the beginning of one of the numbers. That's a fairly typical joke of that kind of Beatle—the kind that a director like Victor Spinetti would do. He would get huge blow-ups of the Beatles and put them there. I'm fairly pleased with that.

DiFRANCO: What I liked was—well, he seemed to be a stereotype dancer, this guy . . .

LESTER: He is—absolutely.

DiFRANCO: I cracked up when I saw that scene.

LESTER: Now, one of these girls was Miss England or something—I don't remember who it is . . . these girls are just big tall nothings.

LESTER: I remembered as I looked through this script—the restaurant. . . .

DiFRANCO: The part with the ketchup on the sleeve. . . .

LESTER: I think you will find make-up sequence—where they have all those beards, is much larger in here—it was cut down. You can tell that Alun is a dialogue writer and all the visuals . . . well, some of them work and some of them don't. One expected the Beatles to have a dance sequence at this point and we cut it out. I ended up doing it with a stop-frame, because I knew I didn't actually want them to dance. Backstage . . . now there—is a gag I didn't use and put into the *Forum*. It always astonished me because I try to think what a man would do to plan his life's career by juggling things, by spinning things into the air . . . because the world is made up of many people doing many things to survive. And I'm going to devote my life to filling my mouth with ping pong balls and spitting them up so that I can keep four of them spinning in the air at the same time. It seemed to me so extraordinary that I had it in about three films. It never works and I always cut it out. There is a little bit of it in *Forum* but it's practicing with this and then being bumped and then offstage hear this cough cough . . . I've got it there . . . it's an A number, which means I just sort of thought of it. The strictly for T.V. people —foreground action—zoom into each because I wanted to do something—Ringo fills cup with dispenser sugar, looks to other table for more, woman comes to clean up and annoyedly takes his cup away.

DiFRANCO: Ringo? The grandfather . . .

LESTER: Well, I gave it to him when we did it. The grandfather goes for sugar, circles round the table behind Ringo and it's a zoom shot—to close-up. Here is one of the extras. This was again set in a studio—the restaurant—lit from the floor. We were rather pleased with that. This was one of the first films I know that refused to use top lighting. And put ceilings on all the sets. All the sets have solid ceilings on them.

DiFRANCO: Seriously though, you just put lights on the sides. . . .

LESTER: And reflected light—bounced light. It was just beginning in those days.

DiFRANCO: I can't imagine that . . . it was five or six years ago . . . a lot of things were new then.

LESTER: I suddenly remember that there wasn't a nine millimeter lens and that people were making black and white films and that there wasn't faster film stock because Ilford was just about to bring out a faster stock and we did a test on it. It has been withdrawn since, its flare factor was so unpredictable—do you know what that is? When you have an area in the screen that is normally exposed and another area that is overexposed, you can produce an effect which creates . . . well, you may remember in *Help* there is a number where people are throwing darts and the figures of the Beatles elongate and stretch into a rather unreal shape. This was because I remembered that this stock produced distorted effects—the bleeding effect when this is f.8 and you are shooting at 2. Ordinary film produces a quite predictable flare, you know where it will be, you know about how far it will go. And if that is 5.6 and we are shooting you at 2, and two stops will be all right . . . But the flare factor means that you will have totally unpredictable effects—this could be only 4 and you are 2 and it would do extraordinary things. And because we didn't know what it was like, I used it in *Help,* but I didn't dare use it here. I was just trying to think how slow the film stock was that we were using. Even in black and white in these days—so think of filmmaking at that time and in this country and there hasn't been much attempt at using technique.

DiFRANCO: What do you generally shoot with? Eastman?

LESTER: Yes, the new Eastman stock—just smashing.

DiFRANCO: Are you shooting anything now?

LESTER: No, I won't be doing anything until March.

DiFRANCO: In one of the articles—I forget what it said you wanted to do, but it said that you were planning something after *Bed Sitting Room*. . . .

LESTER: I had a picture called—*Victorious*, which is a film about racism within government. It had vaguely to do with Rhodesia but in fact it was about the British government. It was people within the government and their racism—examining four different types of racist attitudes. I just couldn't get it set up—nobody would give me money to shoot it. I was four weeks away from shooting it. Had a superb cast—Jeanne Moreau, Ralph Richardson, Timothy Dalton, Dickie Attenborough, you name it . . . it could have been a great film.

DiFRANCO: It would have been very expensive, then?

LESTER: It would have been over two million dollars.

DiFRANCO: What kind of crew?

LESTER: Seventy. We had a hundred and seventy-five every day on *Petulia*. This—looks like the beginning of Ringo going off by himself . . . the river sequence. The only line that was cut out of the film was, "Get yourself knotted."

DiFRANCO: Knotted?

LESTER: Nobody knew, but in fact in the trenches in the First World War, you would tie a knot so you wouldn't have to go to the toilet. Get one of the specialist people who worked on *Curious Yellow* to come in and just do that. It's just like Paul Newman who doesn't do any coughs or laughs in his post-synching. He will post-synch all his dialogue, so the story goes, but if it calls for him to cough or laugh he calls for somebody else to do it. "I was Paul Newman's cougher."

DiFRANCO: My wife dubbed a slave in *Cleopatra* once.

LESTER: She was probably on call for twenty-two weeks.

DiFRANCO: Now we are going to the walk—It was such a lyrical passage—such a nice break for the whole film. Of course, it has become a classic . . . someone said that the talkies have become the walkies.

LESTER: That was the shot where there were those two things that I just grabbed because they were going past.

DiFRANCO: Right. That is 647. There is a cut, too, in the shot. He goes in, we stop motion, and then Ringo comes out immediately.

LESTER: But you can see it, because we were using an Arriflex and we should have had a registered pin camera, but we didn't have a Mitchell on this, we just had Arriflexes. So you do notice it. I remember trying consciously to get a kind of montage quality out of this and somehow to produce in this early thing the way Eisenstein would have cut, that vague look of things . . . I remember trying to make it into a sequence of pure film.

DiFRANCO: I think it does come off as a pure visual experience, until you come to the boys.

LESTER: Yes. We shot with two boys at the same time—one much more than we really wanted to do, who just couldn't speak. Then we got this boy to do it, and he is really too old.

DiFRANCO: And the music for that was thought out before or after?

LESTER: The music was thought out before because it was one of their numbers. It's funny though, isn't it, the man who wrote the score for this, George Martin, who works for the Beatles, was nominated for an award for this film, and he wrote forty-seven seconds of music for this film. That shows you what Academy Awards are worth. Because everything else was Beatles and pre-recorded music. But I put it in and we edited and we dubbed. And it came at the chase right at the end, before the final concert. Where is that cut?—749. As far as I know that is the only music he wrote. And Alun was nominated for the script.

DiFRANCO: What would you say on the script? I mean obviously you know Alun Owen, and you worked with him on it. But did he come to you with some kind of version?

LESTER: He came with an early version which I hated, and I think that first thing gives you an indication. You know, the train and they do their number—well it was still in that tone. Alun is enormously creative. I think the dialogue is excellent. The structure is mine and all the visuals are mine. I think his dialogue was perfect for that, and therefore I think he was a very good choice. He is a very positive writer, and whenever I complained about it he would throw the script on the floor and sulk and say, "You tell me what you want and I will do it. I'm paid as a cheap writer." It was very difficult in those terms because he had always written for television where he had had complete control.

DiFRANCO: He had never done a movie script?

LESTER: I think he had done a re-write for Joe Losey on the—I think that's all he had done. He had never written an original, he had never had to shape a picture. That's where a lot of the arguments came. We were throwing out whole scenes and saying we didn't think they would work. This is still only the second draft. But I'm quite pleased, because he had so many things going for us, like being able to write a whole screenplay in one-liners, as you can see, which is not easy to do. And he understood the feelings that I wanted completely, in other words he knew to leave spaces for lyricism or for exuberance or for that....

DiFRANCO: My feeling about the scenario was that it left so much room for you to work with, and yet provided a structure.

LESTER: We seem to go from there to the pub, which is a series of gags. It's the pub around from here where we used to go.

DiFRANCO: That's very strange, because it comes off as such an alien place. People looking...

LESTER: Well, they were all brought in for that. That man with the beard on 676 is a cartoonist named Bob Godfrey, he makes animated films. I remember trying to re-cut this so it would be comprehensible, and having a lot of trouble. I remember it not working. I'm not sure that it ever did.

DiFRANCO: And then—he throws the dart...

LESTER: The parrot was there.

DiFRANCO: Then there is the cross-cutting to them waiting—...

LESTER: That's the thing about this clock, trying to produce artificially—because it is totally artificial there, quite spurious—the feeling of some urgency in this part of the film, which is the soft part of the film. Once you have done the lyricism, until you get into the chase, you are in a pretty dull patch.

DiFRANCO: But was the cross-cutting done in the editing? Or is it in the script?

LESTER: I think you will find it is in the script. Then Ringo...

DiFRANCO: Oh yes, that hole scene—is great... when she falls into the hole...

LESTER: That was definitely the last shot I did, I'm sure of it.

DiFRANCO: Did you cut to someone else when she fell?

LESTER: No, she actually fell. She was a stunt girl.

DiFRANCO: When you go into the passage in the police station there seems to be a little bit of an attempt at the low angle thing. You build up this ominous quality of the grandfather talking to Ringo, as if the bobbies are going to beat them up and they are really asking if they would like to have some tea...

LESTER: I think that feeling was even in the script. The angles—well, I did that because that was Dragnet to me. This monitor scene—is something—I once did a whole sequence of gags based on that—a sketch for television, when I was in television. I love this changing of dimensions...

DiFRANCO: From television to the real...

LESTER: Yes, so that people—well, one fighting the other and then when this man moves away, naturally he would have the moustache on... So the chase begins. I have a feeling that more is written about the chase than is there. And the stuff with the car is ad-libbed. This is a mate of mine named Don Bluthful who I called and said, "can you come down for a half day's work." I had just thought of the gag the night before, phoned him the night before and asked him to come down.

DiFRANCO: So the stealing of the car will not be in the script?

LESTER: No. There is a big long scene while Ringo goes from the pub, there is a major scene that was cut out of the film, which was eight pages. There is even a re-write with Paul and a young girl actress—that's all out. He didn't do it very well. It was a little piece of lyricism for him. Some of it is nicely written, as I recall. It had nice elements that I liked in it of trying to get that shock of—do you know Pirandello's *Henry IV?* Well, it is all completely in period, they are all in the eighteenth century and then someone takes a cigarette out and lights it up, and zippo—it's like a bomb hits you. Because you had been going for about twenty minutes and then you find it is all a play they have been forced into by the man who is mad, who imagines himself to be in that period and they think he will die unless he keeps up the play, and then you find out later that he knows it's all a game and he is playing along with them. It's just a beautiful thing. And that's like this in that she suddenly takes off the wig—and you know.

DiFRANCO: Do you like the play?

LESTER: No. Funny enough, this—was one of the first scenes that Alun wrote for the film, and I remember saying that it was the best of them. And we all agreed that if we could get the rest of the script up to that standard, we would really have a good thing. And funny enough, out of all that original stuff, that is the only thing that is left.

DiFRANCO: Is that—out also?

LESTER: Yes, I think what that was is a rewrite of some of the pages in there. Because we knew before we were shooting it...

DiFRANCO: Oh, these are all Paul's lines?

LESTER: Yes, we knew that Paul did a very funny Liverpool whore as his party piece. And that is what that is. He did the voice very well.

DiFRANCO: What's interesting was that there is nothing really dirty in the film.

LESTER: Nothing at all. Absolutely pure.

DiFRANCO: That is what is so wonderful about it. This Shake and Norm thing—... it's great.

LESTER: We should be up to just after that . . . there—is Ringo . . . there is exterior street . . . the four little boys in the canal, which we cut down to one, that is the thing by the river . . . that is a bit of mine . . . the chase, you see that is all there is in the chase . . . that certainly, because I remember thinking of the idea and calling up John on the night before and saying come in with Don Bluthful, who appeared in *The Knack* and *Help.* And *Forum*—he is the guy who fell in love with Phil Silvers . . .

DiFRANCO: What about the part with the policeman and the car?

LESTER: That was shot at a school at Nottinghill Gate.

DiFRANCO: The police station . . . the interior steps here . . .

LESTER: Yes—and then you are back into the show.

DiFRANCO: The cutting here—gets frenetic . . . Was the show done in the same place?

LESTER: Yes, the La Scala. I tried to shoot everything that way. I had six cameras going.

DiFRANCO: It was an actual staged show?

LESTER: No. We just hired as many extras and they were hired for the day's work and they would sit there for the day.

DiFRANCO: That show was so real . . .

LESTER: Because we were progressively doing things like adding sweat to the boys to give the illusion that it was like a show. And it was the one thing that I was quite pleased with because it was such a simple thing to do to help the reality. But the terrible fear I had is that when I got the sequence together, I would have to change the order of the numbers. We were just shooting five or six numbers. And I thought if we take a scene and put it there they are going to be very sweaty and then unsweaty and then sweaty again. It was a gamble, but it paid off. We kept the order the way it was. I loved being able to plan the sequence enough musically to know that it would build.

DiFRANCO: When you are directing something that is as involved as this, how many assistants do you use?

LESTER: Just one or two.

DiFRANCO: It must have been very well organized . . .

LESTER: Well, these are very good camera operators and each had his own focus puller and we had three loaders for the six and I gave them all a long briefing of what I wanted. I would give them each a position for each time we went through. We did each number about twice, I should think, and I had three cameras around the stage and three in the audience for the girls and I would give them instructions for the kind of thing I wanted to do for each number, whether they should be moving this way or moving with the zoom or being still, or concentrating and I would say, You get rows, You get close-ups. Then I would just run from one camera to another throughout the whole thing trying to spot something that was getting better, something that was going on and saying get that, get that. We took all the film to look at it and you can imagine we shot twenty-seven thousand feet that one day—I could have gone to New York in less time than it took to see the rushes for that day's work—why look at rushes when for an hour more you could be in New York? Of those six cameras, one operator shot all day like all the others and there is not one foot of his film in the finished product, because he had no feeling for what was going on. Every time something was interesting he would pan off it. It was murder. So really there were five cameras. And then of course there was always the camera that was in the control room with Victor. I tried desperately to get some kind of pattern, knowing that we had already shot all the other numbers, because we shot almost all their numbers in the studio two days before this. We had this place for four days, and this was the last of the four days, so at least we had done the other numbers and knew well, one of them is going to be a slow series of dissolvers, one is going to be that thing all around Paul—"If I Fell In Love With You," for which we suspended a camera from an old piece of rope and then just moved around him . . .

DiFRANCO: That's very nice. Did one of your operators walk around with the camera?

LESTER: I think I did—yes, I did.

DiFRANCO: That's very smooth.

LESTER: By putting pressure on the rope, and sort of walking that way, it slides around...

DiFRANCO: And that was with an Arriflex?

LESTER: Yes. That's all we had was Arriflexes.

LESTER: On this thing—in the control room, the marvelous thing about being able to distort a film picture by changing the gain on the television monitor, which a lot of work is being done on now. A friend of mine from San Francisco has got a grant from the Ford Foundation to shoot a film and then put it on color television and distort the images, because of the distortion that is possible in the image or kind of tubes.

DiFRANCO: Did you use him in San Francisco?

LESTER: Yes. He did the light show for *Petulia* for me, that's how I met him. I remember doing that, distorting the images . . . I don't know what I can really say about this—. Except, in the early stages one couldn't get this kind of reaction until they were quite used to us being there and ignoring us. But these were girls hired to do it.

DiFRANCO: But they were being themselves.

LESTER: Yes.

DiFRANCO: Because of the frenzy that is there with some of them—it is so fantastic, an orgasmic reaction. Here—you have Brambell (Wilfred Brambell, the grandfather) in the audience too—with the handcuffs on.

LESTER: It's trying to make sure that everyone in the picture is also involved in it. One of the things that was very popular about the Beatles in those days was that they used to have jelly babies thrown at them. And we also found that they were throwing pennies as well. I was nearly knocked out during the thing. Really frightening. I was hit hard with a penny. It was hit on the front of the head with it. That slowed me down a bit.

DiFRANCO: Were they throwing things during this?

LESTER: Yes, we have given them jelly babies. I remember this girl who was dubbed the White Rabbit. She was in tears during the whole thing.

DiFRANCO: Yes, she's in 874. What do you mean by the White Rabbit?

LESTER: That was just an expression for her. You can imagine when you have just for that day's work 27,000 feet of material and trying to put it together to form some sort of shape and remember where the bits were ... unbelievable job that. Do you know that this film was fine-cut in two and a half weeks? We started working on the second of March. The film had its premiere in June. So you have six or so weeks for shooting. So you are in the middle of April. It was then fine-cut and dubbed in about five weeks, and neg-cut and the answer print and the whole lot. The whole thing was about three months. From the beginning of shooting till it was in the cinemas.

DiFRANCO: Were you happy with the prints, the negatives?

LESTER: Yes, they were very good prints. I don't know what they were like in America.

DiFRANCO: I have not been able to get a good print.

LESTER: There were extremely good prints in the early days. It's a chance to examine the quality of your local movie screen—to find that little bits of tea and mud and ice cream had been thrown—you know everything is there. It's like a television test card.

DiFRANCO: I think in photographing that you had a problem.

LESTER: Yes, I noticed that you don't have that shot except where it is rim-lit.

DiFRANCO: I'll have to take another look at that. I had not realized it was 360 degrees.

LESTER: It might have been a cut-a-way during it, but certainly we went right round it.

DiFRANCO: Somehow I cannot imagine a cameraman going over 179 degrees—I mean as an establishment man . . .

LESTER: There is no difficulty in this—at all because filming all the lights . . . First of all, it is much easier when you are in a place that justifies showing the position of his lamps. So we said, Put lights like this. He (Gilbert Taylor) had done it for me once before in *It's Trad Dad,* shooting directly into the lamp, a very big lens, and not knowing —I mean you can't really predict what is going to happen.

DiFRANCO: You work very well with him.

LESTER: I did on those terms. Of course, he has the very great advantage of being slightly deaf. He didn't have to hear all this. One of the operators who was in among the girls was so beaten by the noise that it destroyed one of the nerves in his teeth and he lost three teeth, a back tooth and the two beside it. From the sound level. Some of the things you must know about, when the real fans were trying to get in—they sawed through the iron bars of the La Scala theater and broke their way in. At one point I had the tripod of an Arriflex, the boys were behind me, with the points out, because they and I were being pushed down a set of stairs which, if you remember, they go up for the press conference. But they had broken in at the top and were fighting their way down. I grabbed the Arriflex and kept the points up to try to keep them from getting at the boys and myself. It was literally physical survival many times.

DiFRANCO: What about the police? Did they help?

LESTER: As much as they could. We were a bit of a nuisance. They had other things to do than sort us out.

DiFRANCO: You know in New York there is a special force of police that works on movies.

LESTER: Well, there isn't here. If we went out into the streets to shoot, that meant that no traffic could progress for the next two hours. There were never less than a thousand people outside the gates every day. They were here waiting for them because they knew that something to do with the film was here. These gates were locked, there were patrol guards with dogs. What was beautiful was there used to be a great stucco wall on which all the slogans about the Beatles were written. The most wondrous piece of graffiti . . . in fact, I used it in *The Knack.* Where Tolen's room is up at the top of the house, when you went up the stairs there was a whole series of things written all over it. The idea came from this because the walls were just covered with the most marvelous things. Anyway, we get to the end of the show and one wanted a kind of mystical thing—because I think in one of the early versions it said to get back into the car and go and leave—. That is the final sequence. Seventeen minutes is just that. We see the audience streaming in and settling down in their places for the show. As usual, there's the beginning—getting ready. And the grandfather appears. Yes, we changed it from a car to a helicopter for that feeling of release, flight, mysticism, larger-than-life quality that seemed so necessary. And fortunately we did, because in the end we had to do all those shots in the field sequence because we had the helicopter for a full day. There was some vague clock point, I remember. And the helicopter going away.

DiFRANCO: That's—the last shot. What about the end credits?

LESTER: Still Photography did them—Bob Freeman. I didn't do them.

DiFRANCO: I don't have all of them. I went crazy. Every four frames there was a different shot. Just impossible to get them all.

LESTER: That's right. They just threw them down—the pictures. It's amazing how little I remember.

DiFRANCO: I think you remember a lot. If you had to divide this into major scenes or sequences...

LESTER: I would say in general that the first part is the claustrophobic opening leading up to the field. Then there is the television area, which is them doing their actual work. In other words, the first thing is the going in a car, the train, in a hotel room, the night before, the little bit of liberty of being in a club, and all that. And then there is the part after the release of what you do for a living, what they do in the studio, which about two-thirds of the way through leads to the end of that, which is Ringo saying, I'm off, and having his piece of lyricism on his own. And the last third is the chase, which gets you out of that and gets you up for the final shot. I think it was as simply organized as that. I mean there may be some things that you can see better than I can, but certainly we didn't organize it—apart from saying we know we want to have a single quiet scene here because we have bang, bang, bang there.

DiFRANCO: The lyrical part of Ringo ... through the chase?

LESTER: No, I would say that the lyricism of Ringo is the finish of the second third—no, I don't know. It's impossible to say. You have the getting ready, which is the first third, the doing of the television things, the rehearsals, and all that, their work, the ordinary boredom, the make-up room, the waiting around, that is the second third, and the beginning of the third third is Ringo leaving it, having this piece of lyricism and going into the chase....

DiFRANCO: You said something about your past before we started taping, wading through your past...

LESTER: I don't remember, honestly. Oh, we were talking about films being harder to do. As films go on, they get more and more difficult.

DiFRANCO: I just wonder if you have anything special you want to say now.

LESTER: I suppose there is one thing we have not talked about—it was the astonishment when it worked. I don't know if it is telling tales out of school that the producer didn't think the film was going to work at all. He was terribly worried, and I think his pessimism spilled over onto us. It also happened so quickly. And the making of it with such speed and to get through and Oh Christ do this and you can't do that. And having to edit it so quickly. I couldn't think in any objective way if it was going to work or not going to and we zoomed through. And we had a terrible battle with the sound people here about the sound level of the last couple of numbers, the final sequence. In fact, I actually dubbed them, spent another day on the last number, to try to get the sound level up to where it would have some effect. We were having arguments from technicians saying that we couldn't produce that amount of sound on an optical sound system. We then got our optical print and then went back and almost doubled the volume. And I said let's be destroyed for distortion but let's make what happens in their concerts come through.

DiFRANCO: Because that is what happens—the sound level is up high and distorted.

LESTER: Yes and I fought for that. And we got that. And incidentally, when we had the premiere here, they turned the sound right down. And when I went racing up to the box and said, "What happened?" they said, "Well, Princess Margaret is here and we didn't want to offend her."

DiFRANCO: Did Princess Margaret like it?

LESTER: Yes, her husband liked it a lot ... Well, that's what I was trying. Even in those days, '63 or '64, they weren't attempting distortion. But making it and just trying to get it down. But there was a feeling of excitement. We knew we had done the right kind of film and I knew that anyway I hadn't tried to cheat my original feelings. One way or another we didn't try to shirk what we had set out to do. Whether that judgment was right or wrong, we didn't know. The producer was terribly terribly worried about it because he didn't like a lot of it. We were all worried. The editor is a very serious man, and we were all very serious about—have we enough variety, have we enough this, all the things we wanted. We knew we were not pleased with the part of the grandfather. We were disappointed with the way it was working. But you know it was an uncomfortable part and didn't quite work. And we knew it. Its longer version was even worse. But when we finally did it, we had the first showing for the executives at United Artists. They had treated it as an exploitation film for a couple hundred thousand pounds. You know, get it in, get it out quickly. Now during the shooting of it all this madness had built up, and they knew they were onto a good thing. The film was in profit before it opened because the advance sales on the LP were three hundred thousand pounds. That was the United Artists' share, not the Beatles' share—in other words, they had more than the cost of production on the U.A. share of the advance sales of the album before the album had been released. Unbelievable. The first people we showed it to in a rough dub were Arnold Picker, David Picker, Bob Lowenstein and somebody's wife. I sat behind this woman. We had never seen it with anybody but ourselves, and all through the performance there was absolute silence. I mean there were only those three or four in the screening. And scene after scene, I heard tsk, tsk, tsk. And things like if we take this scene out and join it to this... and my mind was just racing. When the lights went up at the end I was sweating and limp and this woman turned around and went tsk, tsk, tsk. I nearly died. And they were all over us. And the film was made. I made it for a tiny salary—no share of the profits. As a kindness, after it was done, Walter Shenson gave me one-half of one per cent.

DiFRANCO: That's too bad, but you couldn't know.

LESTER: Walter Shenson became a millionaire. He owns 50% and the Beatles and Brian had 30%. But I am glad that I made it. I must see it again. I have a very warm feeling towards *Help,* and nobody else does—or not many. Very few people preferred it. Fellini... Zefferelli thought it was one of his favorite films. Renoir loved it. I was delighted.

DiFRANCO: In some of your interviews you talk about living in England after coming from America. Do you think that has any value?

LESTER: Not in terms of this film. I don't think there is anything in it that indicated an attitude of ex-patriotism or of being a foreigner. My value to this film was being able to get on with the Beatles, to try to understand what they represented to this country without prejudice. If that is because I had never been in the class struggle here, then that helped. But I wouldn't make too much of it. You could say the same of an Irishman.

DiFRANCO: You said something in one of your interviews about your being subordinate to the Beatles, and when you died they would say "director of Beatles films. . . ."

LESTER: No, no I didn't say that I was subordinate to the Beatles. What I said was that no matter what I do after this, it's all downhill. In thirty years' time no matter what films I make or what service I do for the community, when I die the placard will read "Beatles director in death drama." And that I think will still be true. When people talk about me, they say you were the one who did those Beatles pictures. No matter what I do that will never change. But it was the Beatles who said they were subservient to me. They said about *Help,* "It wasn't our film. We felt like we were guest stars and extras in our own film." I think that was true. But it had to be true, because not wanting to repeat this film, and still having to make a film about four real people, you had to make a film which didn't deal with their work, which is concerts, television, theater, and all that. We couldn't go into their actual private life, with drinking, marijuana, and all that. That was out. So you had to say, I am making a real documentary in color about people where you can't talk about their work or their private lives. What do you do? You can't expect Ringo to play d'Artagnan. They are not going to play parts. At least not at that stage of Beatlemania, as it was. So it had to be a documentary, but about nothing. So they had to be passive. We had to create this huge baroque fantasy through which they passed. You see, I know all the things that I couldn't do, and they wouldn't let us do correctly, which we wouldn't want to do in *Help,* faced with those problems. I'm very proud of *Help* because I think *Help* is as successful as *Hard Day's Night* in terms of making four people enormously attractive to the audience. I think that a lot of the things that they did and the way they did them, the feeling of it—they were so bloody endearing, and I am saying this now, after having seen it just last week. And my wife and I said, "Oh my God, if they had never changed, if we had all never grown up. If the world was like it was in *Help.* Because you know a lot has happened to mankind since 1964." My wife said, "Why don't you make films like that and stop making all that rubbish that is so serious?" And I said, "I can't laugh any more." Who can laugh? You forget what 1964-1965 was like. You could laugh. You could concentrate your whole energies on creating marvelously positive images of exuberance. And the Beatles seemed to be part of that. Nowadays, they are all separate. John is with Yoko. . . .

DiFRANCO: Such a mess. . . .

LESTER: The mess is the world, not them. The mess is why one makes *Petulia.* If you care at all about the bloody world you can't make *Hard Day's Night* today and you couldn't make *Petulia* in 1963-64. And that is all there is. And there is no good saying let's stop all this and go back to the purity—rubbish. You're stuck with mankind.

DiFRANCO: Well if you are not going to work on this other project on racism, what are you going to do?

LESTER: I am working on a picture—I hope—called *Flashman.* Flashman was the bully in *Tom Brown's School Days.* Do you know the book?

DiFRANCO: No.

LESTER: It's an English classic from which two films were made—one called *Adventures At Rugby,* with Cedric Hardwick, and one of the *Dead End Kids.*

DiFRANCO: Oh, I know what you mean.

LESTER: Tom Brown was Freddie Bartholomew in 1940. Then there was a remake in 1950 with Robert Newton. But the one you would have seen was with Cedric Hardwick as the schoolmaster. Flashman was the bully who picked on poor old Tom Brown, the early Victorian hero. It was about decency and honesty and not lying and being true to your mates and not telling on them; Flashman did all those. And it's his history, carried on when he leaves Rugby and joins the Eleventh Hussars and is caught up in the retreat from Afghanistan, from Kubul through the Khyber Pass in 1842, when 17,000 people were killed and one person survived. The entire British contingent from Afghanistan retreated. They thought there was a threat from Russia through Persia, so they got rid of the actual king of Afghanistan and put a puppet ruler on the throne. Then they cut his money by half so that he couldn't pay all the tribes who used to keep all the passes open. And they eventually threw out the British, through a series of things. And they were all massacred on the way back.

DiFRANCO: That's going to be quite a set.

LESTER: I am going to do it all in the snow. Just getting up out of the absolute whiteness. Looking round and seeing an Afghan coming down. I can't afford the people. Rather I can afford *them,* but not their costumes.

DiFRANCO: Right. Is that why you are reading *Great Regiments?*

LESTER: Yes—all the lot of them. It's really twentieth century attitudes in the nineteenth century. Or, if you like, an examination of Victorian behaviour which had its flowering in the foreign policy of John Foster Dulles. We still have the hangups of Victorian morality.

DiFRANCO: There is a whole re-examination of history in terms of the existential decisions that people made. So many films have been made on the Civil War. And they are all flashy, big violent-type war movies. But none of the films have been made—*How I*

Won The War goes at this in a different way—to express the real situation of what it means to be doing in the seventeenth or eighteenth century something that has a direct correlation to what you are doing now.

LESTER: Flashman behaves as a twentieth-century man, but he still has a sort of Rabelaisian quality about him. What he does not behave as is a nineteenth-century man. The sergeant who goes with him is very much a nineteenth-century man. He believes about God. He doesn't speak to his superior officer in the first person, he wouldn't say "I." And also in a battle, he wouldn't dream of picking up the wounded, not only of the enemy, but of his own regiment. You know it was not until the 1880's that there was an order forcing the British army to give aid and assistance to the other regiments when they were lying dead or dying on the battlefield. That's the code of behaviour that you were dealing with. So that they could look quite callously at the Afghans being slaughtered. But of the 17,000 or 18,000 people who were killed, 5,000 were British. All the rest were seaport troops taken from India into the snow of Afghanistan, with no choice on their part. And all the accounts of the slaughter, and I have read twenty books written about that, seem slightly petulant about the fact that the bloody Indians kept getting in the way of the retreat. They were being slaughtered! These poor people who had nothing to do with conquest or campaign. They were just dragged up as slaves, as it were. They said, "undisciplined rabble that kept getting in the way of our retreat." That's the morality... Flashman is a bounder, a bully, a thief, a rapist, a coward—by their terms. Yet he is absolutely the only man that turns away and can't look when someone is given a gun as a gift, and for target practice he tries it out on a couple of slaves who are forty yards away. It is all true. Everything in the book is documented. Everything in this is actual.

DiFRANCO: You really have subject matter that is unique.

LESTER: Well, it's very funny. He's a sexual athlete who is a true coward. And in the best terms of cowardice he will threaten, he will plead, he will bribe. He will do anything to survive. He says I don't know what we are worried about anyway, the whole thing is a bunch of beans. They were here before us in Afghanistan, and they don't want us here. If we are not going to give them enough money we might as well get out. I am going to get out if nobody else will. And he does everything in his power to do it. He is marvelously like that picture on the book cover. Wondrously elegant as a sexual athlete. Except when things go wrong and he is threatened—then he's crawling around like Keaton. So it has all those qualities. It should be a good project.

DiFRANCO: Who would you have playing the part?

LESTER: Don't know yet—it certainly would be an unknown English actor. Has anyone made a film about the *Pueblo?* That is quite extraordinary. An assistant director talked to me once here about six months ago about writing something for that. Because it does have a lot of basic issues quite tightly knit. He said, and he's quite right, that it should be just a spy ship, but it should be a ship that has a positive weapon on it as well. If it were a nuclear submarine that we were speaking about, that has the means of positive destruction as well, the decision, the dilemma—suppose its rudder gets jammed, or something as simple as that, and it just goes aground on the China coast? What do you do? You have the possibility of firing. It's extraordinary because all that stuff afterwards is marvelous, about the morality of military life. I saw a letter by Matt Morasco, one of the Green Berets. He wrote a letter saying—I'm paraphrasing—I have been killing people in the course of duty, and they are accusing me of murder. It's extraordinary. People who had been killing because of their patriotic duty are now being accused of murder.

DiFRANCO: One of the most incredible things in terms of visual perception of the war is that we are so removed from the war. To say that X amount of people are being killed in Vietnam is equal to saying that six million Jews were killed in Germany. I cannot imagine six million people being killed. But when *Life* magazine takes a picture of a Saigon general holding a gun against a guy's head and shooting him, it really brings the reality home.

LESTER: I was faced with exactly that in *Bed Sitting Room,* which is England with forty million dead. Do you show forty million skeletons? Line them up? You know that the audience would just turn away—reject it. So I've got people sitting on a twelve-foot-high pyramid of boots, army surplus. As a comedy thing. And the whole film is based on that kind of imagery. *Time* magazine gave it the best review I've ever had for any film. And *Newsweek* said I've never felt less seeing any film. I just had no idea what was going on—but the *Time* review was incredible. It was a marvelous review.

DiFRANCO: This is you talking: "I have seen directors who write down a list of scenes for the day and then sit back in a chair while everything is filmed according to plan. I can't do that. I know that good films can be made this way, but it's not for me. I have to react on the spot. For instance, there is a scene in *Help* with Ringo, a girl, and a tiger. What happens in that scene is entirely dependent upon the responses of Ringo, the girl and the tiger. I am a butterfly by instinct. My ideal is a few gags, a few situations, and tremendous mobility in between.The approach is a bit like the technique of a script writer." Oh yes— "... being interviewed makes him giggle." Oh, here's one: "Lester has plans to film, of all things, the life of Jesus, as seen through the eyes of Judas, John the Baptist, and Doubting Thomas, based on the novel *Salt of the Earth."*

LESTER: Phillip Hart.

DiFRANCO: "The happiest—just out and out happiest film I've ever made was *Help.* There is more of me in *Help* than any of the others. Although I think the mass audiences liked *Hard Day's Night* first, and *The Knack* second."

LESTER: And it's all diminishing from there. The film I am least pleased about is *Forum.* Without any doubt. It's a film where I was never speaking with the producer. There were incredible battles. Law suits... the producer locking bits of film away because he said I had stolen one of his gags, that that was a gag he was going to sell to television. I wasn't allowed to work on the script until two weeks before I started shooting. The cameraman and I rewrote the whole screenplay. It wasn't right and we weren't ready—half my screenplay and half the original. The producer was supposed to direct the picture himself, and he had written the screenplay himself. He thought I was a tame director. I had been assigned to do it from *Hard Day's Night* onwards. I had signed to do it and I couldn't get out of it. I thought I could do something with it, but I couldn't. I found a lot of the facts about ancient Rome fascinating, the slum of it—that's why I am looking forward to *Satyricon.* I thought it would be good fun to do it. But that got in the way of this Broadway musical.

DiFRANCO: It seemed as though your own particular style and attitudes really went against the content of the lines. Especially with Zero Mostel, who has the kind of presentation where you have to sit and relax and listen and laugh. Your approach is not literary at all, purely the medium of cinema. All the stuff in *The Knack* is pure cinema. I have all your credits. I can tell you what people categorize you as: overlapping dialogue, direct chronological order, fragmented inverted order—that is, you have a fragmented inverted order as opposed to direct chronological order like Bergman. You are more like Resnais. Have you feeling for Resnais?

LESTER: I liked *Marienbad* enormously. I didn't much like *Muriel.* I liked about half of *La Guerre Est Finie.* I loved *Nuit et Bruillard.*

DiFRANCO: That's another approach, that kind of poetic approach.

LESTER: *Hiroshima* was impressive. I liked *Marienbad* best.

DiFRANCO: Who is your favorite director? Who do you feel closest to?

LESTER: I think probably the people I admire most are not the ones I feel closest to. I think if I were going to the French cinema and there were three new films—one by Godard, one by Resnais, and one by Truffaut, I would go to Truffaut's first, Resnais' second, and Godard's third.

I adore things like *Jules et Jim.* I think *Truffaut's* work is marvelous. Super. I think Fellini is extraordinary. And certain parts of Bergman—*Persona* was a revelation to me.

DiFRANCO: Do you want to give me a five best films list?

LESTER: It's impossible. Keaton first for me.

DiFRANCO: You're Keaton first as opposed to . . .

LESTER: Almost anybody.

DiFRANCO: Oh yes—*The Navigator, The General* . . .

LESTER: Anything. He was a filmmaker. Chaplin had an empty wall and he used to do review sketches with three walls like this. Whereas Keaton was the first man who understood that comedy could be beautiful as well as . . . there was beauty in his films. Ravishing beauty. He was beautiful and he understood, which is a great skill for cinematography, the use of space around the person. It isn't the person being filmed, it's the space between the camera and around the sides. And there will never be anyone like him. He had the knack of putting the camera in exactly the right spot, where two inches further—forward or backward—would have been wrong. And that's why there will never be anyone like him.

DiFRANCO: I agree with you. I loved Keaton for exactly that. Somebody said about you, "strange, unexpected composition, blurred flashes of highly illuminated color, rapid in and out of focus, swift camera movement and positions, wide range of camera angles."

LESTER: Certainly not swift camera movements, because I never move the camera. I try never to. I never track and I never use a crane.

DiFRANCO: The panning you wouldn't characterize as particularly . . .

LESTER: You can pan with your head like this, and you can pan with a camera, but a crane shot which starts there and comes down and moves along and does that as part of the normal action of filmmaking seems to force the audience into movement that it is not used to doing. I let the camera be an eye and you can pan and vaguely shift focus and concentrate on other things and be selective in your composition and your focus. But I don't move the camera itself.

DiFRANCO: This is a semantic problem. Panning would be camera movement.

LESTER: No, I meant movement of the camera, like a helicopter shot, like those marvelous swoops in *Jules et Jim.* And that's what *Hard Day's Night*'s camera thing was. I don't do anything I don't feel is logical to the person sitting in the audience.

DiFRANCO: Did you ever have any of the formal 180 degree angle stuff?

LESTER: Don't cross the line stuff, you mean?

DiFRANCO: Right—the line, the axis . . .

LESTER: Never.

DiFRANCO: You don't deliberately break the rules . . .

LESTER: I just don't have them. Funny, I don't think that I break the rules . . . I certainly do it less than a lot of people. I think I know the rules, but I was never taught them, and I never thought about them. And I was certainly never involved in using them in the early days. I was a television director, and I went out to film inserts for television, which is the first time I had done film. With nobody to tell me what to do, and a bunch of idiots with me, I made my first film with Peter Sellers' own camera and my own money. And we edited it all ourselves and we wrote it all, we did it all, and it was completely amateur, which we had no plans for releasing or doing anything with it. It was completely an amateur exercise. My first feature was shot in two and a half weeks. There was a story of twenty-some pages. Thirty-six musical numbers. It was a real quickie. I think they are called Sam Katzman Quickies. It was all right. The only time I had the opportunity to learn technique is when Joe Losey and I split a series of thirteen half-hours for television, which were made on film, in 1956 or 1957—just the beginning of 1957. There was a bit of technique necessary in those because they were shot in two and a half days—each one. It was practical. It was the only time I ever had to think about technique because it was do half-hour television in two and a half days and get off. And you had to use the sets that the other fellow had before. There was not a more unlikely combination to do them that Losey and myself. He helped me get the job, and I am very grateful to him.

DiFRANCO: There is a problem with schools teaching this kind of rules, and the unions especially—do this and don't do that.

LESTER: In *Petulia* I used to get notes from the head of the sound department saying slate 258, take 3 will be post-synched because of unacceptable level of background noise. And this was my eighth or some film and suddenly getting a note like that after never having any interference in any film before. I used to read these things and say I don't believe it. Who is this man? And I would rip the thing up and send it back. Nonsense.

DiFRANCO: You used to rip it up?

LESTER: You had to. It wasn't their fault, and I suppose it was being a bit cruel. That was what they had been doing for thirty years. They were the arbiters, the judges—and they were judging. I just couldn't conceive of a world where anyone would say, you reshoot this or post-synch that. I mean if I want to do it, I will do it. If it is unintelligible, it is my fault. It's held down to me and not to you. And what are you doing for a living? All those departments are gone now.

DiFRANCO: What do you mean?

LESTER: Well, I can't imagine there is a sound department anymore. Or if there is, there won't be soon.

A HARD DAY'S NIGHT

Directed by

RICHARD LESTER

Screenplay by

ALUN OWEN

1A
XLS
NA
to . . .

EXTERIOR, STREETS OUTSIDE RAILWAY TERMINAL, DAY

Song: *"A Hard Day's Night"*
The film opens with crowds of girls, shot in a sequence of CLOSEUPS, chasing after GEORGE, JOHN and RINGO. The BOYS hare off just ahead of them. They take a turn down a back alley way and the crowd of screaming girls are after them.

EXTERIOR, TERMINAL

They rush on through the narrow cobbled passageway and into the main station [quickly show their tickets at the barrier for the London train] and get on to the platform as hordes of yelling and screaming girls reach the closed gates.*

*Text in brackets indicates material deleted from the original script and not in the finished film.

1B
LS
NA
to . . .

1C
MS
(ending in MCU)
NA

2
LS
NA
PL

3A
XLS
LA

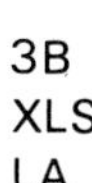

3B
XLS
LA

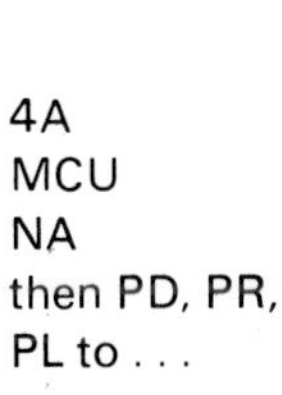

4A
MCU
NA
then PD, PR,
PL to . . .

EXTERIOR, TERMINAL PLATFORM

[We see the fans rushing to the few platform ticket machines, and endless pennies being dropped and tickets torn out in their haste to get on to the platform to see the BOYS.

NORM has been waiting for the BOYS and he hurries them to where all their baggage, instruments and the drums are waiting, piled up to be put into the guards' van. The BOYS turn and see the oncoming stream of girls pushing through the barriers and descending on them with yells and shouts. They grab their instruments, RINGO makes for the drums. NORM plugs into a handy transformer and using their instruments like a gun volley to stop the onrush of females, the BOYS blast fire into a number and start to sing. This stops the girls in their tracks and they settle down on whatever they can to listen to them playing.

As the BOYS are playing, we CUT BACK to the crowds. In the centre we see PAUL struggling and pulling to fight his way through the girls to join the other BOYS. He is dragging a very reluctant old man behind him. The old man seems most disgruntled and we can see by his gestures how unwilling he is to be pulled and pushed forward through all the girls.

At last PAUL reaches the other BOYS. He sits the old man down on a pile of cases and joins in the number to the squeals of delight from the fans. The old man sits aloof and proud, ignoring the whole proceedings. JOHN, GEORGE and RINGO look enquiringly at PAUL who gives a non-committal shrug of the shoulders as if to say "it's not my fault" and the number proceeds.

SHOT of sudden horror on JOHN's face; PAUL follows his eyeline only to see the old man has doffed his cap and is busily collecting money from a disconcerted crowd. PAUL dives hastily into the crowd, and with suitable apologies abstracts the old man, and with a long suffering sigh, drags him back to the group. GEORGE and PAUL hold him firmly as they finish the number, the old man standing there between them.]

4B
MCU
NA
PL

6C
MCU
NA

5
CU
NA

7
LS
NA

6A
MCU
NA
PL to .

8
MS
NA
PU

6B
MCU
NA
PL to . .

9
MS
NA
TL

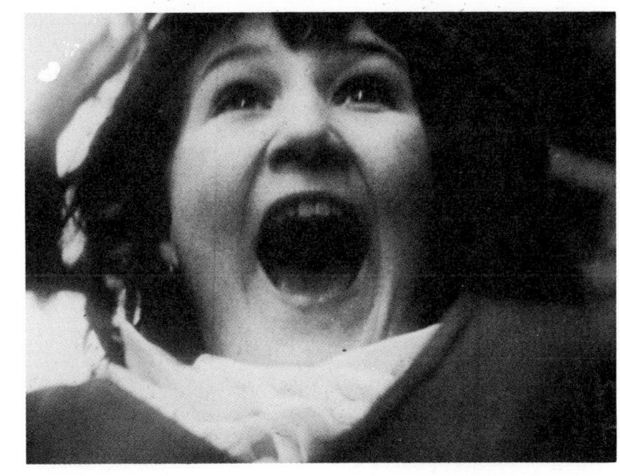

10
CU
LA

11
XLS
NA

12A
MCU
NA
PR to . . .

12B
MCU
NA
PL,
PR to . . .

12C
MCU
LA
PU

13A
MS
NA
TL to . .

13B
MS
NA

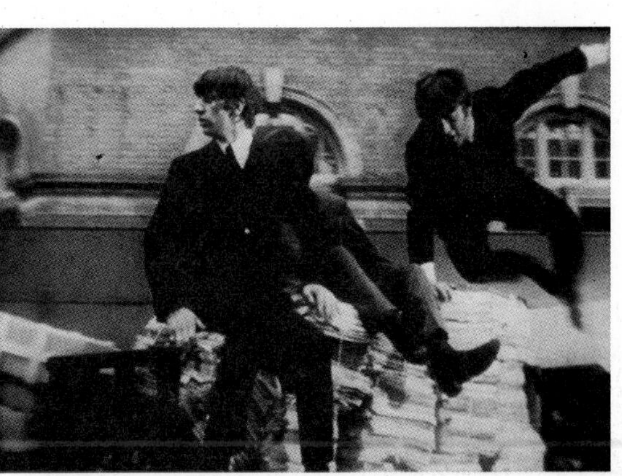

14
LS
NA
PL

15
MS
NA

16
LS
LA
PR

17
MCU
NA

18
MS
NA

19
MS
NA
PL

20
MCU
NA

21A
XLS
NA
PL to . . .

21B
XLS
NA
ZI to . . .

21C
MS
NA

21D
MS
NA

22A
MS
NA
PD to . . .

22B
MS
NA
TD to . . .

22C
XLS
LA
TI

23
CU
LA

24
CU
LA

25
XLS
HA

26
MS
NA
PL,
TL

30A
MCU
NA
PL to . . .

27
MS
NA
TO

30B
MCU
NA

28
MS
NA
TO

31
(PR)
MS
NA
TO

29
MS
LA
TO

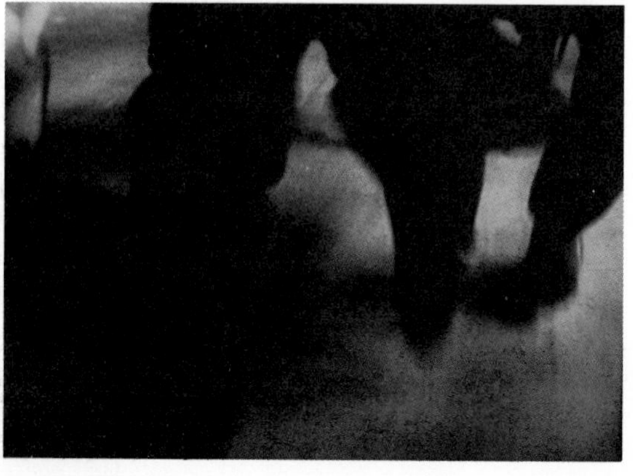

32
MS
NA
TO

33
MS
NA
TO

34
MS
NA
TO

35
MS
NA
TO

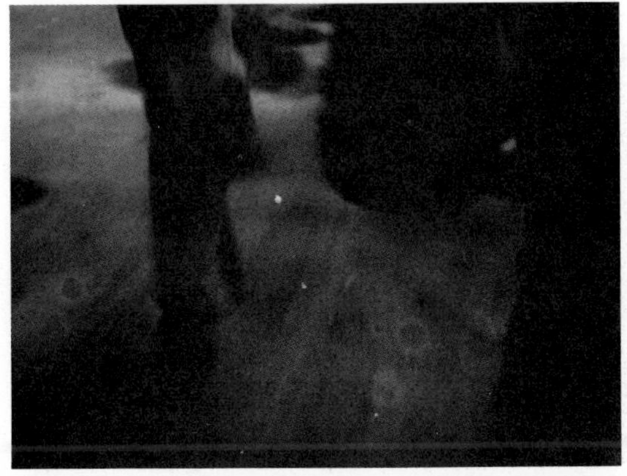

36
MS
NA
TO

As the number finishes and the girls scream and shout with delight, the guard blows his whistle. NORM and SHAKE grab the instruments and the drums, and with the rest pile the lot into the guards' van. The BOYS head into their reserved compartment pursued by the fans but the train moves off. They have successfully repelled all extra boarders.

The BOYS stand and wave to the fans until out of sight line . . . the girls running along to the end of the platform waving and calling out.

37
MS
NA
TO

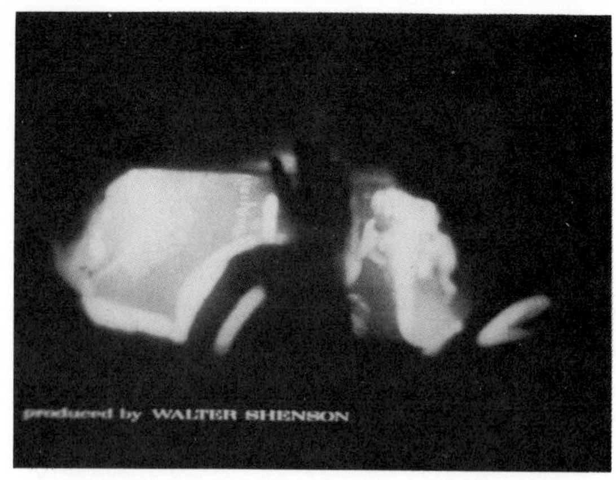

41A
LS
(Bealtes' P. O. V.)
NA

38
MS
LA
TO

41B
LS
(Beatles' P. O. V.)
NA

39
MS
NA
PL,
TL

42
MS
LA
PU,TO

40
MS
NA
PL

43
FS
LA

44
MS
LA

INTERIOR, RESERVED TRAIN COMPARTMENT

The BOYS relax, sitting down on one side of the compartment. They are about to settle down and make themselves at home when first RINGO nudges GEORGE who in turn nudges JOHN. Opposite them is sitting the LITTLE OLD MAN. He is holding himself stiff, erect and very aloof.

The three BOYS look at him enquiringly, but with an elaborate sniff, he looks away from them and out the window.

PAUL catches his eye and winks at the LITTLE OLD MAN. He winks back at PAUL, scowls at the other three then looks firmly out of the window again. The BOYS turn on PAUL.

45
MCU
NA

46
FS
LA

JOHN: Eh . . . pardon me for asking, but who's that little old man?

PAUL: What little old man?

JOHN: (pointing) That little old man.

PAUL: Oh, that one. That's me grandfather.

GEORGE: Your grandfather?

PAUL: Yeah.

47
MS
LA

GEORGE: That's not your grandfather.

PAUL: It is, y'know.

GEORGE: But I've seen your grandfather. He lives in your house.

PAUL: Oh, that's me other grandfather, but he's my grandfather as well.

48
MCU
LA

49
MCU
LA

JOHN: How d'you reckon that one out?

50
MCU
LA

PAUL: Well . . . everyone's entitled to two, aren't they, and this one's me other one.

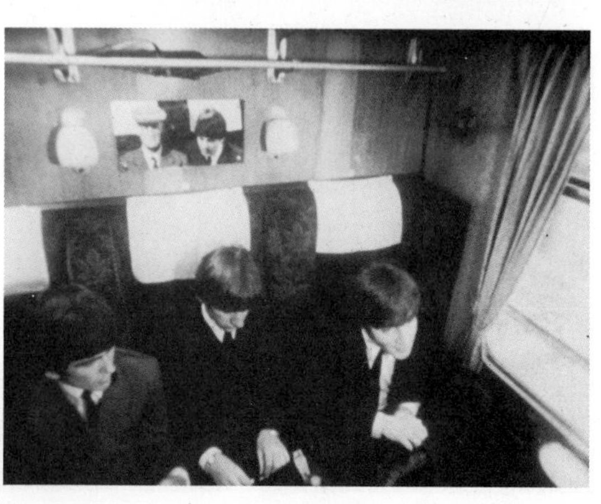

51
FS
HA

JOHN: (long suffering) Well, we know that but what's he doing here?

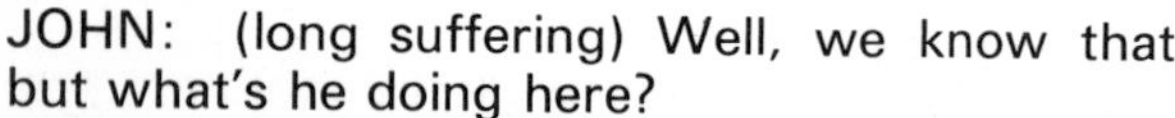

PAUL: Well, me mother said the trip u'd do him good.

RINGO: How's that?

52
MCU
LA

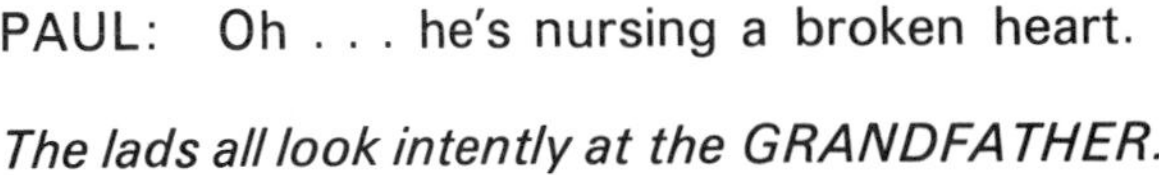

PAUL: Oh . . . he's nursing a broken heart.

The lads all look intently at the GRANDFATHER.

53
FS
LA

JOHN: Aah . . . the poor old thing.

He leans across to GRANDFATHER.

JOHN: Eh, Mister, are you nursing a broken heart, then?

The GRANDFATHER glares at him, in a way that indicates yes.

54
CU
LA

[*He inspects GRANDFATHER carefully.*]

JOHN: (to Paul) Eh, he's a nice old man, isn't he?

PAUL: He's very clean.

They all agree with PAUL.

[PAUL: (whispering) You see, he was going to get married but she threw him over for a butcher.

GEORGE: A butcher?

PAUL: Yeah, she was fickle.

JOHN: Aye and fond of fresh meat and all.

PAUL: (seriously) No . . . it was his sweetbreads. She was dead kinky for sweetbreads. Anyroad, me mother thought it'ud give him a change of scenery, like.

JOHN: Oh, I see.]

55
MS
NA

56
CU
LA

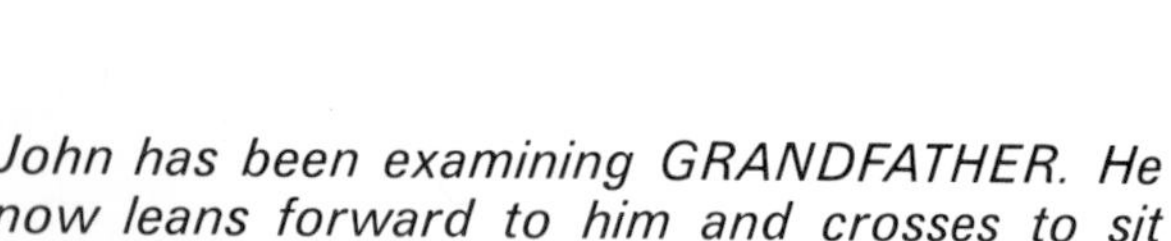

John has been examining GRANDFATHER. He now leans forward to him and crosses to sit beside him.

57A
FS
LA
PR to . . .

JOHN: (in an over friendly voice) Hello, grandfather!

GRANDFATHER: Hello.

57B
FS
LA

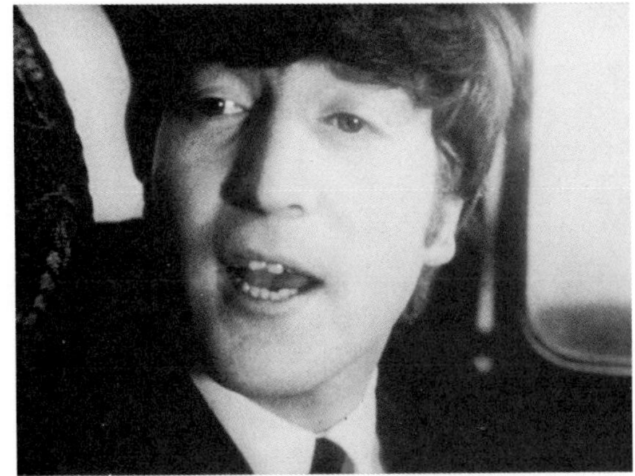

58
CU
LA

JOHN: (delightedly) He can talk then?

59
MCU
LA

PAUL: (indignantly) Course he can talk. He's a human being, like. Isn't he?

60
MCU
LA

RINGO: (grinning) Well . . . if he's your grandfather, who knows?

The lads all laugh.

61
MS
LA

JOHN: And we're looking after him, are we?

GRANDFATHER: I'll look after meself.

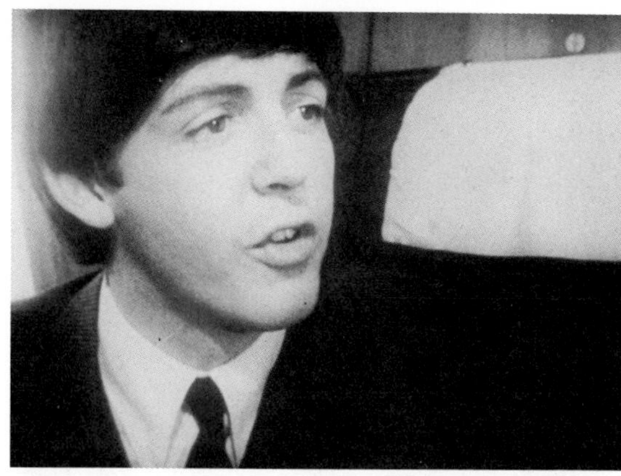

62
MCU
LA

PAUL: (standing up) Aye, that's what I'm afraid of!

JOHN: Has he got you worried?

*(PAUL: (combing hair) He's a villain, and a real mixer and he costs you a fortune in breach of promise cases.)***

GEORGE: (disbelieving) Gerron.

PAUL: (still combing) No, straight up.

[GRANDFATHER: The lad's given you the simple truth. I'm cursed wid irresistible charm, I'm too attractive to be let loose.]

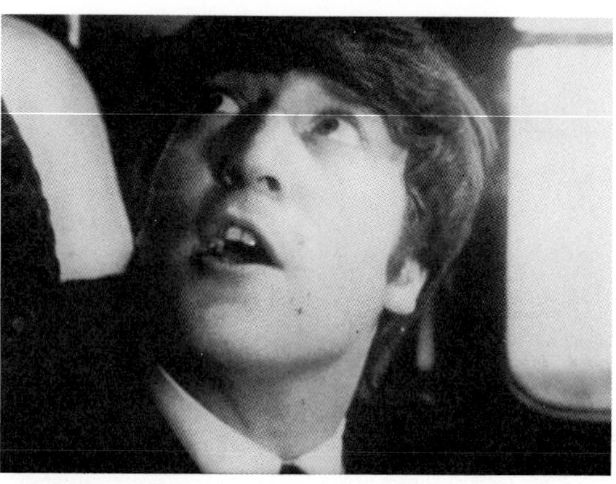

63
CU
LA

**Italicized dialogue in parentheses indicates material added to the original script and thus included in the finished film.

64
MCU
NA

65
FS
LA

At this moment, SHAKE, a tall man who works with the BOYS, pulls open the door of the compartment.

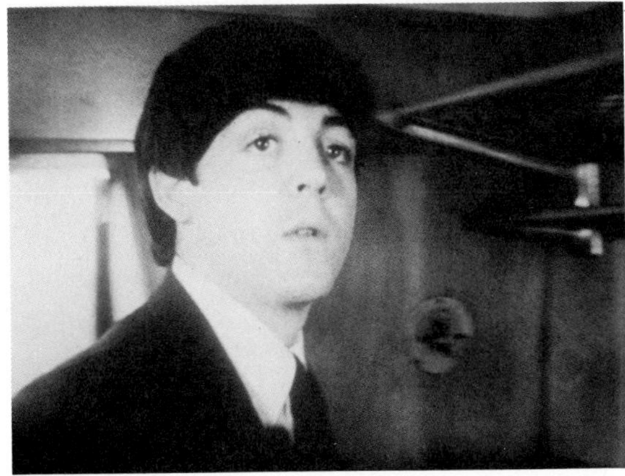

66
MCU
LA
PL

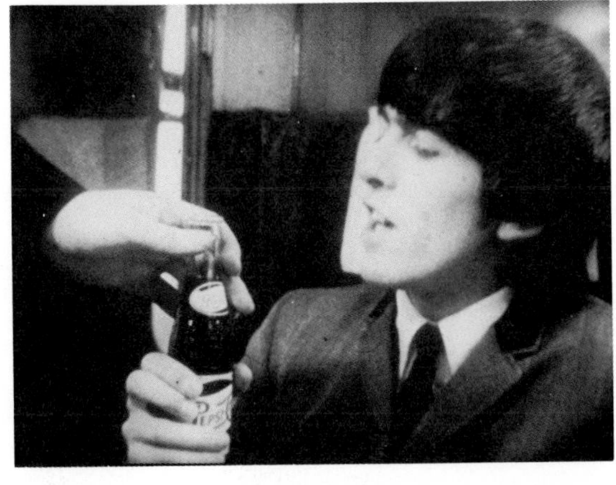

67
MCU
LA

BOYS: Hi, Shake.

68
MCU
LA

SHAKE: You got on alright then?

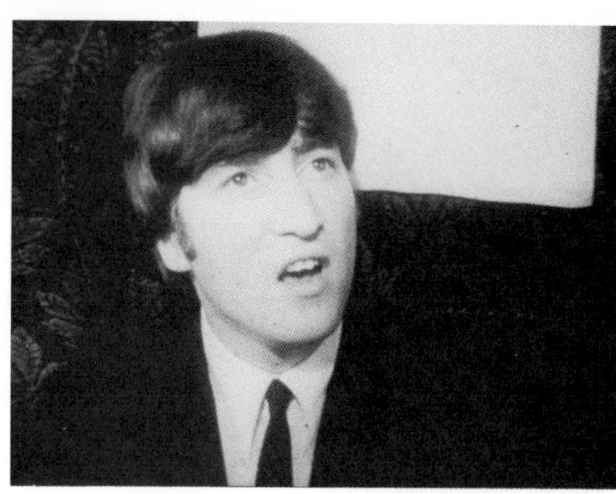
69 MCU LA

(JOHN: No.)

70 MCU LA

SHAKE: We're here.

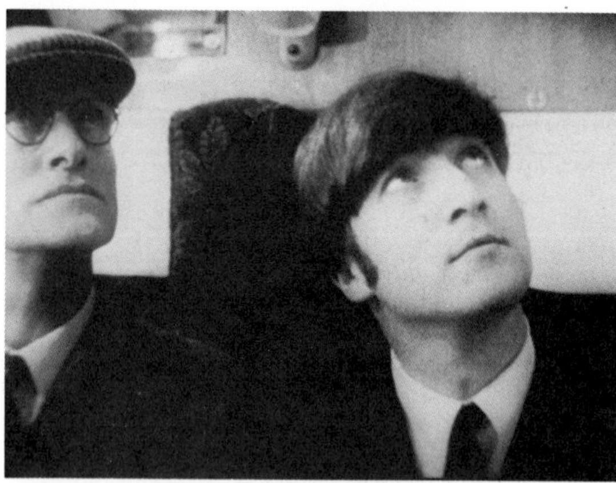
71 MCU LA

—Norm'll be along in a mo' with the tickets.

72 MCU LA

He sees GRANDFATHER.

SHAKE: Who's that little old man?

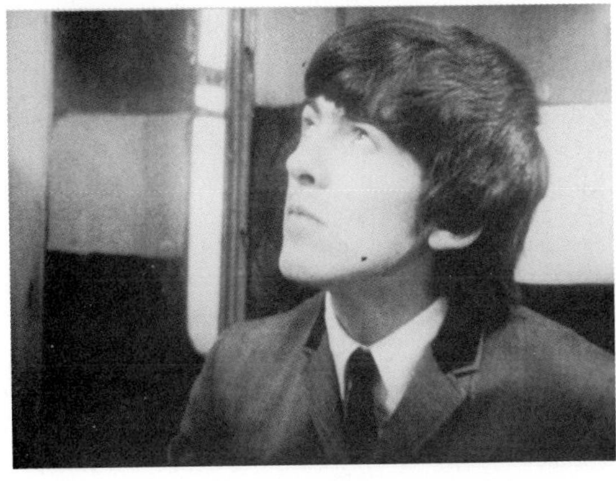

73
MCU
LA

GEORGE: Paul's grandfather.

74
MCU
LA

SHAKE: Oh aye, but I thought . . .

75
MCU
LA

JOHN: (cutting in) No, that's his other one.

76
MCU
LA

SHAKE: That's alright then.

JOHN: (displaying Grandfather) Clean though, isn't he?

77
MCU
LA

SHAKE: Oh yes, he's clean alright.

78
MCU
LA

NORM the road manager appears behind SHAKE.

NORM: Morning, lads.

79
MCU
LA

BOYS: Morning . . . Hi, Norm.

NORM: (checking them quickly) Well, thank God you're all here. Now, listen, I've had this marvellous idea . . . now just for a change, let's all behave —

80
FS
LA

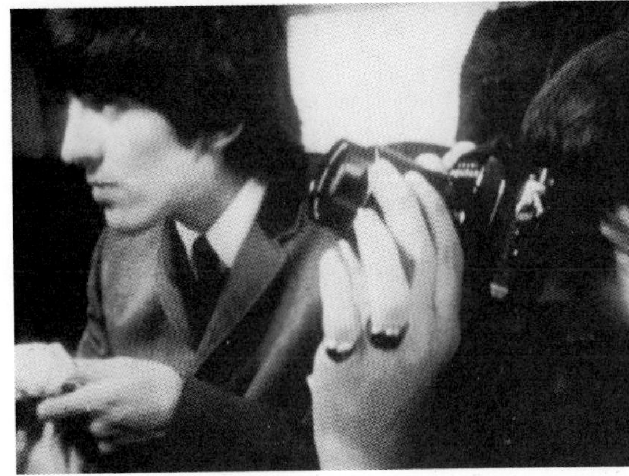

81
MCU
LA

—like ordinary responsible citizens. Let's not cause any trouble,—

82
MCU
LA

—pull any strokes or do anything I'm going to be sorry for, especially tomorrow at the T.V. theatre, because . . .

83
FS
LA

He looks sharply at JOHN who is [polishing his nails.] (sniffing a bottle of Coke). Are you listening to me, Lennon?

84
MCU
LA

85
MCU
LA

JOHN: (off-hand) You're a swine, isn't he George?

GEORGE: (disinterested) Yeah . . . a swine.

86
MCU
LA

87
FS
LA

NORM: (just as indifferent) Thanks.

He sees the GRANDFATHER.

NORM: Eh . . .

88
MCU
LA

BOYS IN CHORUS: . . . Who's that

89
MCU
LA

— little old —

90
MCU
LA

— man?

91 MCU LA

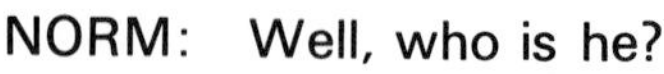

NORM: Well, who is he?

92 MCU LA

RINGO: He belongs to Paul.

93 MCU LA

NORM: (accepting the situation) Ah well, there you go. Look, I'm going down the diner for a cup of coffee, are you coming?

94 MCU LA

PAUL: We'll follow you down.

95
FS
LA

GRANDFATHER rises.

GRANDFATHER: I want me coffee.

NORM: He can come with Shake and me if you like?

PAUL: Well, look after him.—

96
MCU
LA

—I don't want to find you've lost him.

97
MCU
LA

NORM: Don't be cheeky, I'll bind him to me with promises. Come on, Grandad.

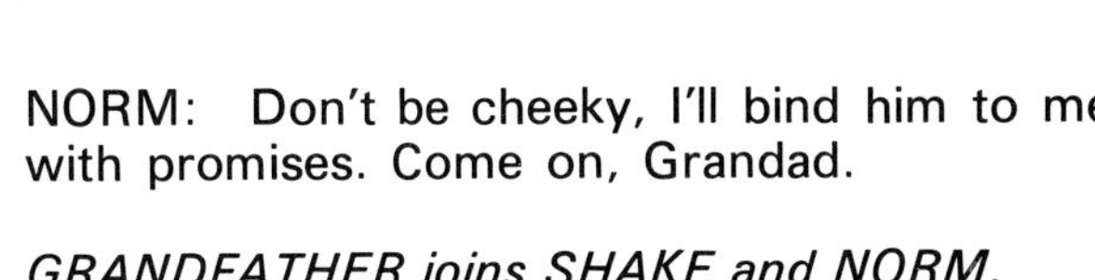

GRANDFATHER joins SHAKE and NORM.

NORM: (over Grandfather's head) He's very clean, isn't he? Come on Grandad.

98
(MS-TI
3/4 S
NA

SHAKE and NORM collect GRANDFATHER and are in the process of leaving the compartment when an upper class city Englishman, JOHNSON, attempts to enter. There is a bit of confusion and they get tangled up with each other.

JOHNSON: Make up your minds, will you!

At last SHAKE, NORM and GRANDFATHER sort themselves out and JOHNSON enters with his case. The other three go to coffee. JOHNSON puts his case up on the luggage rack, then sits down. All his movements are disgruntled . . . he finally picks up his copy of the Financial Times *and burying himself behind it, starts to read.*

99
MCU
LA

100
MCU
LA

101A
MCU
LA

101B
MCU
LA

102
MCU
LA

(PAUL: Morning.

103
MCU
LA

BOYS: All right.)

104
MS
LA

105
MCU
LA

106
MS
LA

After a moment he looks up, notices the compartment window is open. He gets up and without so much as a "by your leave" he closes it, glares at the BOYS and sits down again. The BOYS exchange looks as if to say . . . "Hello, Saucy!!"

107
MCU
LA

108
MS
LA
PDR to MCU

109
MS
LA

(RINGO: Woah!)

110A
MCU
LA

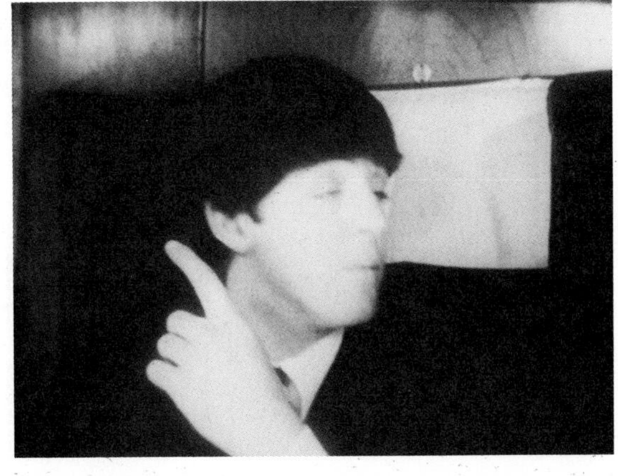

PAUL: (politely) Do you mind if we have it opened?

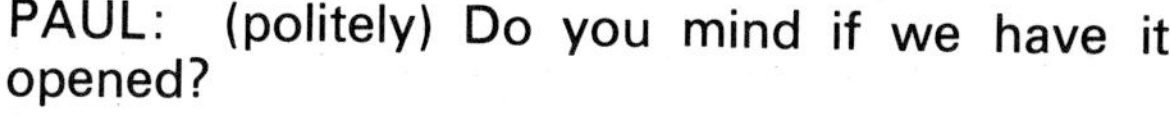

PR to . . .
110B
MCU
LA

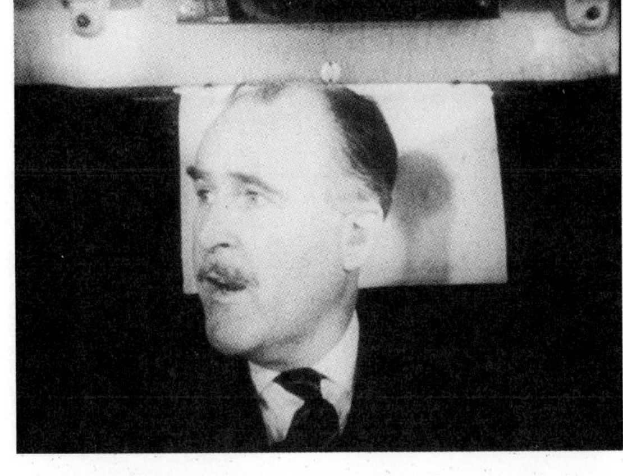

JOHNSON: (briefly) Yes, I do.

PR to . . .
110C
MCU
LA

JOHN: Yeah, but there are four of us, like, and we like it open, if it's all the same to you, that is.

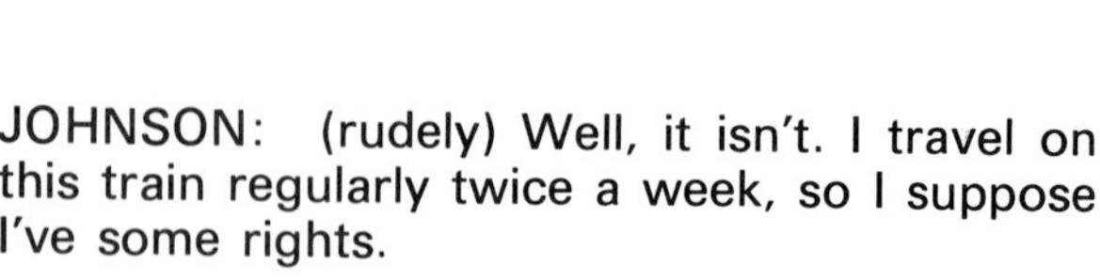

JOHNSON: (rudely) Well, it isn't. I travel on this train regularly twice a week, so I suppose I've some rights.

111
MCU
LA

RINGO: Aye, well, so have we.

112
MS
LA

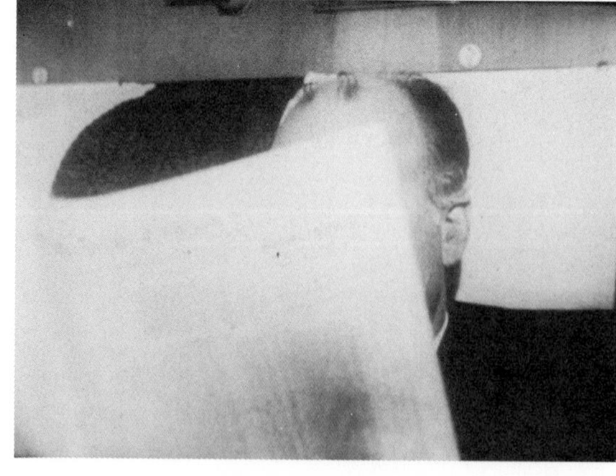

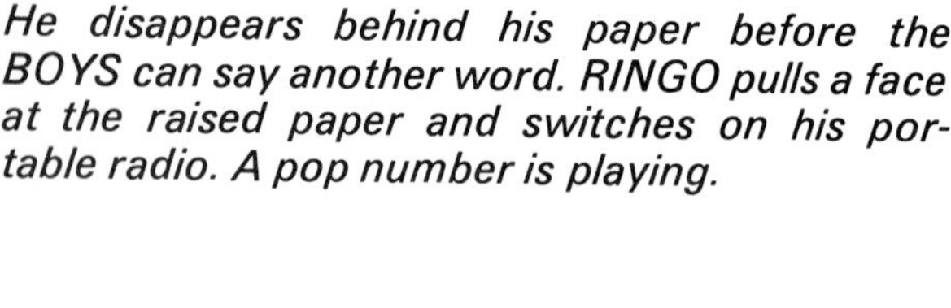

He disappears behind his paper before the BOYS can say another word. RINGO pulls a face at the raised paper and switches on his portable radio. A pop number is playing.

113
MCU
LA

114
(PD)
MS
LA

115A
MCU
LA

JOHNSON puts down his paper firmly.

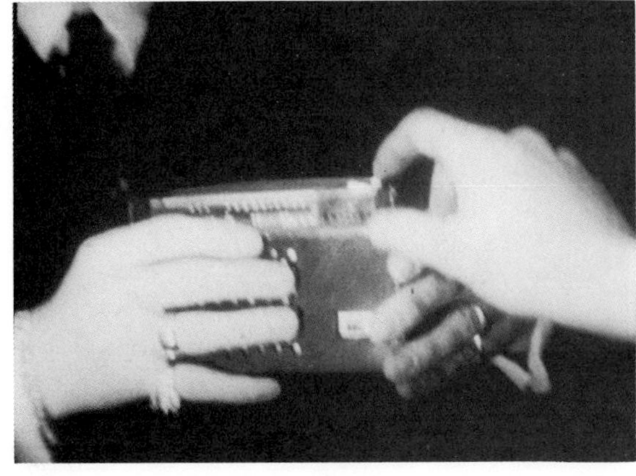

116A
CU
LA
PLU to . . .

JOHNSON: And we'll have that thing off as well, thank you.

JOHNSON leans over and switches it off.

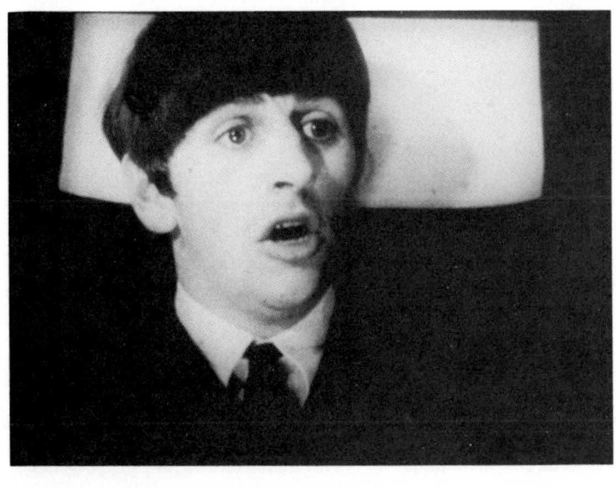

116B
MCU
LA

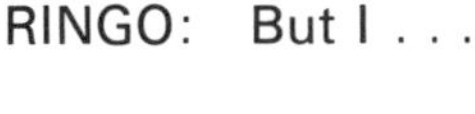

RINGO: But I . . .

117
CU
LA

JOHNSON: An elementary knowledge of the Railway Acts would tell you I'm perfectly within my rights.

He smiles frostily.

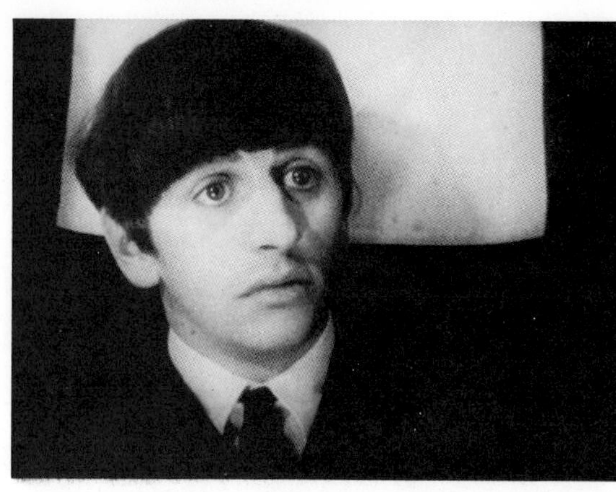

118A
MCU
LA
PL to . . .

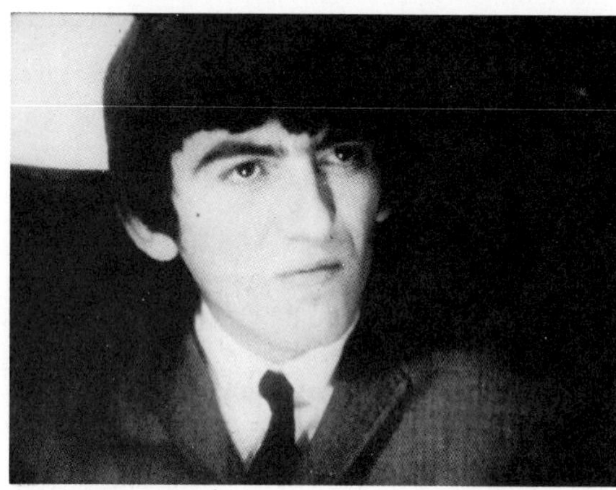

118B
MCU
LA

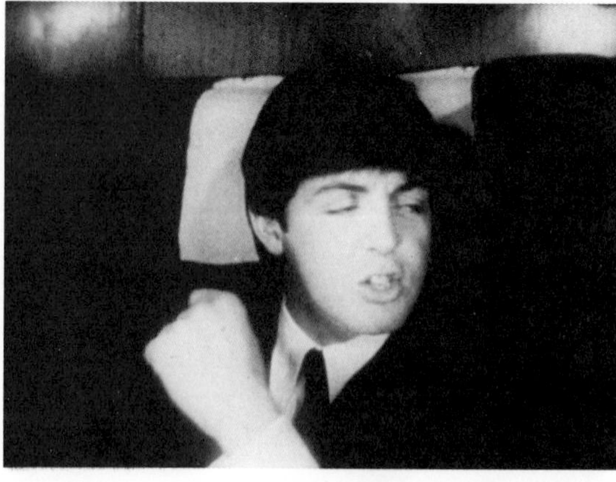

119A
MCU
LA
PR to . . .

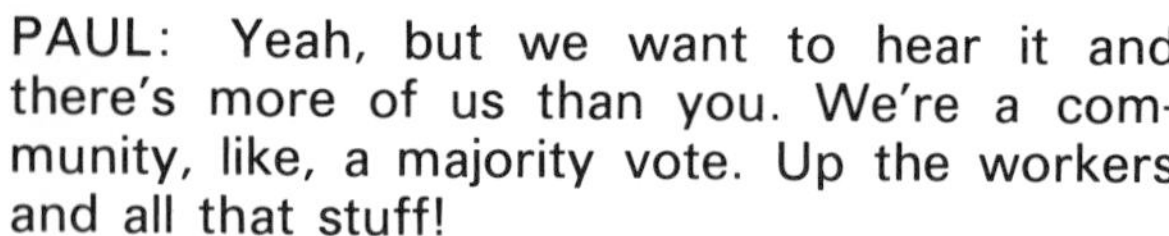

PAUL: Yeah, but we want to hear it and there's more of us than you. We're a community, like, a majority vote. Up the workers and all that stuff!

119B
MCU
LA
PR to . . .

JOHNSON: Then I suggest you take that damned thing into the corridor or some other part of the train where you obviously belong.

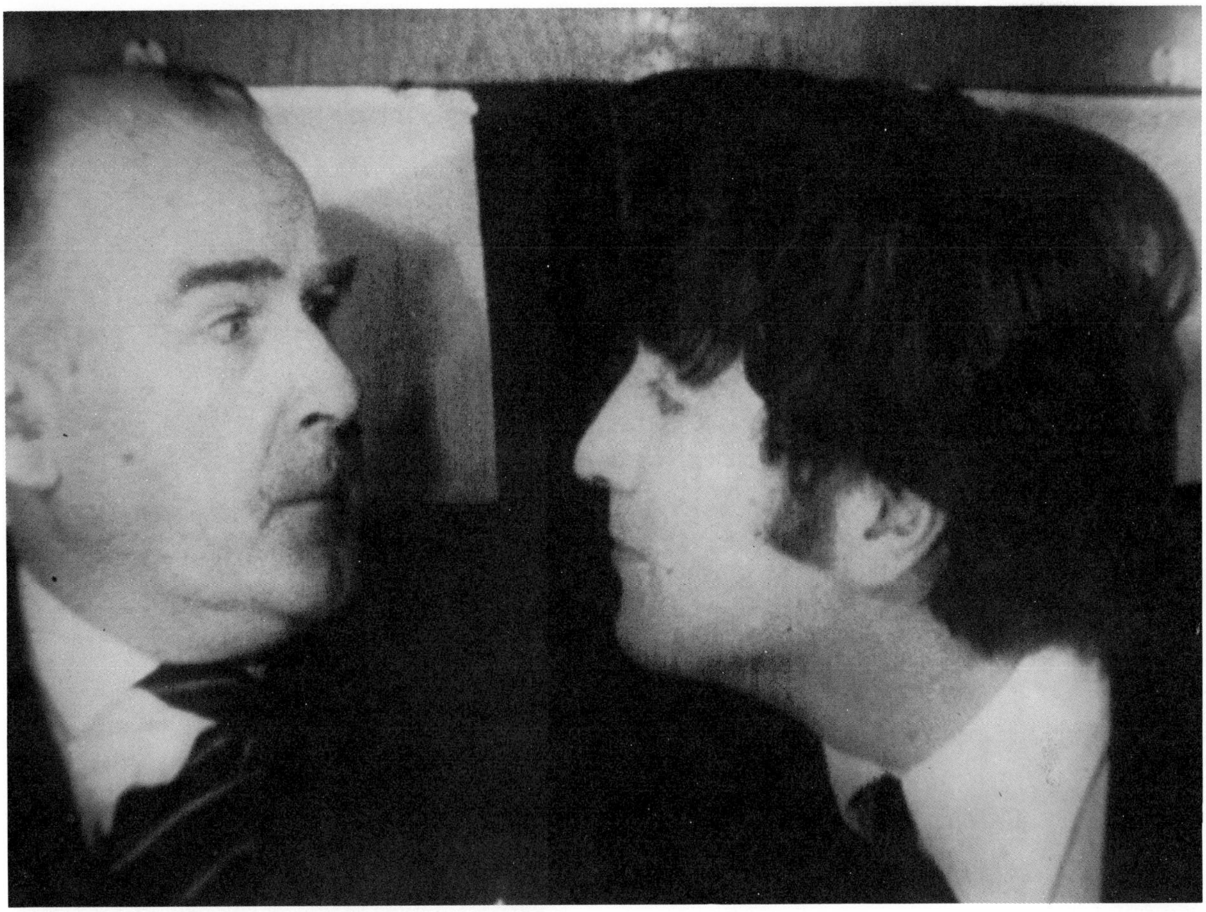

119C
MCU
LA

JOHN: (leaning forward to him) Gie's a kiss!

120A
MCU
LA
PR to . . .

PAUL: Look, Mister, we've paid for our seats too, you know.

120B
MCU
LA
PR to . . .

JOHNSON: I travel on this train regularly, twice a week.

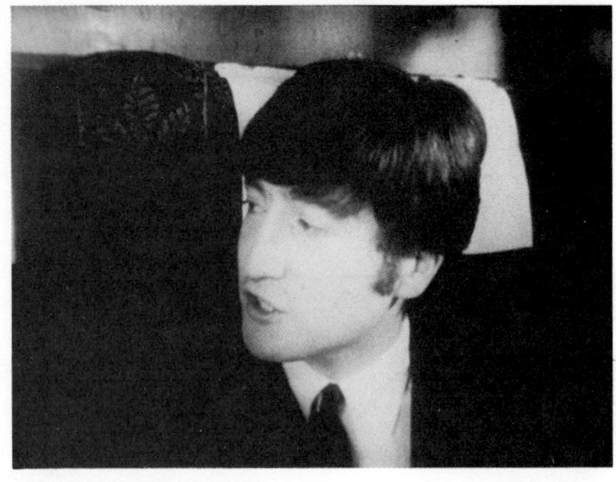

JOHN: Knock it off, Paul, y' can't win with his sort. After all, it's his train, isn't it, Mister?

120C
MCU
LA

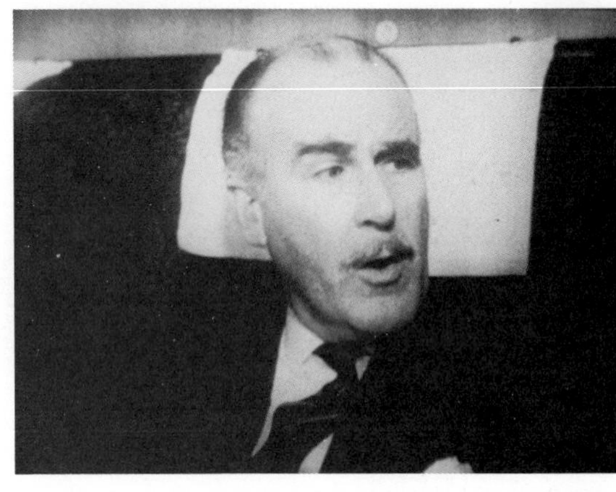

JOHNSON: And don't you take that tone with me, young man!

[GEORGE: But . . .]

JOHNSON: (accusingly) I fought the war for your sort.

121
MCU
LA

RINGO: Bet you're sorry you won!

122
MS
LA

JOHNSON: I'll call the guard!

PAUL: Aye . . . but what? They don't take kindly to insults. Ah, come on, you lot. Let's get a cup of coffee and leave the kennel to Lassie.

123
FS
LA

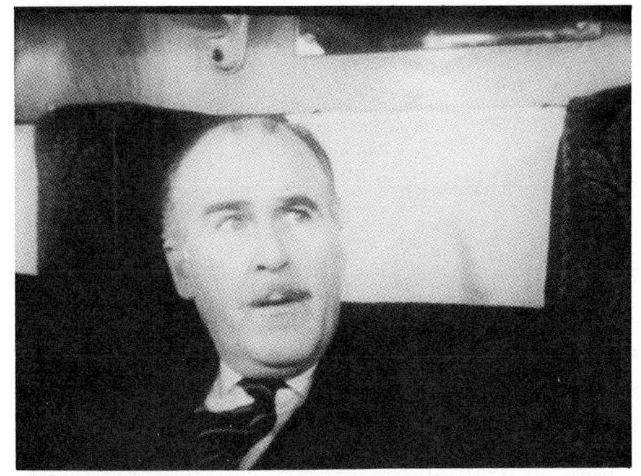

124
MCU
LA

The BOYS troop out of the door into the corridor. JOHNSON smiles triumphantly. He is about to settle down to his paper when there is a tap on the corridor window. He looks up and we see pressed against the window a collection of hideous Beatle faces.

125
FS
LA

126
MCU
LA

PAUL: Eh, Mister . . . can we have our ball back!

[*The man jumps to his feet.*]

(BOYS: Hey Mister . . . can we have our ball back!)

127
LS
LA

[*INTERIOR, TRAIN CORRIDOR*

The BOYS run away like a pack of school boys and disappear round the corner.]

128
MCU
LA

[*INTERIOR, TRAIN CORRIDOR*

From the P.O.V. of the door leading to the restaurant car.

The BOYS come down the corridor in full flight, laughing away like happy idiots. GEORGE and PAUL pull open the sliding doors. The BOYS look inside.]

INTERIOR, RESTAURANT CAR

From their P.O.V. we see the car is half empty and at a table in the centre SHAKE and NORM and GRANDFATHER are sitting. On the table is a pile of photos of the BOYS. NORM and SHAKE are arguing. NORM is being very aggressive, much to SHAKE's discomfort.

129
LS to MS
LA

NORM: Yeah, you want to watch it.

SHAKE: (unhappily) It's not my fault.

NORM: Well, you stick to that story, son.

SHAKE: I can't help it, I'm just taller than you.

GRANDFATHER: (to NORM slyly) They always say that.

130
MS
NA

131
MCU
LA

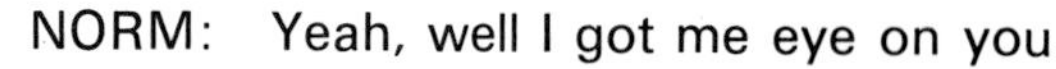

NORM: Yeah, well I got me eye on you.

132
MCU
LA

SHAKE: I'm sorry Norm, but I can't help being taller than you.

133
MCU
LA

NORM: Well, you don't have to rub me nose in it.

134
FS
NA

I've a good mind to . . . (He is about to thump SHAKE.)

JOHN: (enjoying himself) If you're going to have a barney I'll hold your coats.

NORM: He started it.

SHAKE: No, I didn't you did . . .

GEORGE: Well, what happened?

SHAKE: The old fella wanted these pictures and Norm said he couldn't have 'em, all I said was "aw go on, be big about it."

135
MCU
LA

PAUL: And?

NORM: Your grandfather

136
MCU
LA

—pointed out Shake was always being taller than me to spite me.

137
MCU
LA

PAUL: I knew it *he* started it,

138
MCU
LA

139
MCU
LA

—I should have known.

NORM: Y'what?

140
MCU
LA

PAUL: You two have never had a quarrel in your life

141
MCU
LA

—and in two minutes flat he's got you at it.—

142
MCU
LA

—He's a king mixer. [Adam and Eve, meet the serpent. Anthony and Cleopatra, there's your asp. Divide and Conquer, that's this one's motto.]—

—He hates group unity so he gets everyone at it.

143
MCU
LA

The BOYS, i.e. JOHN, GEORGE and RINGO, look at each other then at PAUL.

[PAUL: Aye and we'll have to watch it and all.]

GEORGE: I suggest you give him the photos and have done with it.

144
MCU
LA

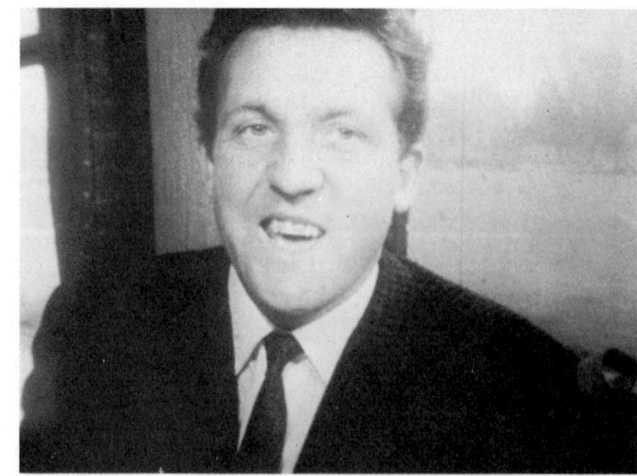

NORM: You're right, here you are old devil.

145
MCU
LA

SHAKE and NORM leave. GRANDFATHER grins triumphantly and collects them, then with a sweet smile he turns to PAUL.

GRANDFATHER: Would you ever sign this one for us, Pauly?

(NORM: Oh, come on Shake.)

146
FS
NA

147 MS LA

PAUL does so automatically but in the middle of signing he gets suspicious. GRANDFATHER smiles at him charmingly so PAUL finishes signing.

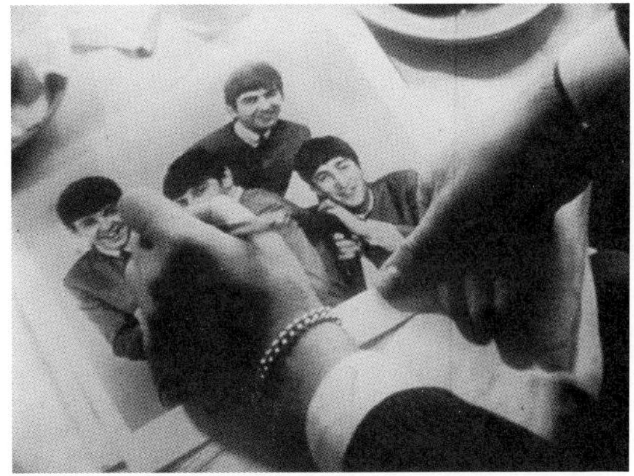

148 CU NA

[JOHN: Come on let's get this coffee.

GRANDFATHER: Before you go, I think it's only fair to warn you about me grandson . . . don't let our Paul have his own way all the time, 'cos if you do he won't respect you!]

[*JOHN, RINGO and GEORGE take this up straight away. They all pretend to be girls, RINGO jumps into PAUL's arms.*]

[GEORGE: (coyly) Oh, Paul, you can't have your own way!

JOHN: (invitingly, in a Marlene Dietrich voice) If I let you have your own way, you little rascal, will you respect me?

PAUL: (choked) I'll murder you, Grandfather!]

[*JOHN waltzes PAUL down to an empty table and the lads sit down.*]

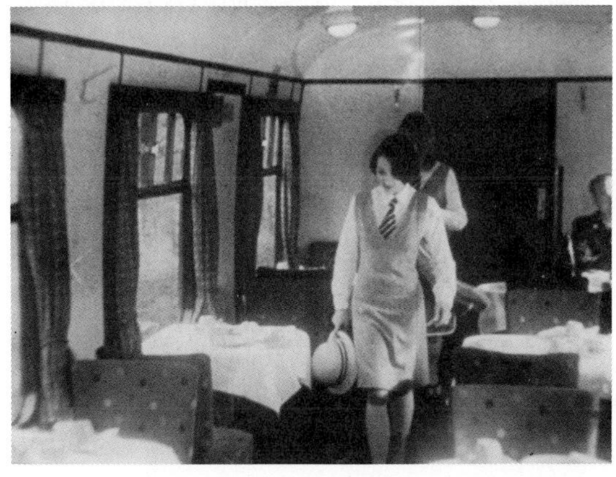

149 (PL) LS NA

GEORGE: Eh, look at that talent.

150 MCU NA

They all gaze across the aisle. From their P.O.V. we see two very attractive young girls, RITA and JEAN, having coffee.

JOHN: Give 'em a pull.

PAUL: Shall I?

GEORGE: Aye, but don't rush. None of your five bar gate jumps and over sort of stuff.

PAUL: Now what's that mean?

GEORGE: (grinning) I don't really know, but it sounded distinguished, like, didn't it?

JOHN: George Harrison, The Scouse of Distinction.

151
MCU
NA
(PR)

152
3/4 S
NA

We follow PAUL as he crosses over to the two girls. He places a bowler on his head.

PAUL: Excuse me, madame. (in posh accent) Excuse me, but these young men I'm sitting with wondered if two of us could join you; I'd ask you meself only I'm shy.

The two girls giggle together. JOHN and GEORGE are about to move over when GRANDFATHER suddenly appears by their sides.

GRANDFATHER: (sternly) I'm sorry, Miss, but you mustn't fraternise with my prisoners.

153
MS
LA

154
MS
LA

JEAN: Prisoners!!

GRANDFATHER: Convicts in transit to Wormwood Scrubs.

155
MS
LA

Typical old lags, the lot of 'em.

THE BOYS: Y'what!!!

[GRANDFATHER: Quiet, you lot, or I'll give you a touch of me truncheon. (He points at Ringo.) That little one's the worst. If we don't keep him on tablets he has fits.]

[RINGO: (protesting) Now look here!!]

[*GRANDFATHER grabs two lumps of sugar from the table and forces them into RINGO's mouth.*]

156
MS
LA

GRANDFATHER: Get out while you can, ladies, [his time's coming round for one of his turns.]

The girls scurry out of the restaurant car. We are not sure if they recognised the BOYS who look in amazement and horror at GRANDFATHER. They are completely flabbergasted. [*GRANDFATHER smiles at them benignly.*]

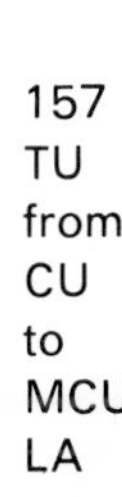

157
TU
from
CU
to
MCU
LA

INTERIOR, TRAIN COMPARTMENT

SHAKE and NORM are seated. SHAKE is buried in a [*science fiction book*] Mad magazine. *NORM looks at his watch, slightly worried.*

NORM: He's been gone a long time.

SHAKE: (without looking up) Who?

NORM: Paul's grandfather.

SHAKE: Oh, I didn't notice, where'd he go?

NORM: Down the . . . er . . .

SHAKE: Oh, down the . . . er . . .?

NORM: Yeah, down the . . . er . . .

SHAKE: Well, give a couple of minutes . . .

He resumes reading. But NORM goes on worrying.

158 LS NA TR

[*INTERIOR, ANOTHER TRAIN COMPARTMENT*

GRANDFATHER is in full flight of conversation with a charming elderly lady, AUDREY, who is listening intently.]

[GRANDFATHER: (proudly) Yes, I'm their manager, I discovered them.

AUDREY: Did you indeed, Mr. McCartney?

GRANDFATHER: Now, Audrey, I told you, the name's John. We show biz people are a friendly lot.

AUDREY: Of course.

GRANDFATHER: Yes, they were playing the queues outside the picture palaces of Liverpool. Scruffy young lads, lacking even the price of a jam roll. Orphans, every Paddy's son of 'em. I saw their potential at once although I had me doubts about the little fella, a savage primitive, that Ringo, but it was him what gave in first. He picked up a brick and heaved it at me and I quelled him wid one fierce flash of me eyes. "Mister, can you spare us a penny copper?" he said. I was disarmed by the grubby little outstretched mauler . . . So, I took them under me managerial banner.

AUDREY: The usual ten per cent?

GRANDFATHER: Oh, not at all, I let them have twenty-five; sure aren't there four of them?

AUDREY: (her eyes lighting up) How fascinating. Do go on . . . (pause) . . . John.

GRANDFATHER: Oh, I'm all heart, Ma'am, all heart . . . Well, I let . . .]

159 MS LA

INTERIOR, TRAIN CORRIDOR

NORM and SHAKE meet with the BOYS as they are returning from coffee.

NORM: Eh, have you got Paul's grandfather?

JOHN: Of course, he's concealed about me person.

NORM: No . . . he's slipped off somewhere.

PAUL: (accusingly) Have *you* lost him?

NORM: Don't exaggerate.

PAUL: You've lost him.

SHAKE: Put it this way, he's mislaid him.

PAUL: You can't trust you with anything, Norm. If you've lost him, I'll cripple you.

SHAKE: He can't be far.

[JOHN: I hope he fell off.

PAUL: (mildly) Don't be callous.]

(NORM: Come lads, lets look up the sharp end.

160
MS
NA

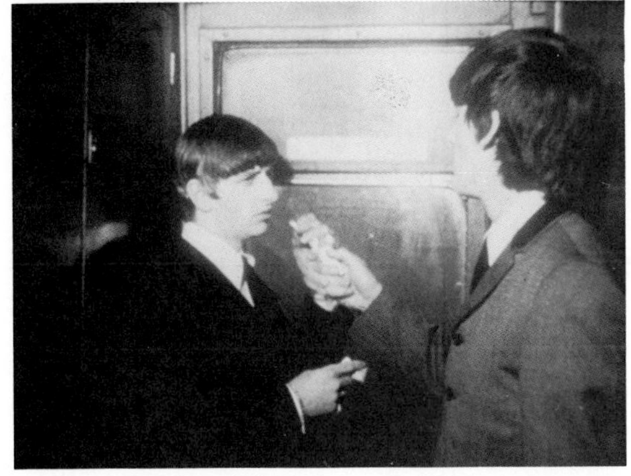

GEORGE: What's the matter with you, then.)

RINGO: His grandfather doesn't like me, honest, I can tell . . . it's 'cos I'm little.

GEORGE: You've got an inferiority complex, you have.

RINGO: Yeah, I know, that's why I took up the drums. It's me active compensatory factor.

161
MS
LA
(TO)

JOHN and PAUL run down the corridor. SHAKE and NORM turn from the door and go in the opposite direction, GEORGE and RINGO follow after the other two BOYS.

162
LS
to
MS
LA

INTERIOR, TRAIN CORRIDOR

PAUL and JOHN look into various compartments. CLOSE SHOT of RINGO looking into compartments in the manner of Groucho Marx.

163
MS
LA
(PU)

In one of the compartments we see from RINGO's P.O.V. the occupant, a glamorous woman, TANIA, with a small lap dog. She is beautifully and most expensively dressed. She looks up and sees RINGO. RINGO smiles at her and she smiles back. She then beckons him to join her. He looks around to see if she means someone else. She nods a negative. RINGO looks back enquiringly then points at himself as if to say: "Who, me?". TANIA smiles enthusiastically. GEORGE has been watching all this.

164
MS
HA

165
MS
LA

166
MCU
NA

167
3/4 S
LA

GEORGE: Are you going in, then?

RINGO: No, she'll only reject me in the end and I'll be frustrated.

GEORGE: You never know, you might be lucky this time.

RINGO: No, I know the psychological pattern and it plays hell with me drum skins.

He blows the glamorous lady a kiss then moves sadly on.

168
MCU
NA

169
MS
LA

170
(PL)
FS
HA

INTERIOR, FURTHER DOWN THE CORRIDOR

PAUL enters a compartment followed by JOHN.

The two girls, RITA and JEAN, from the restaurant car are sitting there.

PAUL: Excuse me but have you seen that little old man we were with?

The girls jump up, surprised.

JOHN: We've broken out, oh, the blessed freedom of it all! (He extends his hands as if handcuffed.) Eh, have you got a nail file

171
MCU
LA

—these handcuffs are killing me.

PAUL: Will you stop it!

He starts to drag JOHN after him.

JOHN: I was innocent, I was framed, I won't go back.

(PAUL: Sorry for disturbing you, girls.)

JOHN is now by the door, he leers at the girls horribly.

JOHN: I bet you can guess what I was in for.

He cackles like a maniac before disappearing, the door closing after him.

A waiter carrying a tray with champagne and glasses on it passes into one of the compartments with the blinds down.

[PAUL: How about that one?]

PAUL moves towards the compartment.

PAUL: (to Ringo and George) Should we go in here?

JOHN: No. I mean, it's probably a honeymoon couple or a company director or something.

PAUL: Well, I'm going to broaden my outlook.

PAUL opens the door of the compartment.

172
MS-LS
LA

173A
FS
NA
ZI to . . .

173B
CU
NA

INTERIOR, TRAIN COMPARTMENT

From the BOYS' P.O.V. we see GRANDFATHER and the elderly lady, AUDREY, sipping champagne and nibbling caviar on toast.

GRANDFATHER: (looking up) Congratulate me, boys, I'm engaged.

PAUL enters and crosses over to him.

PAUL: Oh no you're not.

174A
MCU
NA
DK
ZO to .

Not this time.

—[You've gone too far this time . . . and who's paying for all this?]—

[GRANDFATHER: It's all taken care of. It's down on our bill.

PAUL: Oh, well that's alright (Realising) What?

AUDREY: Young man, kindly moderate your tone when you address my fiancee.

PAUL: I'm sorry, Missus, but the betrothal's off. (He grabs Grandfather by the arm.) I'll refuse me consent, he's over-age!]

[*AUDREY grabs GRANDFATHER's other arm and pulls back.*]

[AUDREY: Leave him alone, after all he's done for you is this the way you repay him.]

[*A tug of war now starts between PAUL and AUDREY.*]

[PAUL: (pulling) Him? He's never done anything for anybody in his life.

AUDREY: (pulling) You dare to say that when even those ridiculous clothes you are wearing were bought when you forced him to sell out his gilt edged Indomitables!!]

[*JOHN and GEORGE jump on the seat egging PAUL and AUDREY on.*]

[JOHN: Come on, auntie, you're winning.

GEORGE: Get in there, Paul, she's weakening.]

[*RINGO attempts to interfere.*]

RINGO: Look, Missus, this is all a misunderstanding, you see, he's . . .

AUDREY: Keep away from me, you depraved lout, I know all about your terrible past.

RINGO: Y'what?

[*She hits RINGO with her handbag and continues struggling with PAUL for GRANDFATHER. RINGO grabs her handbag to stop her from hitting him.*]

[RINGO: He's given me a bad character, blackguarding me name to all and sundry. He's got to be stopped. It's not fair.]

[*RINGO pushes out into the corridor, forgetting that he is holding the woman's handbag. A voice shouts off from outside.*]

[VOICE OFF: That's one of them . . . stop thief!]

[*INTERIOR, TRAIN CORRIDOR*

From RINGO's P.O.V. we see down to the right the city man, JOHNSON, approaching with a GUARD. RINGO turns the other way to the left when he is joined by three other BOYS. From their P.O.V. down the corridor we see the two girls, autograph books in hand, followed by ten girls from the same school.

Both groups are closing in on the BOYS. There is no escape.]

[RINGO: (looking down at the handbag in his hand) Oh Mother!!]

174B
FS
NA
DK
(PR)

INTERIOR, TRAIN LUGGAGE VAN

Very dark, and behind bars we see GRANDFATHER. He is sitting crouched up on a wooden box tea chest and looks pretty miserable. He turns towards the CAMERA; in the foreground of the SHOT we see PAUL standing. [In the background an impassive GUARD is reading a paper which he does throughout the scene.]

GRANDFATHER: (bitterly) And to think me own grandson would have let them put me behind bars!

PAUL: Don't dramatise.

The CAMERA PULLS BACK and we see GRANDFATHER in the luggage compartment of the guards' van. In with him are [a crate of chickens and] a dog. [The chickens peck at him, GRANDFATHER moves listlessly away.]

PAUL: Let's face it, you're lucky to be here. If they'd have had their way you'd have been dropped off at Stafford.

[*GRANDFATHER proudly turns away from PAUL, who dodges round so he can still see his face.*]

PAUL: Well, you've got to admit you've upset a lot of people.

175A
MCU
LA
DK

—At least I can keep my eye on you while you're stuck in here.

175B
MCU
LA
DK

[*GRANDFATHER turns away again.*]

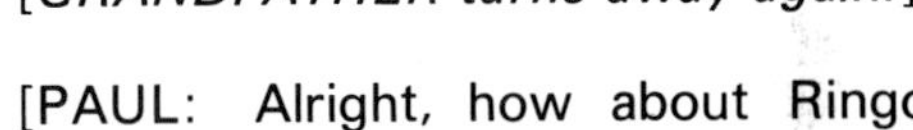

[PAUL: Alright, how about Ringo? I mean . . . he's very upset, you know . . . and as far as your girlfriend, little Audrey's concerned, she's finished with men for the rest of her natural, and another thing . . .

GRANDFATHER: (cutting in) You're left-handed, aren't you, Paul?

176
MCU
LA
DK

PAUL: Yeah . . . so what?

GRANDFATHER: Why do you always use your left hand?

PAUL: Well, don't be daft, I've got to.

GRANDFATHER: And I take a left handed view of life, I've got to.]

PAUL grins. After a moment of looking at him, PAUL opens the door of the luggage compartment and joins GRANDFATHER on a box.

177
(ZI)
MS
NA
DK

PAUL: Shove up!

GRANDFATHER produces a penny.

GRANDFATHER: Odds or evens?

PAUL sighs.

PAUL: Odds.

GRANDFATHER flips the coin.

The guards' van door opens and JOHN, GEORGE and RINGO come in,[*with them are the girls, RITA and JEAN.*]

178
MCU
LA
DK

JOHN: (as he sees PAUL behind the bars) Don't worry, son, we'll get you the best lawyer green stamps can buy.

PAUL: Oh, —

—it's a laugh a line with Lennon. (to Ringo) Anyroad up . . . It's all your fault.

179
(TR)
LS
NA
DK

RINGO: Me? Why?

(PAUL: Why not?)

[GEORGE: Bag-snatcher.

GRANDFATHER: That's right; convict without trial . . . Habeus corpus.

JOHN: (casually) Every morning.]

JOHN has been looking around the guards' van.

JOHN: Gaw, it's depressing in here, isn't it?—

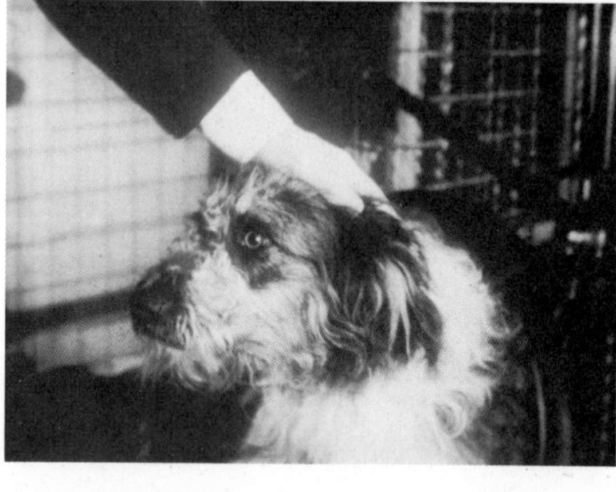

180
MCU
LA
DK

—Funny . . . (he pats the dog.) 'cos they usually reckon dogs more than people in England, don't they?—

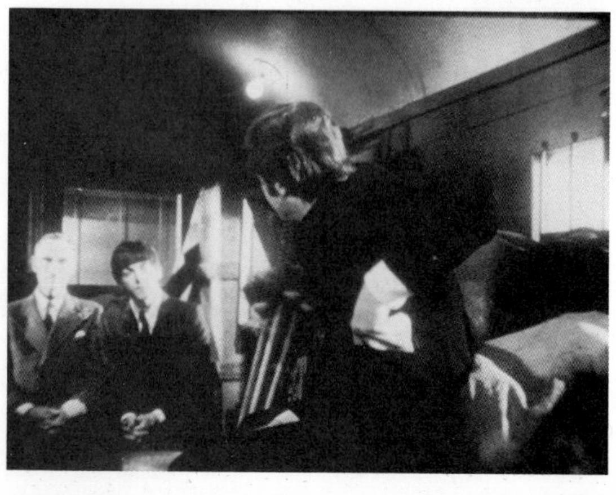

181
FS
LA
DK

—You'd expect something a little more palatial. (He shudders.) Let's do something, then.

PAUL: Like what?

[JOHN: Well, I've got me gob stopper. (He produces his mouth organ.) Look, a genuine Stradivarius, hand tooled at Birmingham.]

182
MCU
LA
DK

(JOHN: Mmm.

183
MCU
LA
DK

PAUL: Okay.

184
LS
NA
DK

GEORGE: God, it's the girls.

185
(PR + PU)
MCU
LA
DK

RINGO: I'll deal.

JOHN: Aye, aye, the Liverpool shuffle.)

Song: *"I Should Have Known Better"*

[*And to RINGO's beat on a tea chest they are off, PAUL and GEORGE improvising other sounds, much to the girls' delight. During the number, GRANDFATHER quietly lets the latch off the chicken crate and chickens begin to wander through the scene.*]

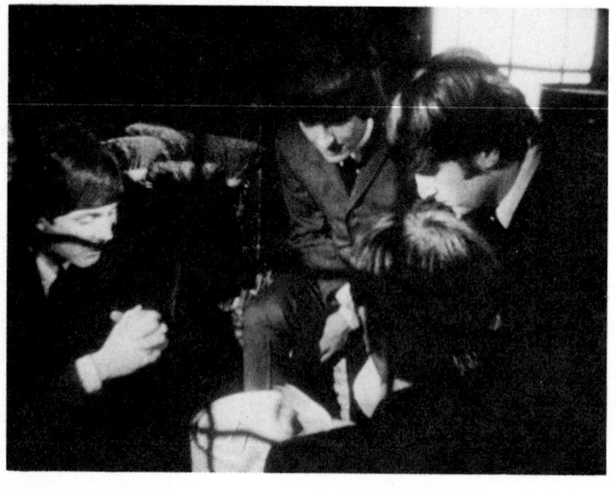

186
FS
NA
DK

187
MCU
NA
(PR)
DK

188
MCU
NA
DK

189
MCU
NA
DK

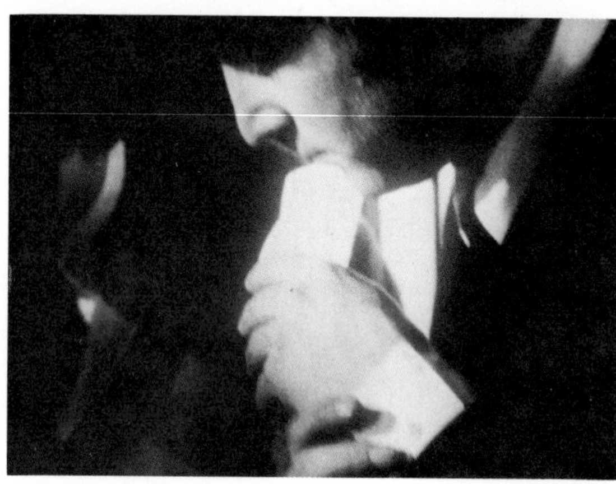

190
MCU
PD
to
CU
LA
DK

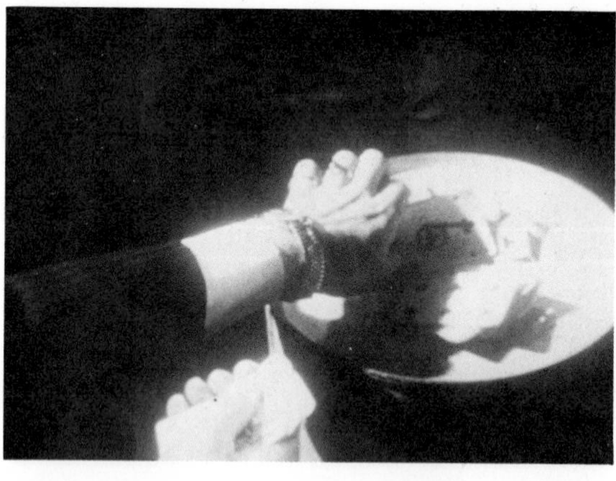

191
(PD)
MCU
NA
DK

192
CU
LA
DK

193
LS
NA
DK
(TR)

197
MS
LA
DK

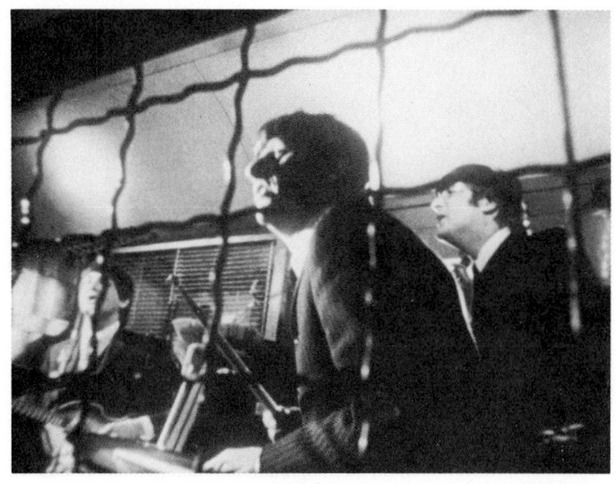

194
MS
LA
DK

198
CU
LA
DK

195
CU
LA
DK

199A
MCU
LA
DK
PL to . . .

196
MCU
LA
DK

199B
MCU
LA
DK

200
MCU-MS
LA
DK

204
CU
LA
DK

201
MCU
LA
DK

205
MC
LA
DK

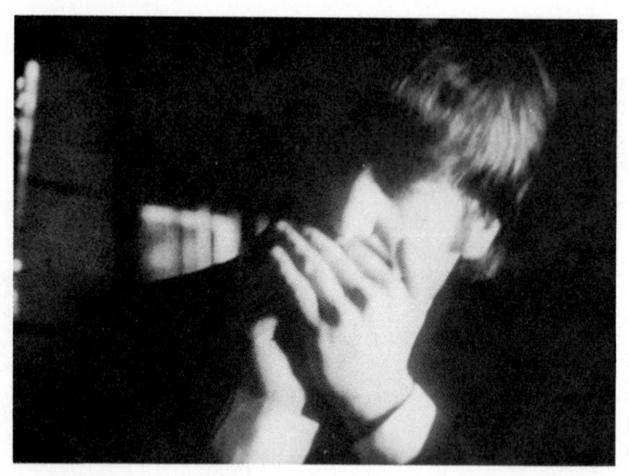

202
MCU
LA
DK

206
LS
NA
DK
(TR)

203
CU-MCU
LA
DK

207
CU
LA
DK

208
MCU
NA
DK

211B
CU
LA
DK

209
XCU
LA
DK

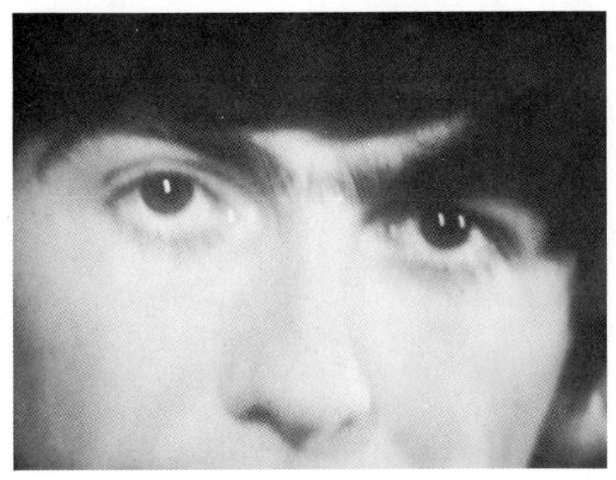

212
XCU
LA
DK

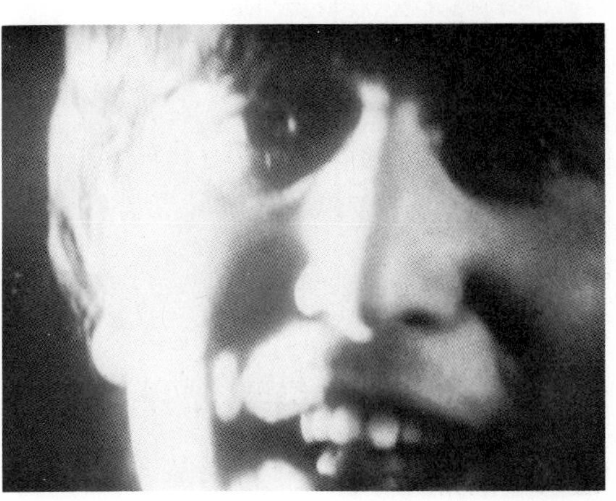

210
CU
LA
DK

213A
MCU
LA
DK
PU to

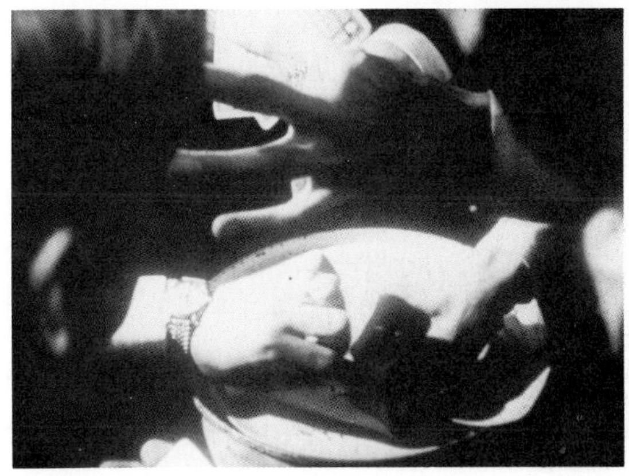

211A
MCU
LA
DK
(Focus Change)
to . . .

213B
MCU
LA
DK

214
MCU
LA
DK

215
MCU
LA
DK

(GEORGE: He's wearing his lucky rings.

RINGO: All mine!

JOHN: They can't buy you happiness, my son.)

216
MCU
LA
DK

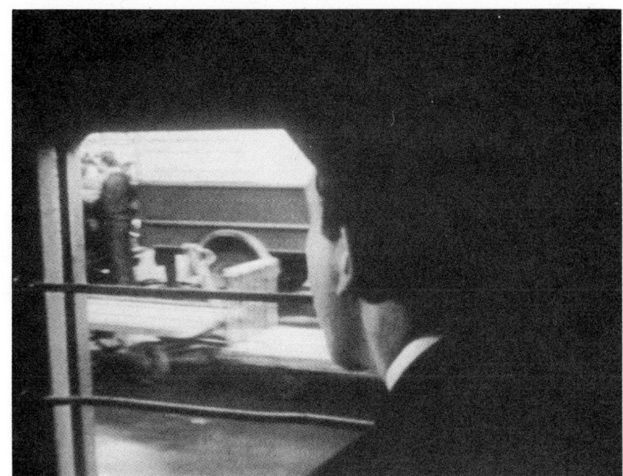

217
LS
NA

218
XLS
NA
(TI)

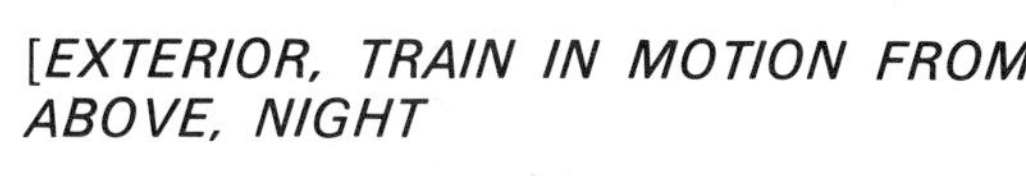

[EXTERIOR, TRAIN IN MOTION FROM ABOVE, NIGHT

While the number is progressing, the train is getting nearer and nearer to London.]

EXTERIOR, PLATFORM TERMINUS

SHOTS of the station full of GIRLS waiting for the BOYS.

219
LS
NA
DK

INTERIOR, GUARDS' VAN

[By the time the number finishes the train pulls up with a sharp halt that sends all the passengers sprawling, BOYS and girls.]

NORM enters the guards' van.

NORM: Don't move, any of you.

220
MCU
LA
DK

—They've gone potty out there. The whole place is surging with girls.

JOHN: Please, can I have one to surge with?

[NORM: No.

JOHN: Ah, go on, you swine.]

221
MCU
LA
DK

NORM: No, you can't. Look, as soon as I tell you, run through this door

222
MCU
LA
DK

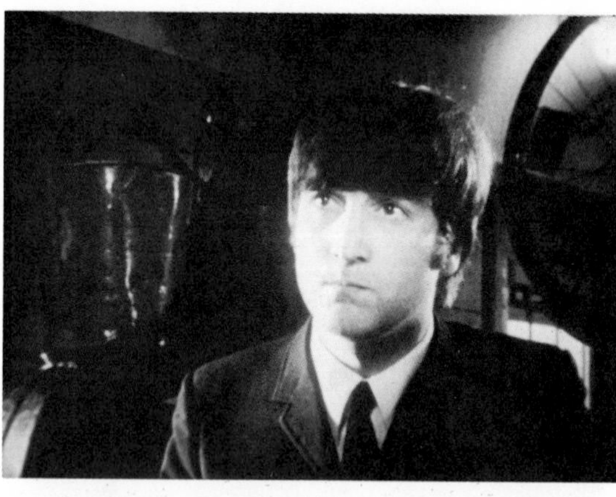

—and into the big car that's waiting.

223
MCU
LA
DK

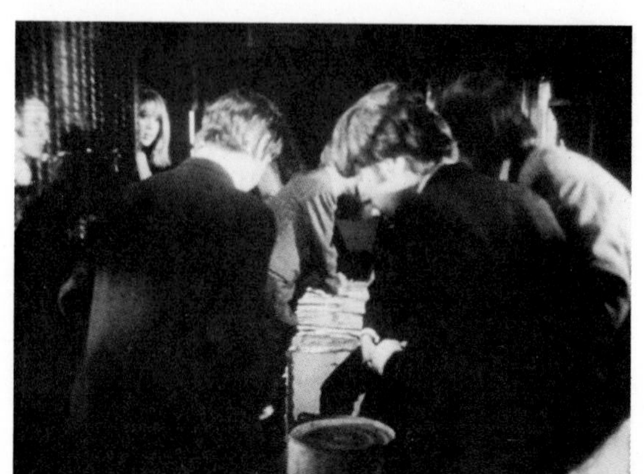

He points and we see a big car parked across the road. The BOYS prepare to depart, lining up with GRANDFATHER at the door.

224
FS
NA
DK

225A
LS
NA
(P. O. V.)
TI to . . .

225B
LS
NA

EXTERIOR, PLATFORM TERMINUS

Just as they are ready to go a line of taxis draws up parallel to the train and now separates them from the big car waiting for them.

[NORM: Oh no!]

[*GRANDFATHER pushes past the BOYS, holding his coat closed.*]

226
XLS
NA

227
MS
NA

(NORM: Come on lads, come on.)

[GRANDFATHER: Alright, lads, follow me.]

[*And before NORM can stop him, he darts out of the door, PAUL after him. The fans further down the platform see PAUL and charge forward . . . in a panic NORM and the others follow, JOHN just having time to kiss both the girls.*]

[JOHN: Vive l'amour!]

[*NORM drags him away.*]

228
XLS
HA

229A
MS
NA
DK
PR to . . .

EXTERIOR, RAILWAY STATION

[*The BOYS manage to follow GRANDFATHER by leaping onto a motorized luggage carrier, GEORGE driving and the other three posing as a frozen tableau on the back.*] *GRANDFATHER has arrived at a taxi door. He flings it open and runs through, opening the other door, thus making a safe bridge to the car.*

The BOYS follow. They run towards GRANDFATHER's taxi. The FANS have followed the BOYS and we see streams of GIRLS piling through all the taxis [*one of which contains JOHNSON the city man, opening and shutting the doors to get through, much to the indignation of the TAXI DRIVERS.*]

229B
MS
NA
DK

[*INTERIOR, BIG CAR*

NORM is sitting in front with the DRIVER FRANK, the four BOYS and GRANDFATHER are squashed together in the back.]

[NORM: (to the driver) Go like the clappers, son!

FRANK: (smoothly) That was my entire intention, sir.]

[*EXTERIOR, RAILWAY STATION*

The car moves off surrounded by the FANS; from a height we see them converge on the car but it moves forcefully out of the station and off. It moves into the traffic in the main road and the journey to the hotel begins.]

230
XLS
HA

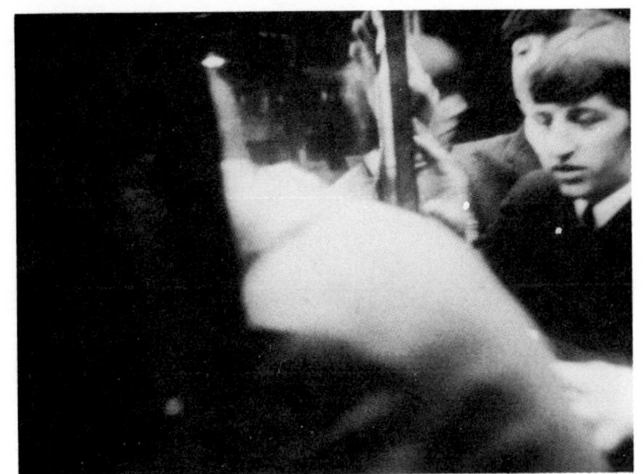
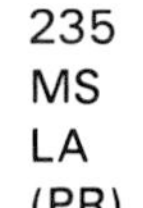

231
(PL)
MS
NA

235
MS
LA
(PR)

232
LS
LA

236
XLS
NA
(PR)

233
MS
LA

237
MS
NA

234
XLS
HA

238
LS
NA
(PR)

INTERIOR, HOTEL SUITE

There is a reception room and off it lead rooms that are presumably bedrooms, bathroom, etc. JOHN is lying sprawled out on a settee [listening to a transistor radio, demolishing a basket of fruit.] PAUL is sitting at an upright piano and GRANDFATHER is mooching about the room. One of the doors opens and GEORGE enters followed by RINGO, none of the BOYS are wearing coats.

239A
CU
NA
ZO to . . .

239B
MS
NA
PD + PL to . . .

RINGO: I don't snore.

GEORGE: You do—repeatedly.

239C
MS
NA
PL to . . .

RINGO: (to John) Do I snore?

JOHN: (eating a banana) You're a window rattler, son.

RINGO: Well that's just your opinion. Do I snore, Paul?

PAUL: (stopping playing) With a trombone hooter like yours it'ud be unnatural if you didn't.

239D
LS
NA

240
3/4 S
NA

GRANDFATHER: Don't mock the afflicted, Pauly.

241
MS
LA

PAUL: Oh for Pete's sake, it's only a joke.

242
3/4 S
NA

GRANDFATHER: Well, it may be a joke, but it's his nose.—

243
MS
LA

— He can't help —

—having a hideous grey hooter, it's the only one he's got.—

244
3/4 S
NA

—And his poor little head's trembling under the weight of it.

245
MS
LA

NORM enters with three piles of fan mail and places them in front of JOHN on a table. RINGO is almost in tears, examining his nose in a mirror.

NORM: Paul, John, George—

246
(ZO)
MS
NA

—get at it.

247
MS
LA

248A
3/4 S
NA

JOHN: Hello the income tax have caught up with us at last.

PAUL and GEORGE gather round the low table. RINGO is left out of it.

RINGO: None for me, then?

NORM: Sorry.

He hands RINGO a single envelope.

JOHN: That'll keep you busy.

GRANDFATHER: It's your nose, y'see. Fans are funny that way . Take a dislike to things. They'll pick on a nose . . .

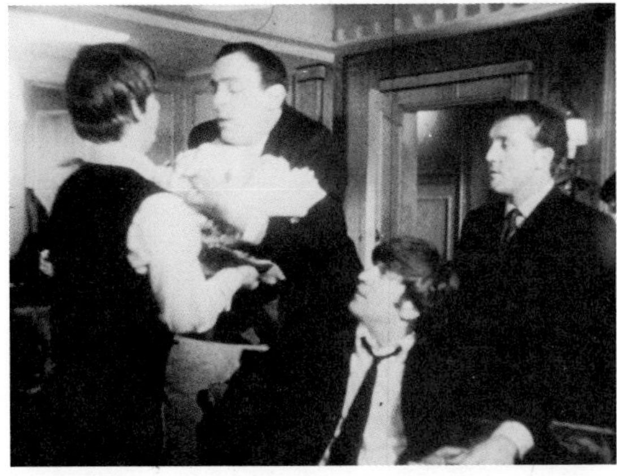

248B
3/4 S
NA

RINGO: You go and pick on your own.

SHAKE enters with a stack of mail about three times larger than all the others put together.

(SHAKE: Hey, here.)

JOHN: Is that yours?

SHAKE: For Ringo.

He dumps it in RINGO's arms who staggers into an armchair. The BOYS send him up.

JOHN: That must have cost you a fortune in stamps, Ring.

249
MCU
NA

GEORGE: He comes from a large family.

250
FS
LA

RINGO: (dumping the letters) Well.

RINGO opens his letter and reads it. It contains a large embossed card.

251
MCU
NA

RINGO: Eh, what's [Boyd's Club] *(Le Circle Club?)*

The lads gather round him and PAUL takes the card from him and reads.

252
MS
LA

PAUL: "The Management of Le Circle Club takes pleasure in requesting the company of Mr. Richard Starkey,—

253
MCU
NA

—that's you, in their recently refinished gaming rooms.—

254
MS
LA

—Chemin de Fer. Baccarat, Roulette, and Champagne Buffet."

255
MCU
NA

RINGO: (surprised) And they want me?

JOHN: Oh it's got round that you're a big spender.

256
MS
LA

NORM: (snatching the card) Well you're not going.

257
MS
NA

RINGO: Ah.

258
(ZI)
MCU
LA

GRANDFATHER: (taking card from Norm) Quite right, invites to gambling dens full of easy money and fast women, chicken sandwiches and cornets of caviar, disgusting!

He pockets the card himself.

259
MCU
NA

RINGO: That's mine.

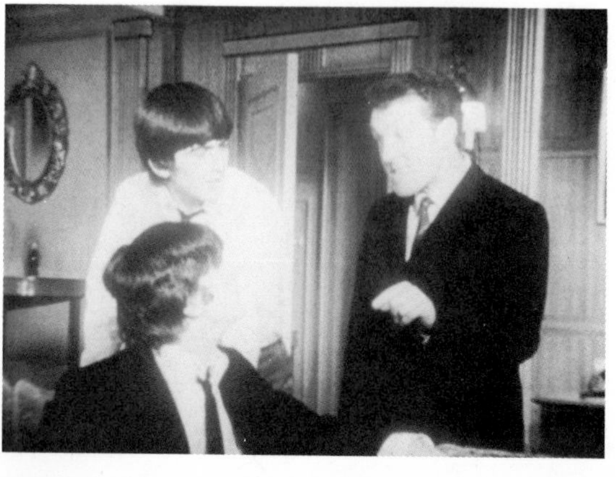

260
(ZI)
MS
LA

NORM: Have done, and you lot get your pens out.

BOYS: Why?

NORM: It's homework time for all you college puddings. I want this lot (He indicates the fan letters.) all answered tonight.

261
MCU
NA

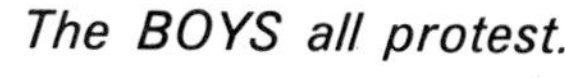

The BOYS all protest.

(RINGO: I want to go out.)

262
MS
LA
(ZO to LS)

NORM: I'll brook no denial!

JOHN: It's all right for you, you couldn't get a pen in your foot, you swine.

NORM: [Come on, Shake, we'll leave 'em to their penmanship.] *(Babble on, babble on, but a touch of the writer's cramp will soon sort you out.)*

He goes followed by SHAKE. There is a pause and JOHN deliberately rises slowly and crosses to his coat. He puts it on and walks to the door.

263
MCU
LA

(GEORGE: Where are you going?)

264A
LS
LA

JOHN: [While the swine's away the piglets can play.] *(He told us to stay here, didn't he?)* Well come on, what are we waiting for?

With a whoop PAUL, GEORGE and RINGO collect their coats and head for the door.

[GRANDFATHER: What about all these letters?

BOYS: Read em!]

They disappear. After a moment GRANDFATHER takes out RINGO's card.

GRANDFATHER: [And a free champagne buffet.] (He grins to himself.)

264B
3/4 S
LA

At this moment a waiter enters with a tray. (WAITER: I'll clean up, sir.)

264C
3/4 S
LA
ZI to . . .

He is clad in tails and GRANDFATHER eyes them longingly, measuring himself the while alongside the startled waiter. He leaves us with no doubt in our minds what he wants, i.e., the waiter's suit.

264D
MS
LA
ZI to . . .

264E
MCU
LA

INTERIOR, DANCING CLUB

Song: *"I Want To Be Your Man"*
The club is the latest in modern decor and full of teen-agers all enjoying themselves. The CAMERA wanders around the club till it finally picks out JOHN, PAUL, GEORGE and RINGO all crowded around one small table. The music is blaring away from a juke box and the BOYS join the dancers. They are recognised and given smiles and nods of encouragement by all the other customers. During this scene we CUT AWAY.

267
MS
LA
DK

265
FS
NA

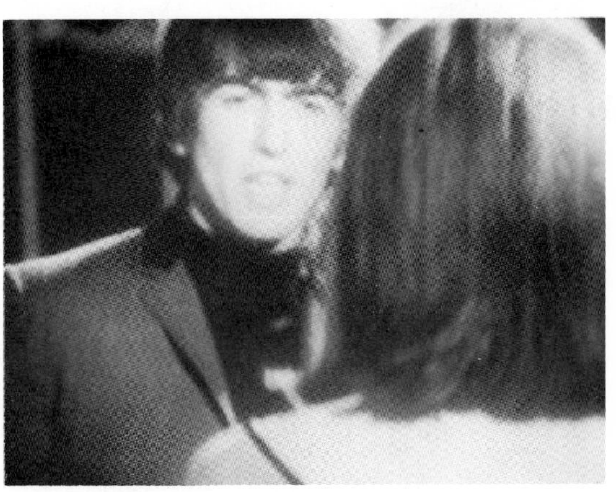

268
MCU
NA
DK

266A
CU
NA
DK
PR to . . .

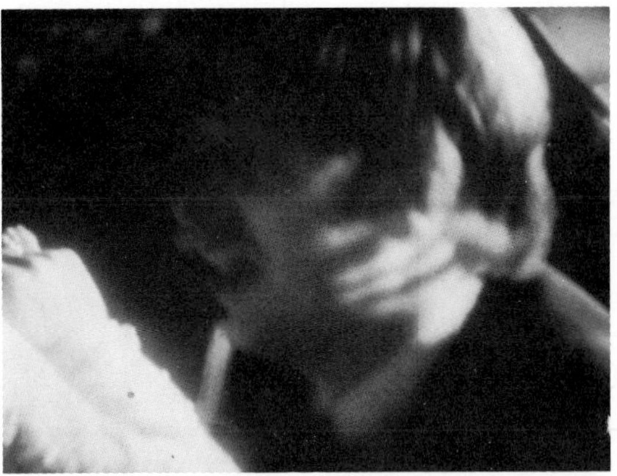

269
MCU
NA
DK

266B
MCU
NA
DK

270
CU
NA
DK

271
LS
LA
DK

272
MCU
NA
DK

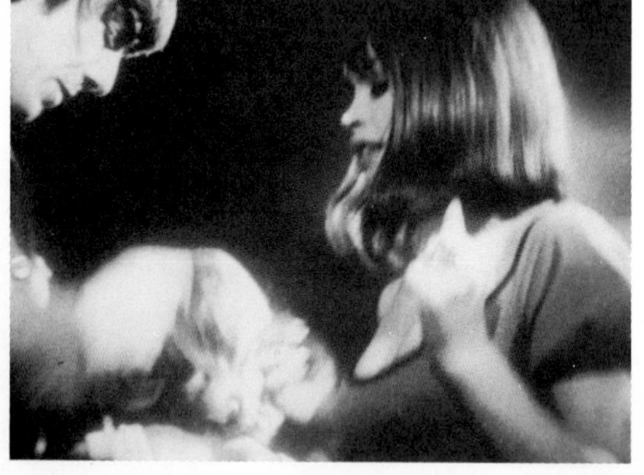

273
MS
LA
DK

274
MCU
NA
DK

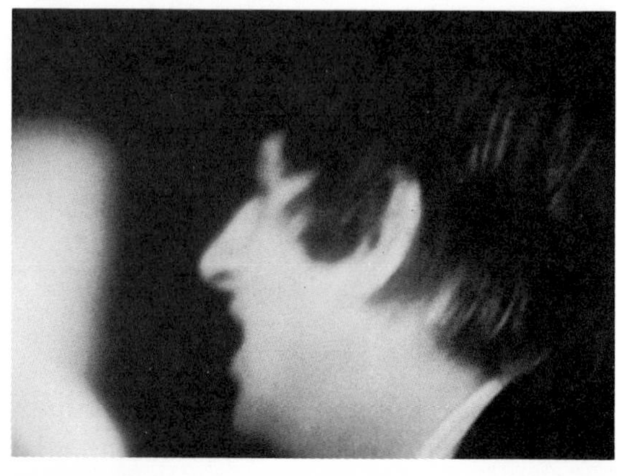

275
CU
LA
DK

276
MLS
NA

INTERIOR, LE CIRCLE CLUB

The whole atmosphere is of quiet elegance and loud wealth. Around the baccarat table the rich, bored customers sit barely moving a face muscle as they languidly murmur "suivez" and "banco" to the dealer as he operates the shoe. The manager of the club is beaming with satisfaction as he surveys his customers. One of these customers is clad in evening dress and he has his back to us. The rest of the players (male) are in suits. By each of them is standing a lush lady with a bored sophisticated face that looks as if it has been painted on. From the REVERSE of the LAST SHOT we now see the solitary evening dress player is GRANDFATHER. He looks around him and wipes off his look of enjoyment and elaborately out-bores everyone in the room.

277
MS
LA

278
3/4 S
NA

279
MS
LA

DEALER: Alors, M'sieur?

280
3/4 S
NA

GRANDFATHER: (nonchalant) Souflée.

281
MCU-MS
NA

He turns to the buxom BLONDE, who is dripping over him.

GRANDFATHER: I bet you're a great swimmer. My turn? Bingo!

282
MS
LA

CROUPIER: Pas "Bingo," M'sieur . . . Banco.

283
3/4 S
NA

GRANDFATHER: (taking cards) I'll take the little darlings anyway.

He takes up the cards and can't understand that they are unnumbered.

GRANDFATHER: Two and one is three, carry one is four.

The buxom BLONDE leans over him.

[BLONDE: Lay them down.

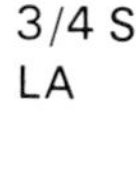

284
3/4 S
LA

[GRANDFATHER: (disturbed by his eyeline) Eh?]

[BLONDE: Lay them down.]

[GRANDFATHER: We'd be thrown out.]

[BLONDE: Your cards . . . lay them down . . . face up.]

[*He does so.*]

CROUPIER: Huit . . . et sept. (He pushes chips and box to Grandfather.)

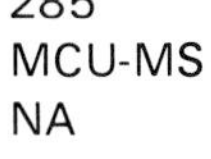

285
MCU-MS
NA

[BLONDE: You had a lovely little pair, y'see

GRANDFATHER: *I* did?]

[*CROUPIER taps impatiently on box (shoe).*]

[BLONDE: They're yours.

GRANDFATHER: They are?

BLONDE: The cards . . . you're bank.]

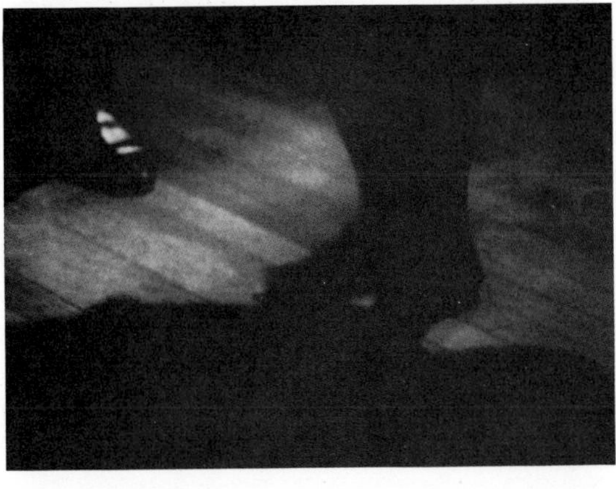

286
CU
LA
DK

INTERIOR DANCING CLUB

Song: *"Don't Bother Me"*
The BOYS are having a rare old time and the place is really moving.

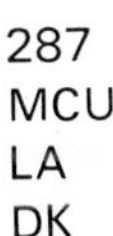

287
MCU
LA
DK

288
MS
LA
MS

289
MS
HA
DK

290
MS
HA
DK

291
MS
HA
DK

292A
MCU
NA
DK
PR to . . .

292B
MCU
NA
DK

[*INTERIOR, LE CIRCLE CLUB*

GRANDFATHER is playing and a waiter is checking the requirements of the players.]

[GRANDFATHER: Bingo!

CROUPIER: (wearily) M'lord dit "bingo."

WAITER: (to Grandfather) A little light refreshment.

GRANDFATHER: (lordly) A glass of the old chablis to wash down a gesture of gibblets wouldn't go amiss. (He resumes his game.) Souflée, chop chop.]

[*The CROUPIER uses the spatula to pick up a card. GRANDFATHER grabs it and scoops some sandwiches off a passing tray.*]

293
MS
LA

294A
(PU)
MS
NA

294B
MS
NA
PL to . .

INTERIOR, LE CIRCLE CLUB

GRANDFATHER is looking worried at the call of the card he loses and we see that all his chips have gone. He notices the waiter delivering snacks and champagne to a couple, so quick as a flash, he places a handkerchief over his arm and writing a bill out on a piece of paper, presents it to the couple and collects payment in chips. He then resumes playing.

294C
LS
NA

295
MS
NA

296
(PR)
MS
NA

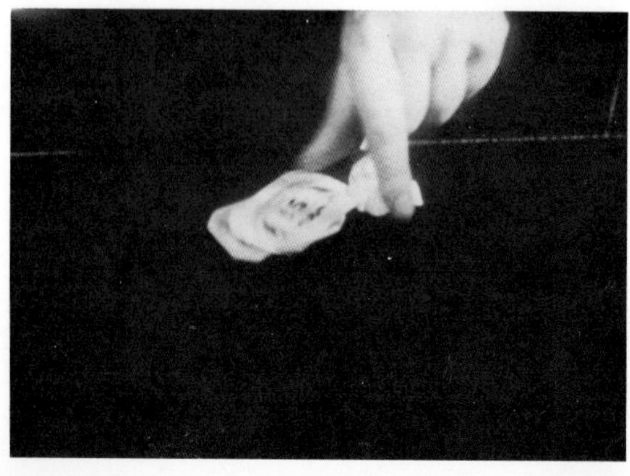

297
CU
NA

298
MS
NA

GRANDFATHER: Bingo!

299A
CU
NA
DK
ZO+PL to . . .

INTERIOR, DANCING CLUB
Song: *"All My Loving"*

299B
LS
NA
DK

300
MS
LA
DK

301
MS
LA
DK

302
MCU
LA
DK

303
MS
LA
DK

304
MS
NA
DK

305
LS
LA
DK

306A
(PR + ZI)
MS
NA
DK
ZO to . . .

The BOYS are at their table again laughing and enjoying themselves, when suddenly their faces freeze. From their P.O.V. we see NORM standing glowering down at them, with him is SHAKE. Reluctantly the BOYS rise and follow NORM out.

306B
LS
NA
DK

307
MS
LA
DK
(ZI)

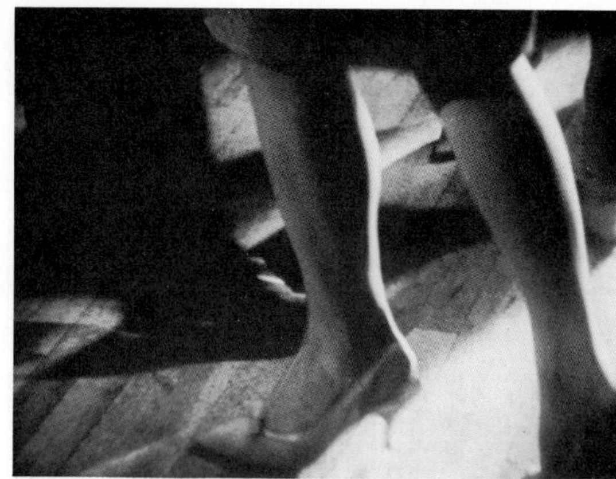

308
CU
LA
DK

309
CU
LA
DK

310
MCU
LA
DK

INTERIOR, HOTEL ROOM

Waiter is sitting on chair in underclothes, reading. He hears a noise, says "The manager!" and hides in outer clothes closet. NORM and the BOYS enter saying:

311A
LS
NA
PR to . . .

311B
LS
NA
PR to . . .

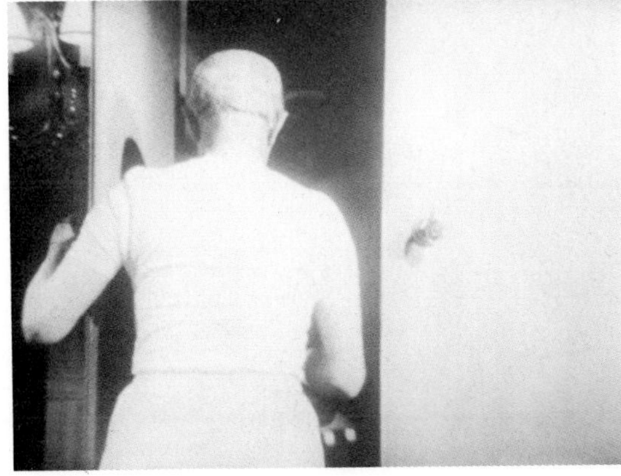

311C
MS
NA

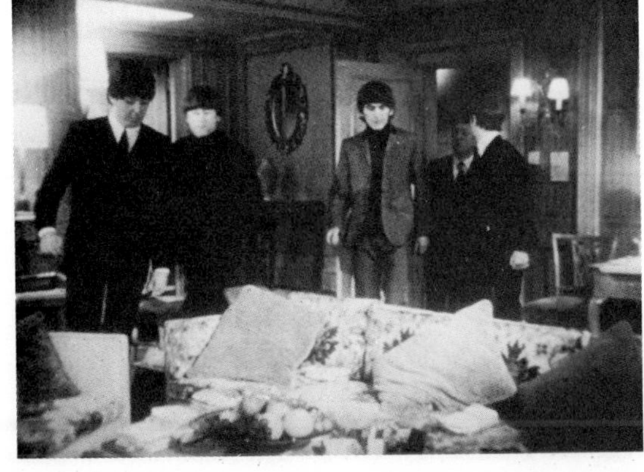

312A
LS
LA
PR + ZI to . . .

NORM: Now get on with it.

JOHN: We were going to do it.

NORM: Aye, well, now! (He goes through bedroom.)

RINGO goes to hang up coat in closet. He does so, then crosses to rest.

RINGO: Any of you lot put a man in that cupboard?

ALL: A man? No.

312B
MS
LA
PL + ZO to . . .

RINGO: Well somebody did.

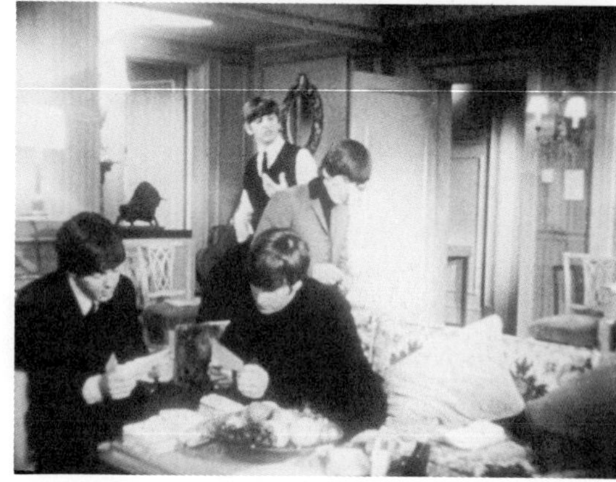

312C
LS
LA
PR + ZI to . . .

GEORGE goes to cupboard.

312D
MS
LA

We see the waiter from his P.O.V.

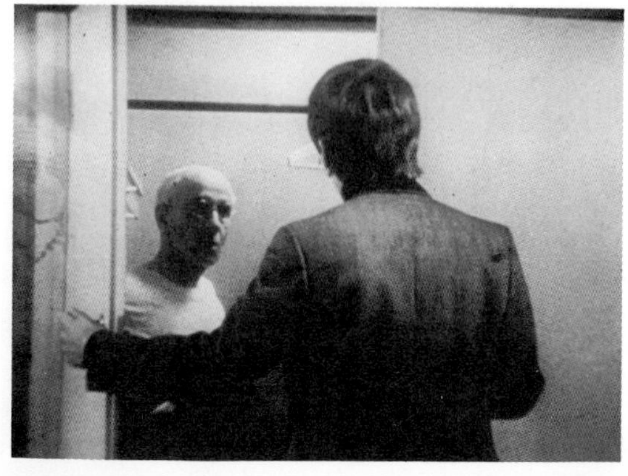

312E
MS
LA

312F
MS
LA
PL + ZO to . . .

He closes door, returns to group.

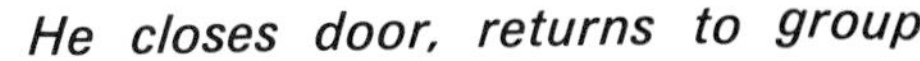

312G
LS
LA
PR + ZI to . . .

GEORGE: He's right, y'know.

BOYS: (disinterested) Ah well, there you go.

SHAKE enters front door, goes to hang up coat and drags waiter out.

312H
MS
LA
PL + ZO

SHAKE: Eh, what's all this?

PAUL: Oh, him . . . He's been lurking.

JOHN: Aye, he looks a right lurker.

SHAKE: (to waiter) You're undressed. Where are your clothes?

313A
CU
NA
PL to . . .

WAITER: The old gentlemen borrowed them to go gambling at Le Circle.

[PAUL: No!]

313B
CU
NA

RINGO: Oh, he's gone to my club, has he?

314
(PR)
MS
LA

PAUL: (turning on Ringo) Yeah, it's all your fault, getting invites to gambling clubs. He's probably in the middle of an orgy by now.

315
(ZI)
3/4 S
LA

JOHN: Well, what are we waiting for?

[SHAKE: Aye, come on, honest, that grandfather of yours is worse than any of you lot.]

(WAITER: What about me?

JOHN: Too old.)

316
MS
NA

INTERIOR, LE CIRCLE CLUB

GRANDFATHER is drinking champagne [*in locked arms*] *with BLONDE.*

WAITER: Encore de champagne, Monsieur?

GRANDFATHER: Yes, and I'll have some more champagne as well.

He takes another swig of his glass.

317
MS
LA

MANAGER: (beaming) Lord John McCartney, he's the millionaire Irish Peer, filthy rich of course.

CUSTOMER: Oh I don't know, looks rather clean to me.

[*The MANAGER comes to GRANDFATHER's side.*]

[MANAGER: Play is about to resume, m'lord.

GRANDFATHER: (handing him a chip) Lead me to it, I've a winning itch that only success can pacify.]

[*He takes his place at the table. The MANAGER watches for a moment then moves away from the table towards the club reception desk.*]

318A
(PR)
MS
NA

INTERIOR, LE CIRCLE CLUB RECEPTION DESK

JOHN, PAUL, GEORGE, RINGO, NORM and SHAKE are trying to gain entrance.

(NORM: Come ahead you lot. Try to act with a bit of decorum—this is a posh place.

JOHN: We know how to behave, we've had lessons.)

ATTENDANT: I'm sorry sir, members and invited guests only.

[PAUL, GEORGE, RINGO, JOHN: I've got to get in. It's urgent and important. I've had an invite. Take me to your leader.

NORM: Shurrup.]

(NORM: Well, uh . . .

318B
MS
NA

ATTENDANT: Oh, yes.

318C
MS

SHAKE: I'm with them, I'm Ringo's sister.)

The BOYS enter and meanwhile the MANAGER has walked into SHOT. He recognises the BOYS and welcomes them with false enthusiasm. They all start to enter the main room.

NORM: Have you got a little old man in there?

MANAGER: (pleasantly) Do you mean Lord McCartney?

319
LS
NA

PAUL: He's at it again, look, I'm his grandfather . . . I mean . . .

320
3/4 S
NA

BLONDE: (standing next to Grandfather) Oh, it must be the dolly floor show.

321
MS
NA

[JOHN: Stay where you are everybody this is a raid and we want him.]

322
MCU
LA

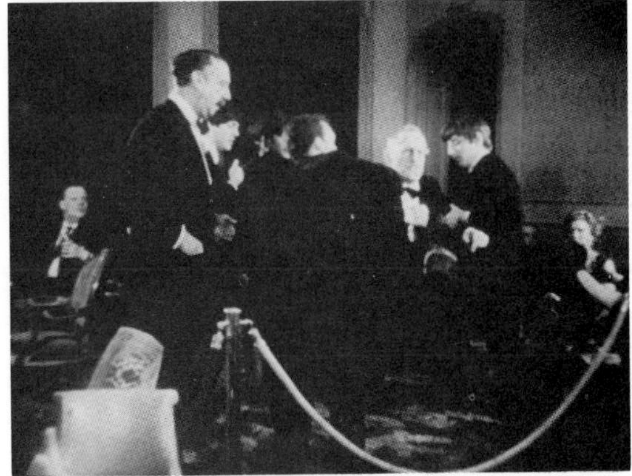

323
LS
NA

GRANDFATHER: Who are these ruffians? . . . I've never seen them before in my life! . . .

They grab the protesting GRANDFATHER and drag him into the reception area. He keeps trying to return to BLONDE and table. [GEORGE and RINGO each take an end of the velvet cord hanging between the two stanchions. They exchange ends and re-hook it, thus encircling GRANDFATHER by the entrance desk.] They then go to settle up.

324
MS
NA

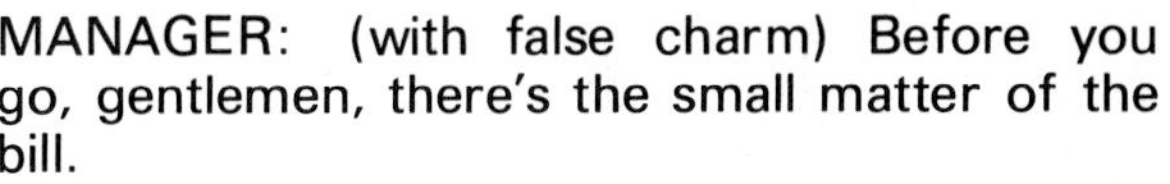

MANAGER: (with false charm) Before you go, gentlemen, there's the small matter of the bill.

325
MCU
NA

326
MS
LA

[He snaps his fingers and a waiter hands him the bill.]

NORM: (taking it) I'll settle that.

He glances at it.

NORM: A hundred and eighty quid!

MANAGER: (icily) I beg your pardon, guineas.

At that moment a WAITER appears with a tray full of pound notes.

WAITER: Your winnings, my lord, one hundred and ninety pounds.

The MANAGER tears up the bill and takes the money.

327A (ZI) MS NA

GRANDFATHER: How about me change?

MANAGER: Cloak room charge.

He hands GRANDFATHER his old mackintosh.

RINGO: (brightly) Ah well, easy come, easy go. (The others glower at him.) Well.

327B MS NA

INTERIOR, LARGE HOTEL BATHROOM, DAY

The bath is full of bubbles and the bubbles are high over the top of the bath. After a moment, JOHN's head appears out of the bubbles; he is wearing his leather cap and in his hands are a toy merchant ship and a toy submarine. He begins to play an elaborate game of U-Boat hunting of British ships; he conducts the game in pig German, barking orders. GEORGE now enters, he is dressed in his undervest and trousers, and he is carrying a sponge bag and hand towel. Behind lumbers SHAKE.

328A MS NA

JOHN: Guten morgan, mein Herr. Kanen sie nach ein tea haben? Ah, the filthy Englander, gootey morgee.

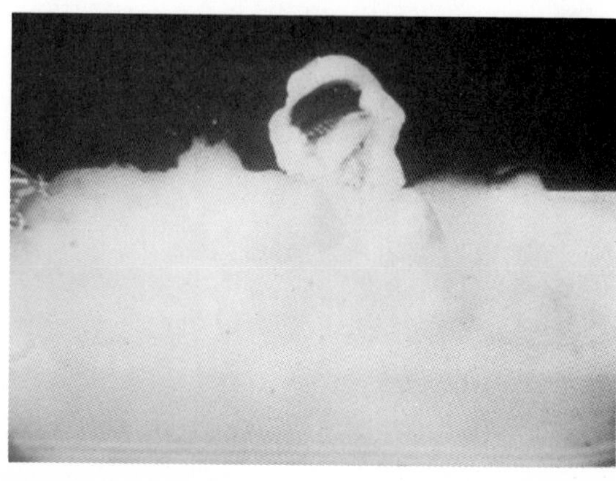

328B MS NA

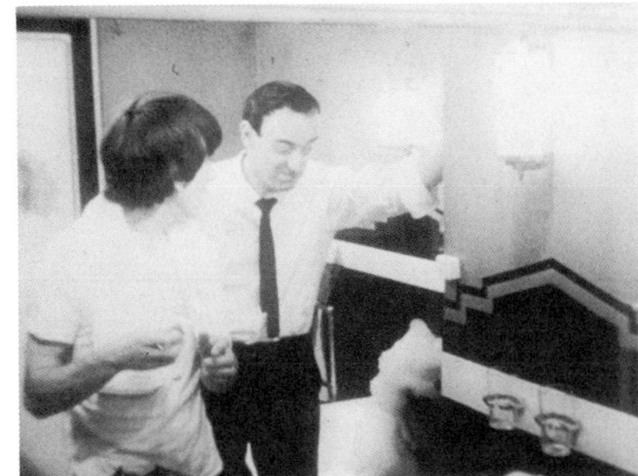

329
MS
NA

SHAKE: Aw go on George.

GEORGE: Don't be ridiculous.

SHAKE: You said I could.

GEORGE: Honest, me mind boggles at the very idea. A grown man, and you've never shaved with a safety razor.

SHAKE: It's not my fault, I'm from a long line of electricians.

GEORGE: Well, you're not practising on me.

SHAKE: All right. Well, show us then.

GEORGE: (long suffering) Oh, come on then.

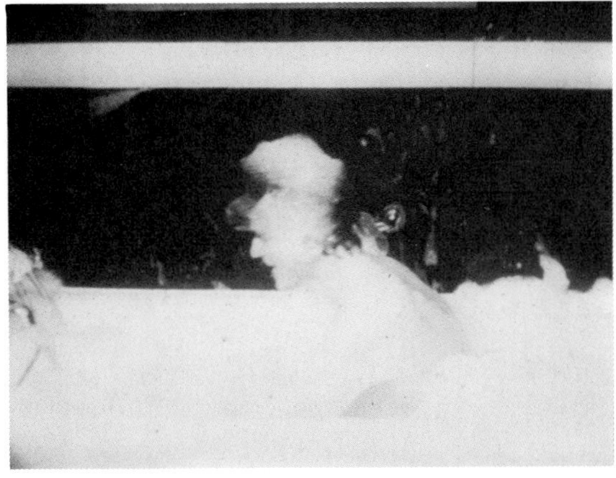

330
MS
NA

GEORGE has unpacked his razor and can of lather. He now has an idea, and instead of lathering his face, he lathers SHAKE's image in the mirror and to demonstrate shaving, he shaves the image. [He, however, pulls all the appropriate faces of shaving on his own face followed closely by SHAKE.] In the background JOHN continues the North Atlantic sea-war.

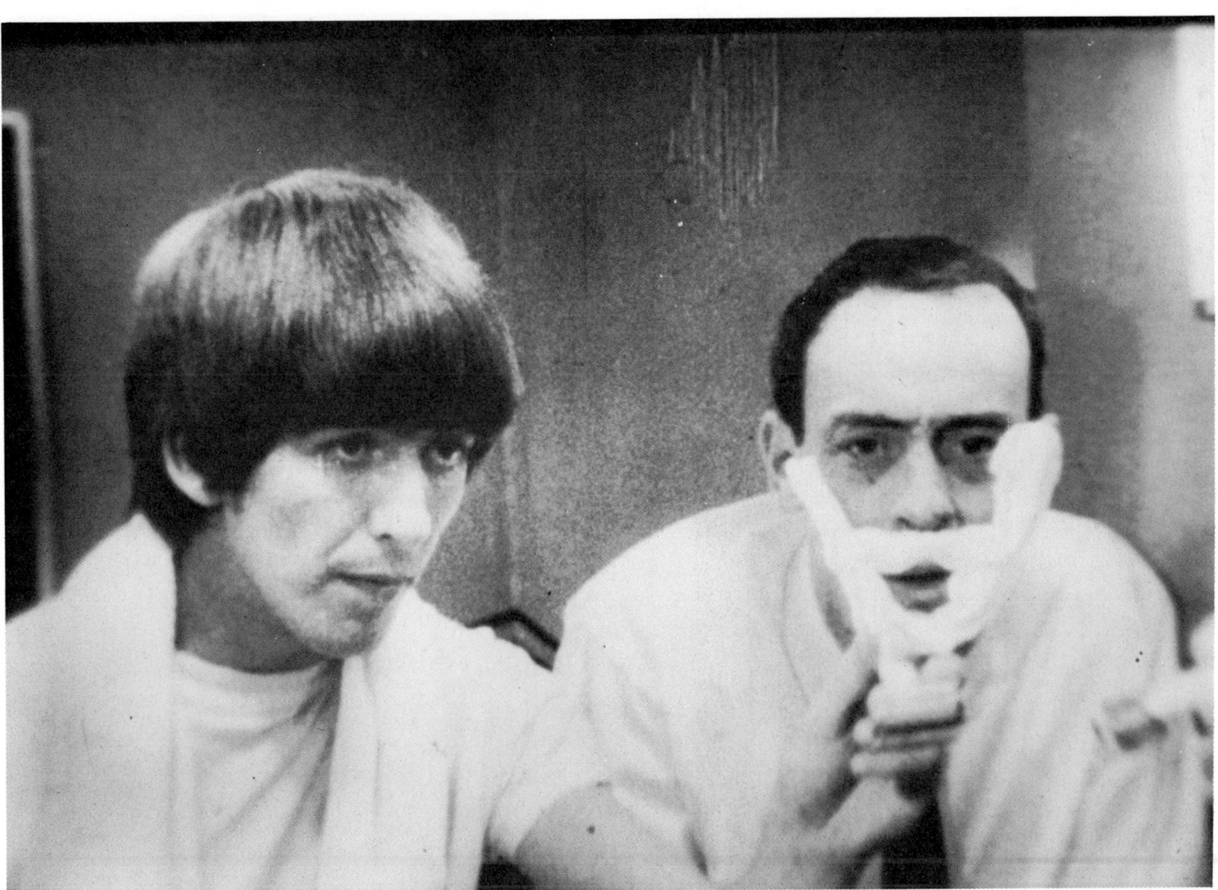

331
MS
NA

JOHN: Rule Britannia, Britannia rule the . . .

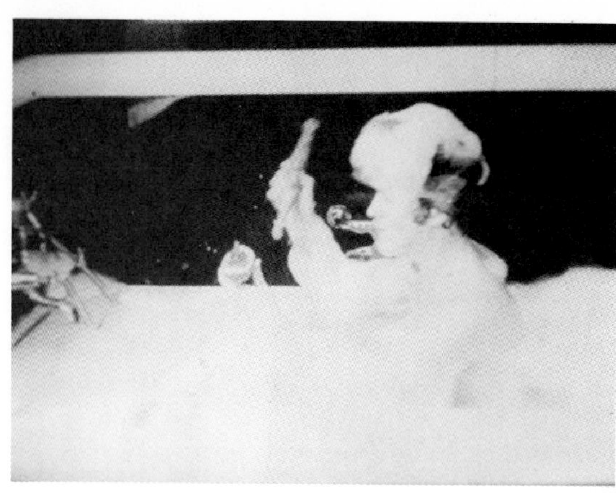

332
MS
NA
(PR)

GEORGE: Put that tongue away, it looks disgusting hanging there all pink and naked—one slip of the razor and . . .

CLOSE UP SHAKE as he hastily withdraws his tongue with a gulp. At this moment there is a loud sound from JOHN, then a cry of:

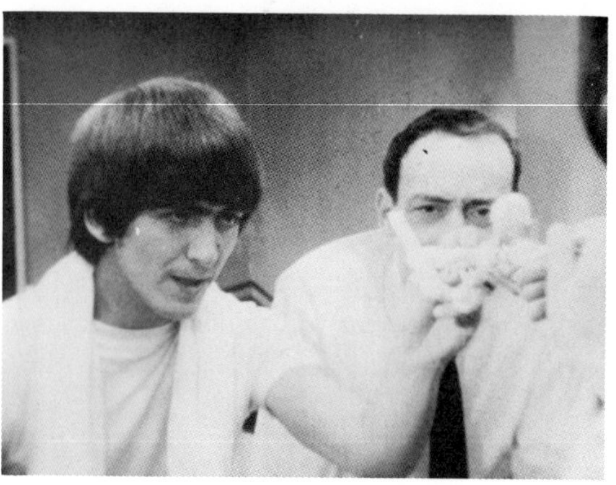

333
MS
NA

JOHN: Helpt uns helpen. Help!

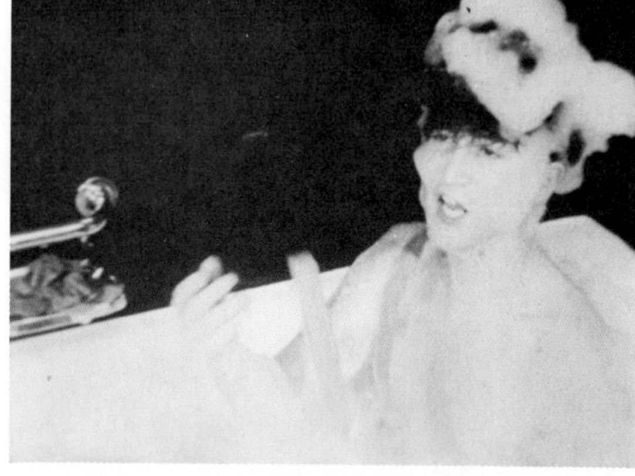

334
MCU
NA

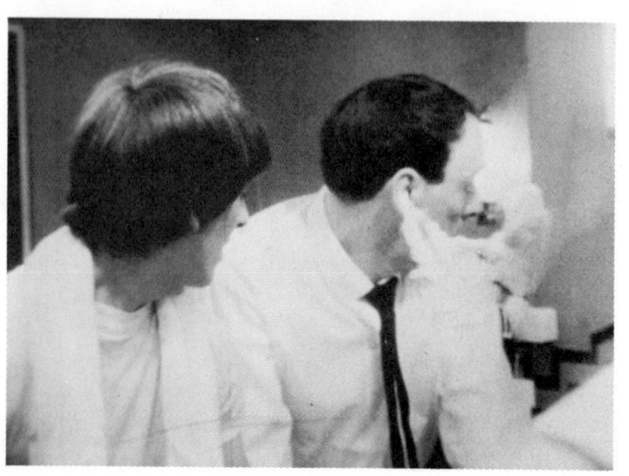

335
MS
NA

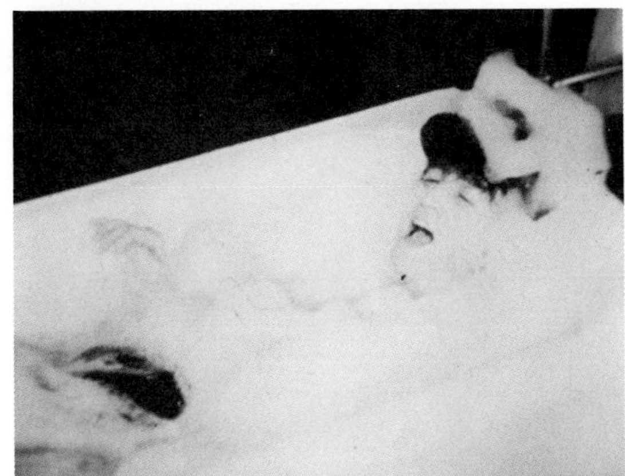

336
MCU
NA

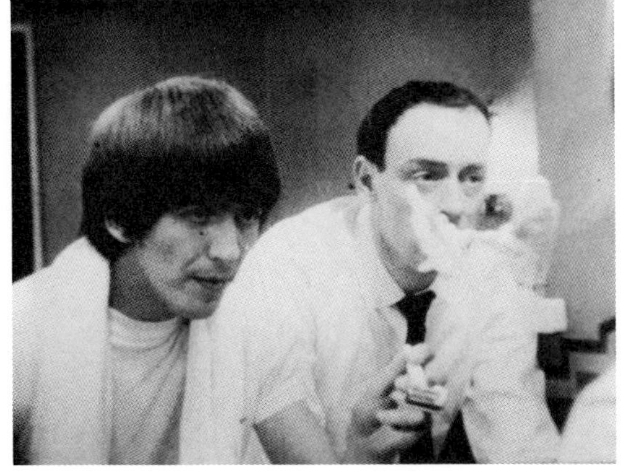

337
MS
NA

SHAKE AND GEORGE rush to the bath side just in time to see JOHN disappear below the surface of the bubbles.

GEORGE: (to Shake) Torpedoed again.

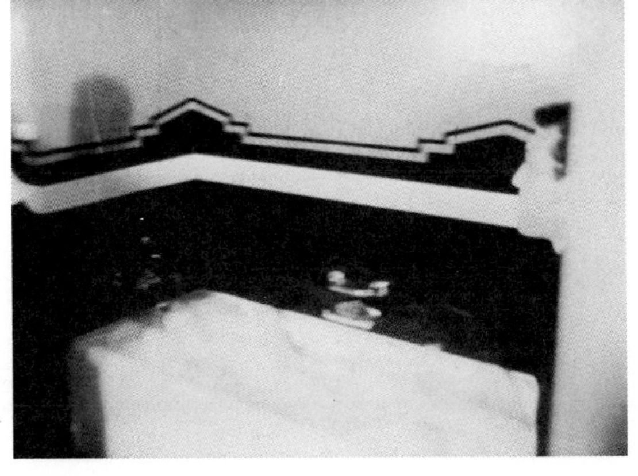

338A
FS
HA
PL to . . .

They are about to resume the shaving lesson when NORM enters.

NORM: [And what's all this? Do you know there's a dirty great car waiting to take you lot to the television place? (He bundles SHAKE and GEORGE out of bathroom.) Where's John?] Come on lads, there's a car waiting to take you to the studio. Where's John?

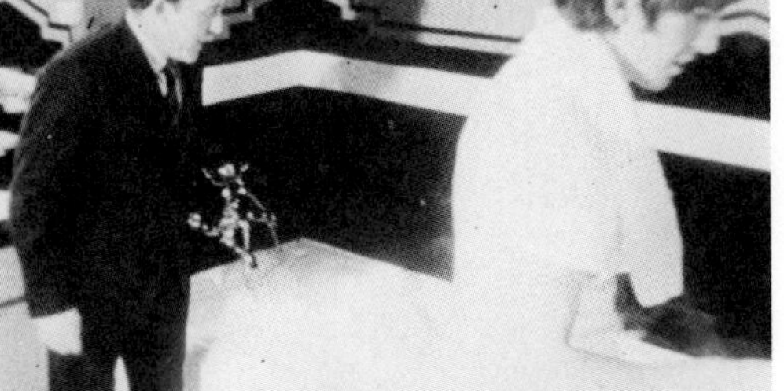

338B
FS
HA

GEORGE: (as he exits) In the bath.

NORM crosses to the bath.

[NORM: Right you are Lennon.]

NORM: All right, Lennon, let's have you.

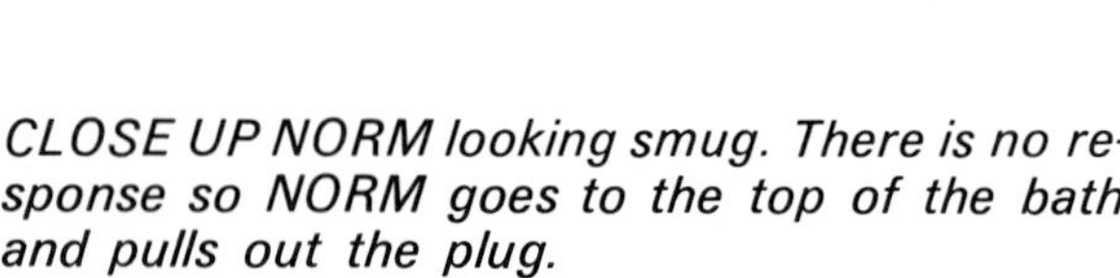

CLOSE UP NORM looking smug. There is no response so NORM goes to the top of the bath and pulls out the plug.

339
MCU
LA

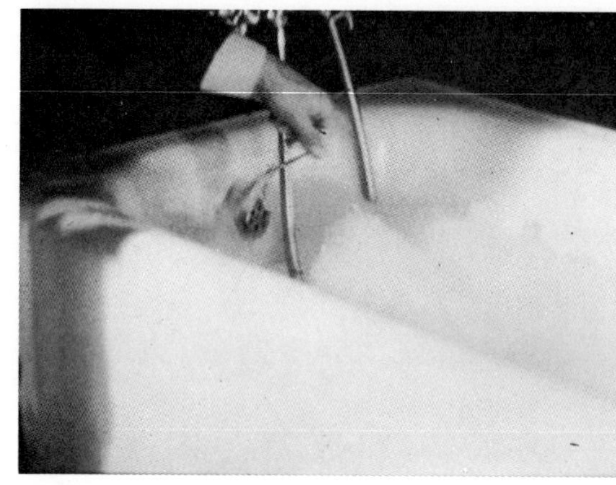

NORM: Come on John, stop lurking about.

340
MS
LA
(PR)

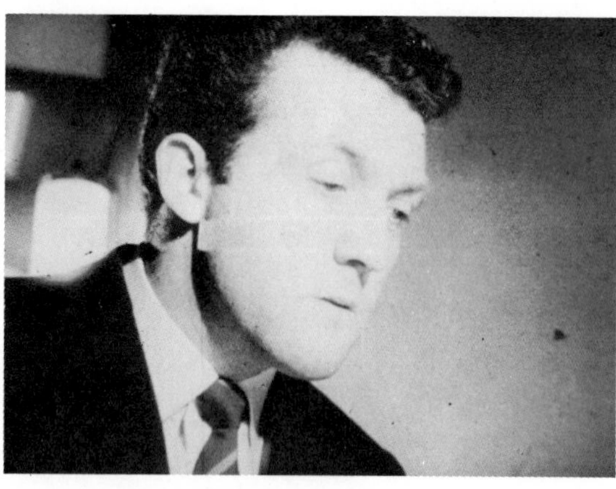

NORM waits a moment then turns to the bath, a look of horror comes over his face and we see the bath is empty.

341
MCU
LA

NORM: John! John!

We CUT from bath to NORM, still amazed, and JOHN's head comes into frame.

JOHN: [I wonder how I did it!] What are you messing around with that boat for—there's a car waiting, come on!

342
(PU)
FS
HA

[*INTERIOR, BIG CAR MOVING ON WAY TO STUDIOS*

The BOYS have settled down.]

[JOHN: Should I say it?

GEORGE: Follow your impulse.

RINGO: It'll only get you into trouble.

JOHN: (to RINGO) Aah, shurrup, misery!]

[*JOHN slouches forward.*]

[JOHN: (urgently) O.K. Driver, follow that car!]

[*The driver is an urbane man in a handsome grey uniform.*]

[FRANK: (indicating the traffic) Would you like to be a little more precise, sir?

JOHN: Well, that's the wrong line for a start.

FRANK: Sorry? (meaning: "I beg your pardon.")

GEORGE: Oh, don't pay any attention to him, he was just fulfilling a life long ambition.

FRANK: I see.

JOHN: Yeah, you know, "O.K. Buster, follow that car, there's a sawbuck in it for you if you get real close!"

FRANK: Oh, yes, now I'm with you. But, gee, Mister, I've got my license to think of . . . we're doing a hundred now . . .]

[*The car is stopped in traffic behind a bus. JOHN gets out of car and walks to the front. JOHN leans in window delightedly, he flashes his wallet. The car starts again.*]

[JOHN: (walking alongside) Ever seen one of these before?

FRANK: Ah . . . a shamus, eh?

JOHN: I see you go to the night court.

FRANK: I've made the scene.

JOHN: (jumping into car) Well, remember, it's Leathery Magee up ahead in that convertible, so cover me in the stake out.

GEORGE: I don't think that bit's right.

JOHN: What do you expect from an ad lib . . . Raymond Chandler?]

[*EXTERIOR, STREET*

As the big car overtakes a company director's Rolls, JOHN lowers his window and the BOYS let out an imaginary hail of bullets at the executive in the back. He reacts violently and starts to shout at them. As he does so, he presses the button of his window, so that we hear only part of it. But what we do hear is unpleasant. He immediately presses the button and the window rises.

RINGO and PAUL jump out of the car. RINGO takes two drumsticks from his coat pocket and using them as bandilleros, inserts them with style into the radiator grill (V.O. "Ole" from the BOYS). PAUL then using his coat as a matador's cloak, does a butterfly pass at the car which has just started up, narrowly missing him but he keeps in the matador position.]

[*INTERIOR, CAR*

NORM: Will you all stop it, you're like a gang of school kids. I knew this was going to happen one day.

JOHN: (as Ringo and Paul climb in) Well, you shouldn't have had bacon for your breakfast, you cannibal.

FRANK: (to Norm) We're nearly there, sir.

JOHN: Eh . . . don't call him sir, he's got enough delusions of power as it is.]

[*CLOSE SHOT of a long suffering NORM.*]

[NORM: And I was happy in the bakery. I'll never know why I left.]

EXTERIOR, OLD VICTORIAN MUSIC HALL THEATRE which has been converted to the T.V. studios.

There are a few groups of GIRL FANS standing outside the front of the theatre, but against the curb of the pavement is a night-watchman's canvas hut and brazier. The car approaches.

343
XLS
NA

INTERIOR, CAR

NORM: Get ready John, open the door and as it draws up, out you go and straight in.

344
MS
NA

JOHN nods and opens the door. The FANS start to swarm 'round them. To escape, the BOYS dash into the night-watchman's canvas hut, pick it up and run with it to the stage door, revealing the night-watchman, staring in astonishment.

At the door the BOYS put the hut down and enter the theatre.

345
LS
NA

346
MS
LA

347A
LS
NA
TL to . . .

INTERIOR, [STAGE DOOR ENTRANCE] HOTEL LOBBY

As the BOYS enter, two P.R.O. men in dark suits, stiff white collars and old school ties step forward and smile menacingly.

FIRST P.R.O. MAN: (menacingly) Press conference, they're waiting for you.

NORM: (jovially) Give us a couple of shakes to get our breath.

FIRST P.R.O. MAN: (more menacingly) They're waiting now!

347B
FS
NA
PU to . . .

(JOHN: Give us a shout when it's over.

RINGO: I've got a suit just like him, you know.

PAUL: This lot means it. They're even taking hostages.

JOHN: I don't like the handkerchief. I always have the handkerchief in me trouser pocket.

347C
FS
NA

You can't blow your nose on it up there, you know.)

[And without more ado they grab an arm each and march the protesting NORM towards the stairs that lead to the Dress Circle.]

The BOYS, SHAKE and GRANDFATHER rush after the rapidly disappearing NORM, who by now is half way up the stairs.

348
3/4 S
LA

INTERIOR, [DRESS CIRCLE LOUNGE] BALLROOM

[It is empty except for two BARMAIDS poised ready to serve, standing behind trestle tables full of drinks and sandwiches.] The dark-suited MEN enter with NORM and close behind them follows GRANDFATHER, SHAKE and the BOYS. The group arrives at the centre of the lounge and have time to look about and see the food but before they can get to it, from all directions NEWSPAPERMEN and PHOTOGRAPHERS converge upon them.

Now begins an elaborate tug-of-war between various PHOTOGRAPHERS using their flash attachments and REPORTERS to capture a Beatle and in the midst of this running battle a man with a portable recorder is trying to interview them. Together and singly the BOYS are pushed about the room and while this goes on a hard core of NEWSPAPERMEN are busily devouring sandwiches and pouring themselves drinks, to the annoyance of the BARMAIDS.

Every time one of the BOYS attempts to get a sandwich or a drink, it is either too late, the plate is empty, or they are intercepted. The single and constant thing we see in the scene is the pushing and pulling, heavy impersonal handling; the BOYS are just things to be placed like still life in one advantageous position after another. During the scene these individual exchanges take place:

349
LS
HA

[SOUND REPORTER: What's your philosophy of life?

JOHN: I'm torn between Zen and I'm alright Jack.

REPORTER: Has success changed your life?

RINGO: Yes.

REPORTER: Do you like playing the guitar?

GEORGE: Next to kissing girls it's favourities.]

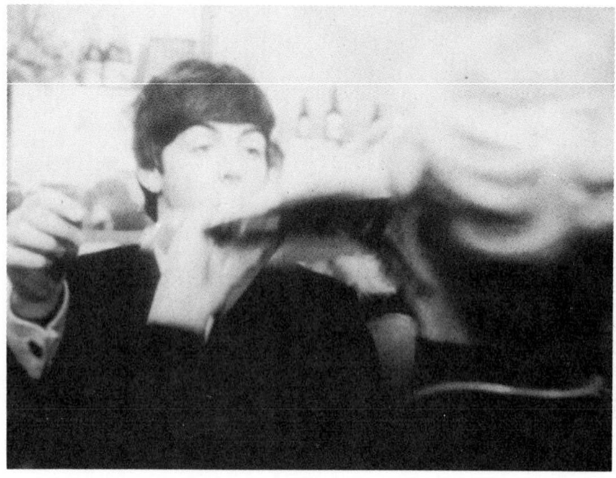

350A
(PR)
MS
NA
TR to . . .

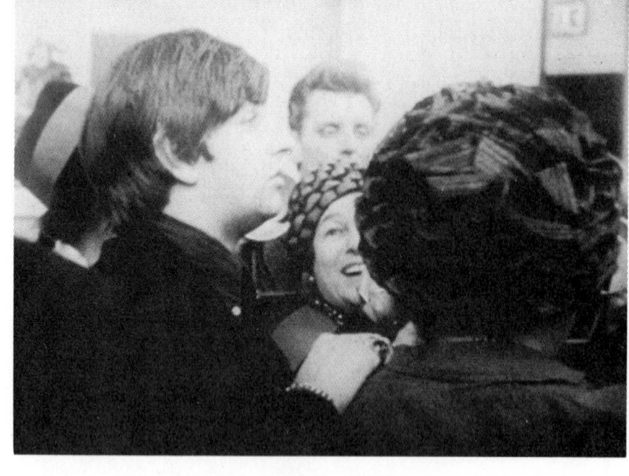

350B
MS
NA
(TR)

351
CU
NA

(REPORTER: . . . highbrow music?

GEORGE: I've always liked that question.

352
CU
LA

353A
DISSOLVE
to . . .

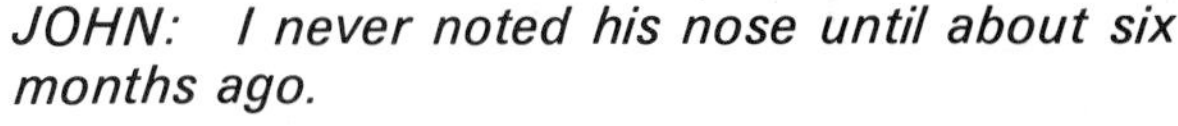

JOHN: I never noted his nose until about six months ago.

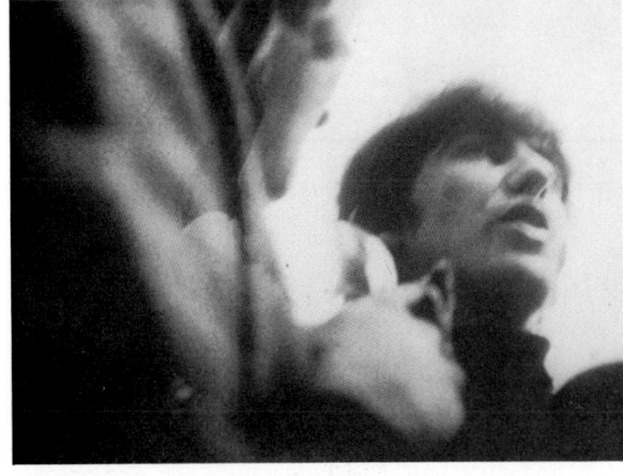

353B
MCU
LA

354A
DISSOLVE
to . . .

GEORGE: And me mother asked me before we left for America if we wanted any sandwiches.

354B
CU
LA

355A
DISSOLVE
to . . .

355B
CU
LA

356A
DISSOLVE
to . . .

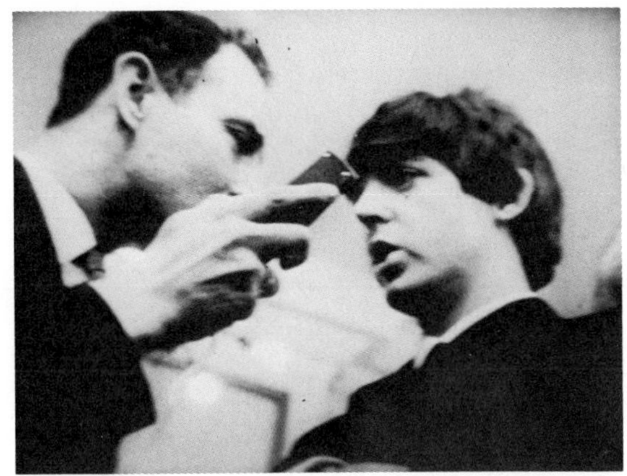

356B
MCU
LA

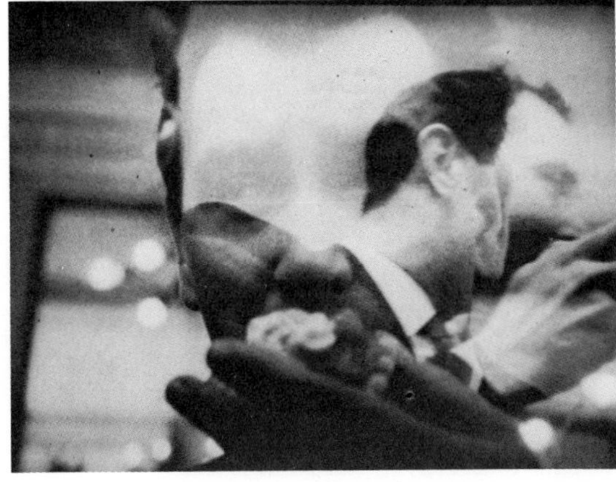

357A
DISSOLVE
to . . .

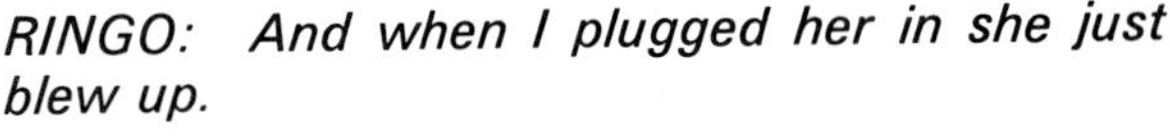

RINGO: And when I plugged her in she just blew up.

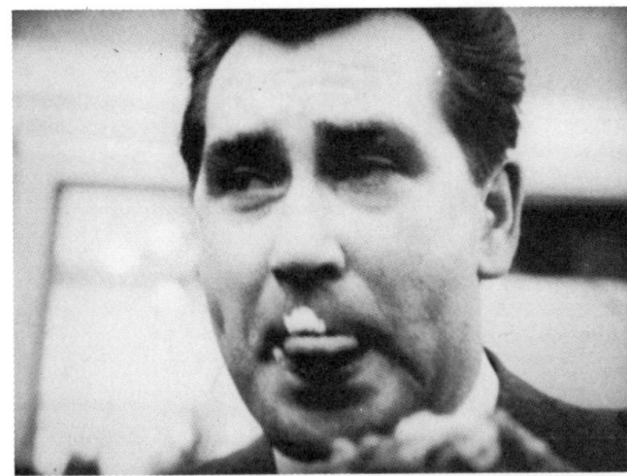

357B
CU
LA

358
359
DISSOLVE
to . . .

359
360
DISSOLVE
to . . .

360
MCU
NA

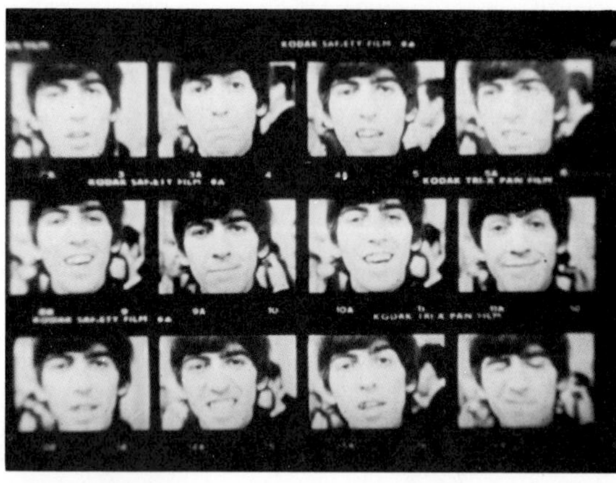

361 A-L
(Each frame appears within the shot one at a time.)

362
MCU
NA

363
MCU
NA

REPORTER: Tell me, how did you find America?

JOHN: Turn left at Greenland.

364
MCU
NA

REPORTER: Has success changed your life?

GEORGE: Yes.

365
MCU
NA

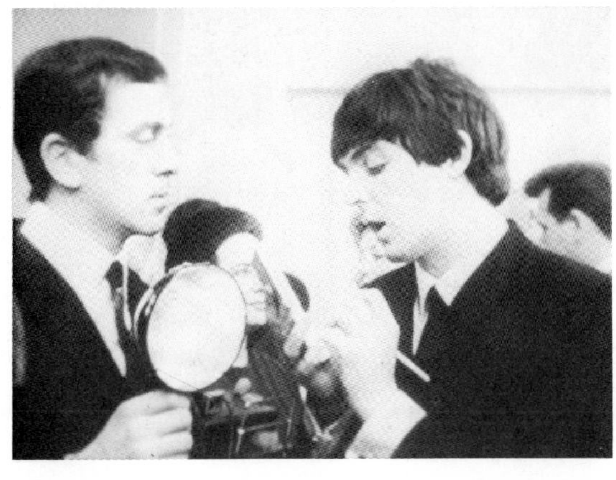

PAUL: I'd like to keep Britain tidy.

366
MCU
NA

REPORTER: Are you a mod or a rocker?

RINGO: Uh, no, I'm a mocker.

367 MCU NA

REPORTER: Have you any hobbies?

368 MCU LA

PAUL: No, actually, we're just good friends.

369 MCU NA

REPORTER: Do you think these haircuts have come to stay?

RINGO: Well, this one has you know, stuck on good and proper now.

REPORTER: Frightfully nice.

370 MCU NA

REPORTER: What would you call that hairstyle you're wearing?

GEORGE: Arthur.

371
MCU
NA

PAUL: *No, actually, we're just good friends.*

372
MCU
NA

RINGO: *Yours are brown, aren't they?*

REPORTER: *What do you call that collar?*

RINGO: *A collar.*

373
MCU
NA

REPORTER: *Do you often see your father?*

PAUL: *No, actually we're just good friends.*

374
MCU
NA

REPORTER: *How do you like your girlfriends to dress?*

RINGO: *(laughs))*

375A
MCU
NA
PR to .

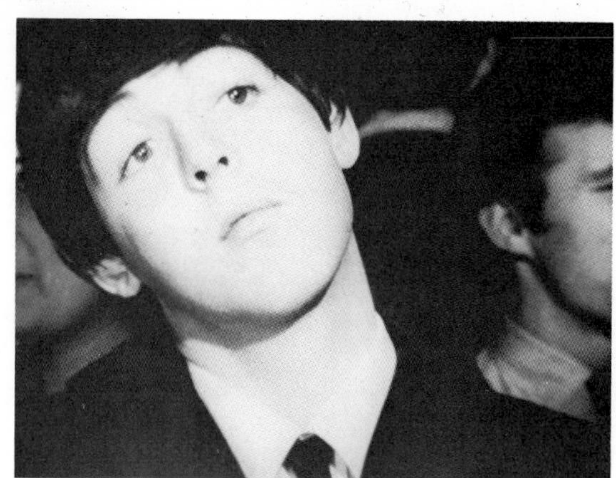

376
CU
NA

375B
MCU
NA

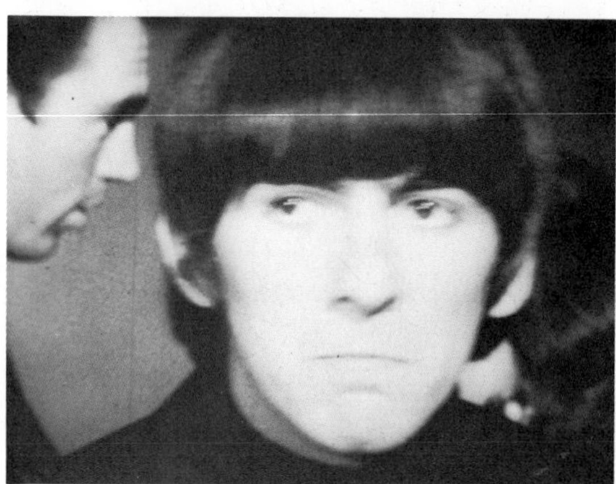

377
CU
NA

378
MCU
NA

379
LS
HA

HIGH SHOT of the press reception and we see the BOYS ease their way out [until they get to the curtained entrance to the Dress Circle. Completely unnoticed, they slip through.]

380
FS
LA
DK

INTERIOR, THEATRE DRESS CIRCLE

The BOYS come up the stairs into the Dress Circle proper. GRANDFATHER and SHAKE are sitting there having a picnic of beer and sandwiches.

PAUL: (ironically) Anything to spare?

GRANDFATHER: We've just finished, Pauly. George, write us your John Henry on this picture.

[GEORGE: Sure.]

PAUL: Eh, look at that. That's our set down there!

381
XLS
HA
DK

He points, and from PAUL's P.O.V. we see on stage, the setting up of the show, scenery and lights, cameras and sound equipment are being put into position by a small army of studio staff. DANCERS and SINGERS are milling about as well.

[PAUL: Let's go and muck in.]

JOHN: Well, should we go down and have a go?

382
LS
LA
DK
(PR)

They exit to rows of the Dress Circle and go through the entrance down the narrow stairs to the stalls and on to the stage that is built and extended right into the stalls, which are partly covered up.

(JOHN: Look at the birds.)

383A
3/4 S
LA
DK
PR to . . .

(JOHN: Just passing through, lad.)

383B
MS
NA
DK
PR to . . .

INTERIOR, STAGE
Everyone is so busy that they hardly notice the BOYS, who wander about examining the studio equipment. A load of three drum sets are being brought on stage and a voice shouts out:

[VOICE: Here, what about these electric guitars?]

SHAKE: Where are they?

VOICE: On the stage, down here.

383C
FS
NA

[SHAKE: (going towards the voice) I'm coming.]

RINGO is busy setting up his drums, and MEN are setting up the other sets. He drops a stick and the FLOOR MANAGER retrieves it and is about to tap the drum. The FLOOR MANAGER is a languid young man.

384
LS
LA

385
(PD + PU)
3/4 S
NA
HK

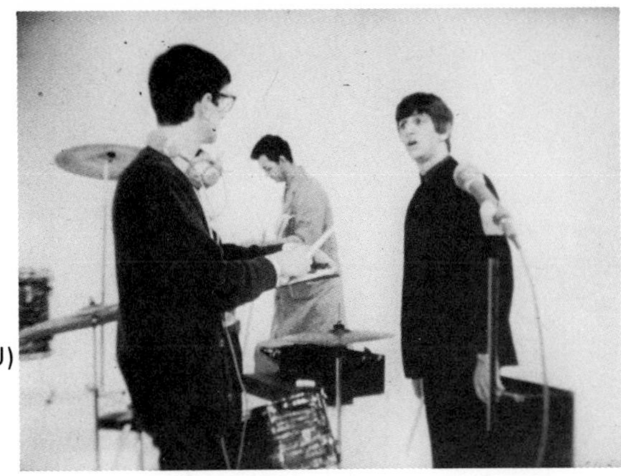

RINGO: Leave them drums alone.

FLOOR MANAGER: Oh, surely one can have a tiny touch.

RINGO: If you so much as breathe heavy on them, I'm out on strike.

FLOOR MANAGER: Aren't you being rather arbitrary?

RINGO: That's right retreat behind a smoke screen of bourgeois cliches.

386A
MCU
NA
HK
PL to . . .

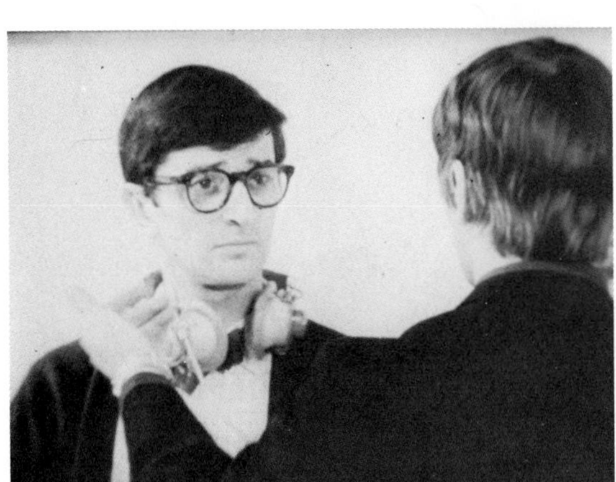

I don't go round messing about with your earphones, do I?

FLOOR MANAGER: Spoil sport!

RINGO: Well!

386B
MS
NA

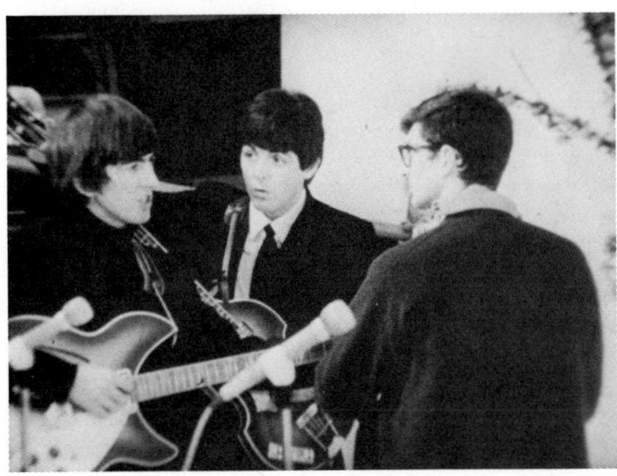

RINGO fusses like a mother hen clucking over his drums. The FLOOR MANAGER is furious.

GEORGE: He's very touchy about those drums. They loom large in his legend.

RINGO gives his drums a defiant crash and JOHN and PAUL stop what ever they are up to and hurry over.

PAUL: What's up?

GEORGE: (pointing) He's sulking again.

387A
MS
LA
HK
PL to . . .

JOHN: I'll show him.

Song: *"If I Fell"*
[*He picks up a set of drum sticks and bashes back at RINGO, who does a more complicated drum roll. GEORGE now joins in and to PAUL's encouragement a drum duel starts completely naturally and improvised. During this encounter the work proceeds around them and the guitars are brought on and SHAKE sets them to working order. PAUL first, then JOHN and GEORGE take up their own instruments and out of the drum duel emerges one of their numbers.*]

389B
MCU
LA

387B
3/4 S
LA
HK

390
MS
NA

388
LS
HA
HK

391
LS
HA
(PD)

389A
CU
LA
PU to . . .

392A
MS
NA
ZO to . . .

392B
LS
HA
HK

393A
MS
LA
HK
PL to . . .

393B
MS
LA
HK

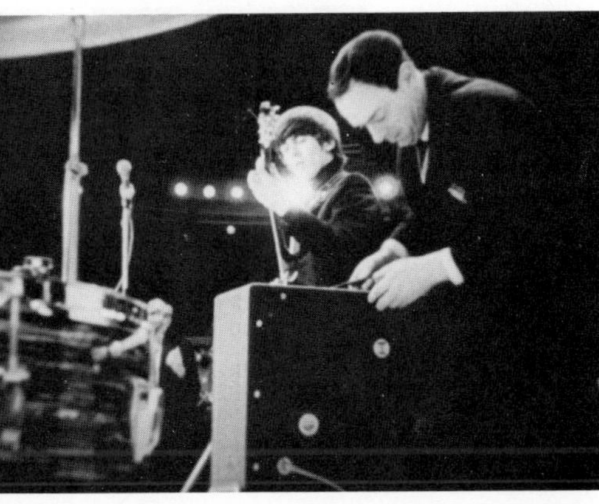
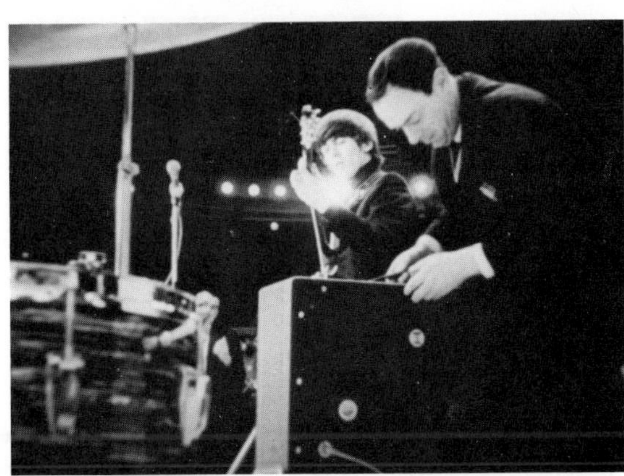

394
FS
LA

395
LS
HA

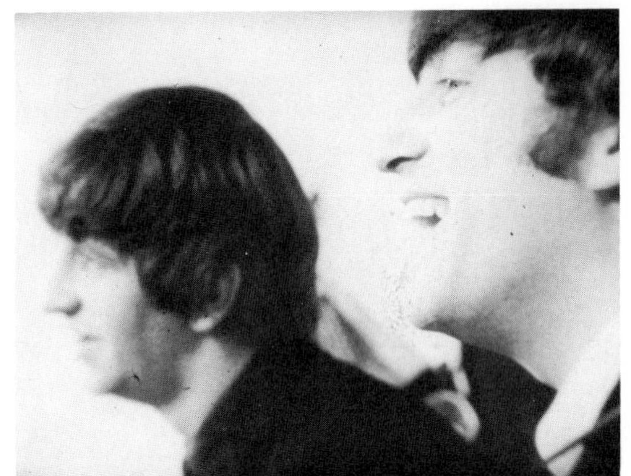

396
MCU
NA
HK

397A
MCU
LA
HK
PL to . . .

397B
CU
LA
HK

398A
MCU
HA
HK
ZI to . . .

399B
CU
LA
HK

399A
MCU-MS
LA
HK
PD to . . .

398B
CU
HA
HK

400A
MS
NA
HK
ZO to . . .

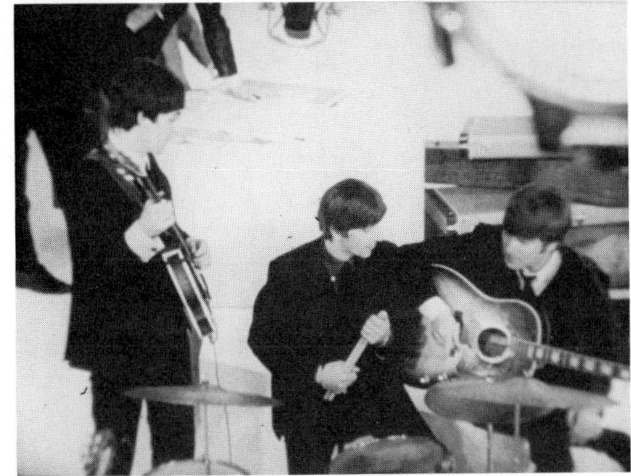

400B
FS
HA
HK

(JOHN: Pardon, excuse, I'd like more drums, third.

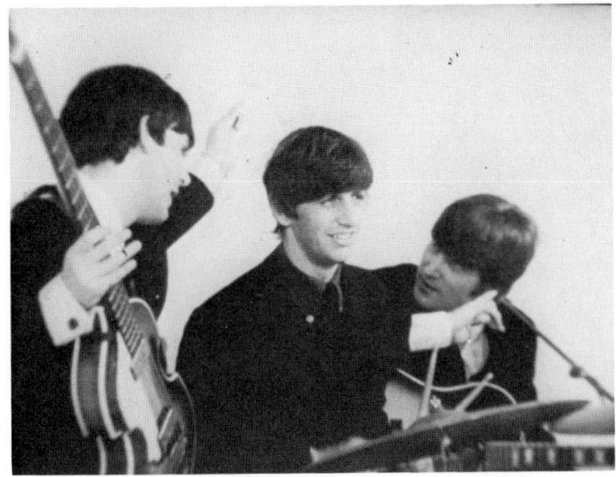

401
MS
LA
HK

PAUL: I think it's on the third bit . . .)

402A
LS
NA
DK
TR to . . .

INTERIOR, RAMP

As the number finishes a baldheaded man, (he is the T.V. DIRECTOR) storms down the ramp that leads from the control box under the Dress Circle.

DIRECTOR: (with over-exaggerated calm) Alright I'm sorry and let's hear no more about it. If that's your opinion you're probably right. Look, if you think I'm unsuitable let's have it out in the open, I can't stand these back-stage politics.

402B
MS-3/4 S
LA

By the end of this speech he is standing in front of JOHN who takes the scene in his stride.

JOHN: Aren't you tending to black and white this whole situation?

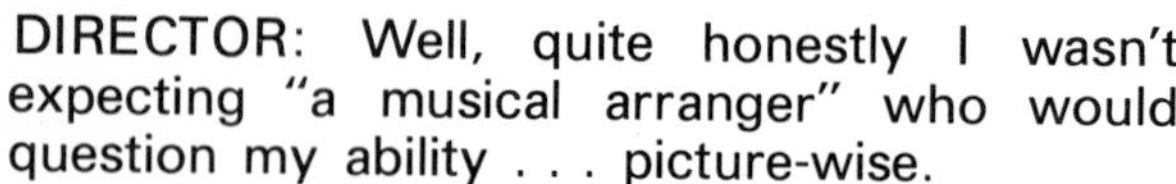

DIRECTOR: Well, quite honestly I wasn't expecting "a musical arranger" who would question my ability . . . picture-wise.

403
MCU
LA

JOHN: (to the others) I could listen to him for hours.

404
MCU-MS
NA

PAUL: What's all this about a musical arranger?

405
MCU-CU
NA

DIRECTOR: Mr. McCartney Senior!

The BOYS have a giggle at the very idea and at this moment GRANDFATHER appears from behind the DIRECTOR.

GRANDFATHER: Pauly, they're trying to fob you off wid this musical charlatan but I've given him the test.

406
MS-3/4 S
LA

407
MCU-CU
NA

DIRECTOR: (bravely) I'm quite happy to be replaced.

408
MCU-MS
NA

GRANDFATHER: (indicating the director) He's a typical buck-passer.

409
MCU
LA

DIRECTOR: I won an award.

JOHN: A likely story.

DIRECTOR: It's on the wall in my office.

410
MCU-MS
NA

At this moment NORM comes on the stage, confident, cigar in mouth and serene.

NORM: Hello our lot, everyone happy?

411
FS
NA

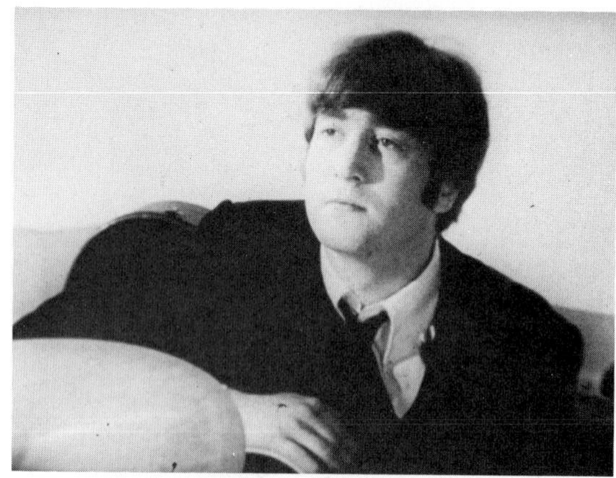

412
MCU-MS
NA

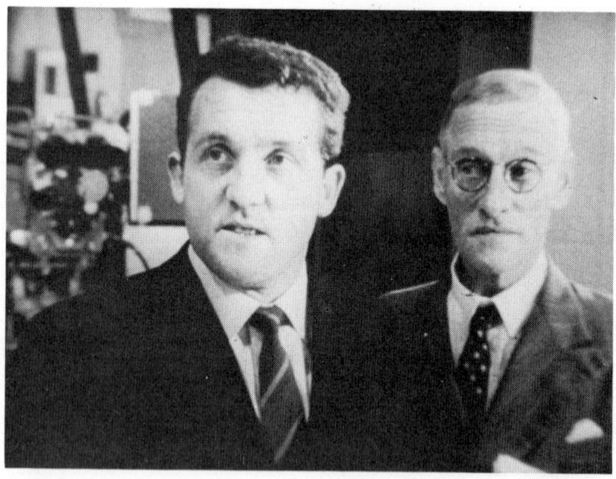

413
MCU
NA

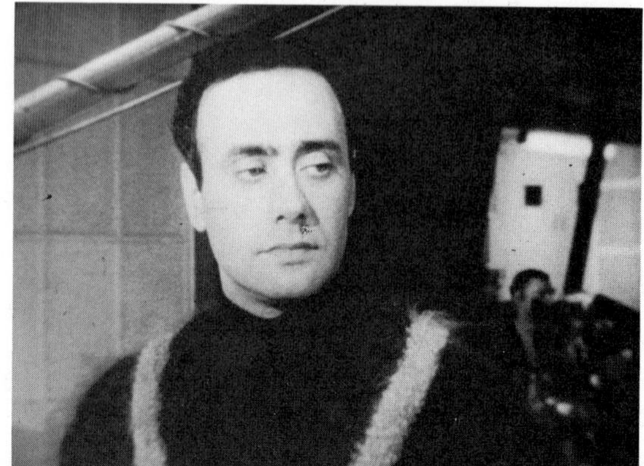

The BOYS, the DIRECTOR, FLOOR MANAGER and GRANDFATHER turn on him and stare silently.

NORM: All right,

414
MCU
NA

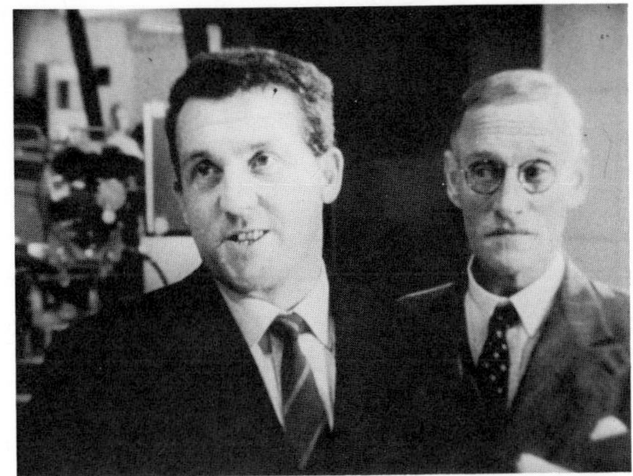

415
MCU
NA

all right. If you don't need this lot, I'll lock 'em up in the dressing room till you do.

416A
MCU
NA
PL to . . .

DIRECTOR: Please do, I'll not need them for half an hour. Thank you.

He glares at GRANDFATHER who glares right back. The DIRECTOR walks away with the FLOOR MANAGER pacifying him.

416B
MS
NA

DIRECTOR: Give me a bottle of milk and some tranquilizers. Oh, it's a plot, I see it now, it's all a plot.

(FLOOR MANAGER: Tranquilizers . . .)

They go left towards the backstage.

417
MCU
NA

NORM: (producing key) Now, come on, I've got the key.

He leads the lads off right. RINGO is last as he is putting his drum sticks down safely.

NORM and the BOYS turn on him.

NORM: Come ahead, Ringo.

[JOHN: Come on speedy!

PAUL: Ringo!

GEORGE: Wake up!]

RINGO glares at them and follows quickly. As the BOYS move off after NORM, they pass the next act waiting for rehearsal. It is an elegant man in full tails suit meticulously adjusting his cufflinks. Beside him is a free-standing sign reading "Leslie Jackson and his ten disappearing doves." The BOYS pass him and go through the door. GRANDFATHER stops and looks at the performer with respect.

GRANDFATHER: Leslie Jackson! I saw your father in the old empire in 1909. If you're as good as him son, you're all right.

He slaps the man on the back with happy camaraderie. There is the sound of a dove, a few feathers fall out of the sleeve of the man's coat and he and GRANDFATHER look down at the floor. The man glares at GRANDFATHER takes out a pen from his pocket, crosses out "10" on his sign, and writes "9" in its place, puts the pen back in his pocket [and starts towards the centre stage putting on a false performer's smile as he does.]

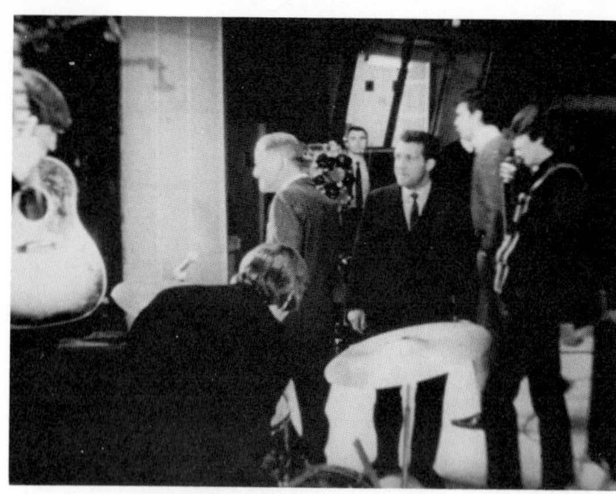

418
FS-LS
NA

419
3/4 S
LA

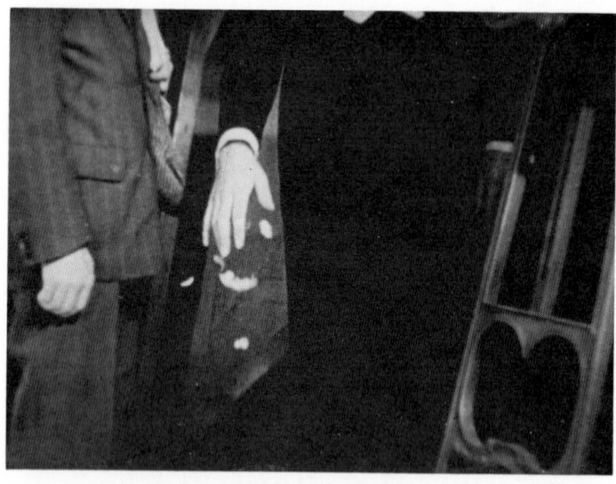

420
MCU
NA
(PD)

421
MCU
LA

422
FS
LA

INTERIOR, BACKSTAGE THEATRE CORRIDOR

423A
3/4 S
NA
DK
PL to . . .

The BOYS move down the narrow stairs and out of the ground floor dressing rooms streaming with a steady flow of costumed actors and actresses. They engulf the lads and force them against the wall—the actors are all making for the stage door. As the actors push past the BOYS we see the BOYS' excited faces, their mouths watering for the costumes. JOHN touches the costume on one actor.

JOHN: (to actor) Gear costume!

ACTOR: (eyeing him) Swop?

(JOHN: Cheeky.)

423B
3/4 S
NA
DK

424
MS
HA
DK

NORM: Right, first floor and no messing about.

NORM, leading the way, goes up the stairs but as they turn the first corner they are confronted by a group of girls; a game of manners starts: "After you," "No, after you." NORM who is ahead of the group looks down on them in disgust.

NORM: Lennon, put them girls down or I'll tell your mother on you. And stop messing about.

425A
MS
NA
DK
TO + PR to . . .

The BOYS let the girls pass and resume the journey, always surrounded by people.

(NORM: Stay in there until that rehearsal. I'm going to keep you even if I have to put the key in the lock and turn it.)

425B
MS
NA
DK

INTERIOR, DRESSING ROOM AND CORRIDOR

RINGO's attention is caught by a door. He crosses and opens it, looking out to a fire escape. The others join him and the four BOYS step through the door and onto the fire escape.

(RINGO: We're out!)

426
FS
LA

EXTERIOR, TOP OF FIRE ESCAPE

Song: *"Can't Buy Me Love"*
From the BOYS' P.O.V. we see down below [into the property yard behind the theatre. It is a long narrow yard full of old coaches, motor cars and all the general debris of hundreds of sets from past theatre shows. Through the piles of heaped high junk there are a couple of narrow alleyways.]

427
LS
LA
(PD)

The BOYS scamper down the fire escape.

428
LS
LA

432
MS
NA

429
LS
LA
Pan Around

433A
LS
LA
Pan Around,
PL+TL to...

430
MS
LA

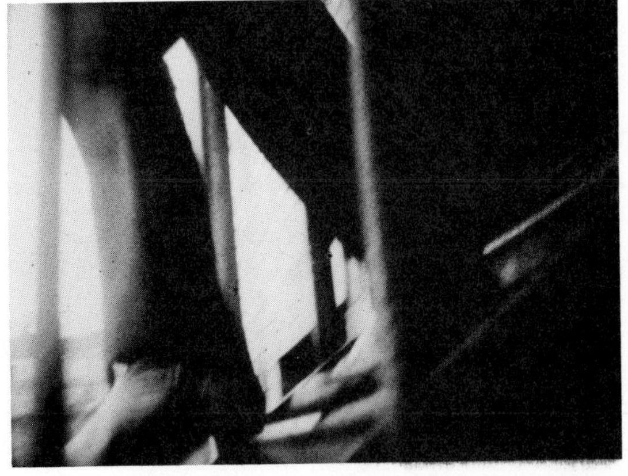
433B
MCU
LA
TL

431
LS
LA
Pan Around

434
LS
NA

[When they reach the bottom there is a large door. They open it and look through.]

From their P.O.V. we see a large green field quite empty. The BOYS step through the doorway into the field. We now see from a HELICOPTER SHOT the four BOYS standing together surrounded by space. It is the first time they have been alone and unconfined all day. They look at each other and grin . . . then first GEORGE and PAUL let out a whoop and run towards the centre of the field; after a moment JOHN and RINGO follow them. [The BOYS pick up some loose straw and insert it under JOHN's cap and sleeves, turning him into a scarecrow.]

The four BOYS dash about madly calling out to one another and generally horsing around. Out of this emerges an imaginary game of soccer and although there is no ball the game is fast and furious. RINGO is goalkeeper. GEORGE is the referee. JOHN has his name taken by the referee. PAUL takes the penalty kick. RINGO dives the wrong way and disgustedly kicks the imaginary ball into the back of the net. After a few moments the long shadow of a man falls across the grass.

436B
XLS
HA
(Accelerated Moti

436C
XLS
HA
(Accelerated Motic
PD to . . .

435
XLS
NA
(Accelerated
Motion)

437
XLS
NA

436A
XLS
HA
TR
(Helicopter
Shot)

438
XLS
HA
(Helicopter Shot)
(Accelerated Motior

439
LS
NA
(Accelerated
Motion)

441C
MS
NA
TO

440
Cu
NA

442
LS
NA

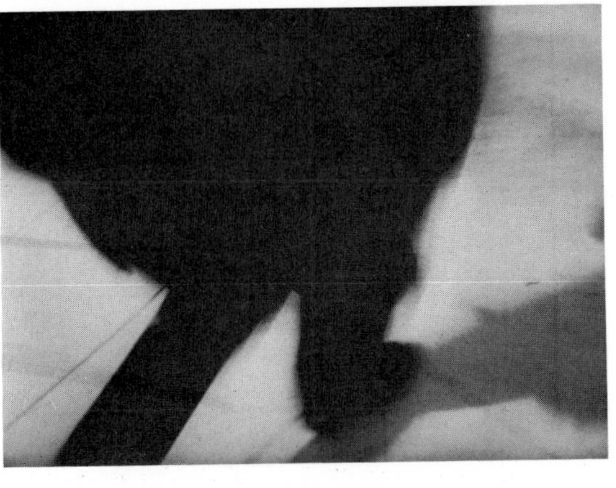
441A
MS
NA
PD, in circle
PU to . . .

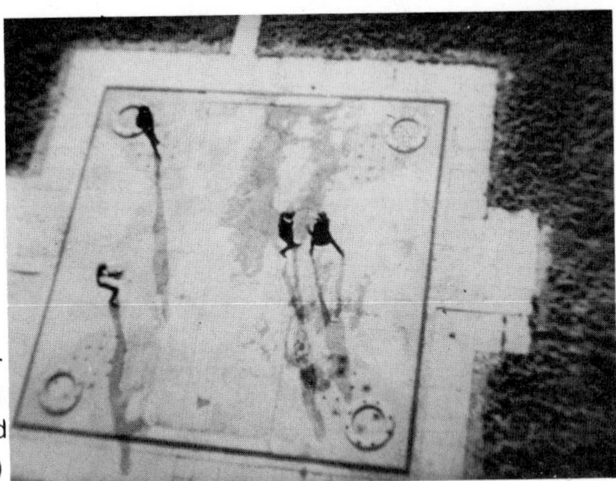
443
XLS
HA
(Helicopter
Shot)
(Accelerated
Motion)

441B
LS
NA
PD to . . .

444
XLS
LA
(Accelerated
Motion)

445
XLS
HA
(Helicopter
Shot)
TL+TO to
XLS

448
FS
LA
PD
(Slow Motion)

447
FS
LA
PD
(Slow Motion)

446
FS
LA
PD
(Slow
Motion)

449
LS
NA
(Slow Motion)

450A
XLS
HA
(Helicopter Shot)
(Accelerated Motion)
TO to . . .

452A
XLS
HA
(Helicopter Shot)
(Accelerated Motion)
TR to . . .

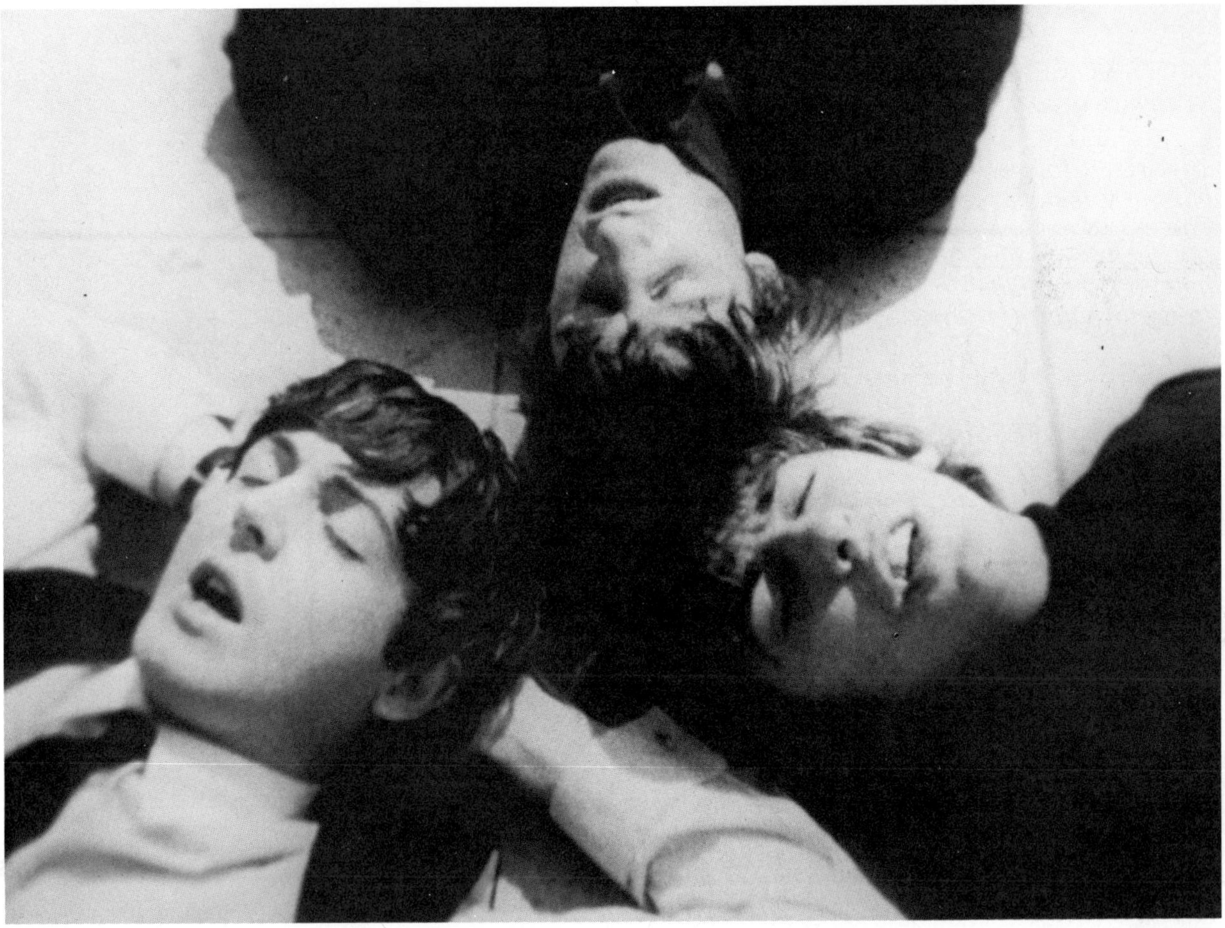

451
CU
HA

450B
XLS
HA
(Helicopter Shot)
(Accelerated Motion)

452B
XLS
HA
(Helicopter Shot)
(Accelerated Motion)

453
XLS
HA
(Helicopter Shot
(Accelerated Mo
TL+TO

MAN'S VOICE (off): I suppose you know this is private property.

The BOYS freeze. From their P.O.V. we see a big burly middle-aged man glowering at them. The BOYS exchange rueful glances and, under the big man's eye, mooch back towards the gateway they came in by. GEORGE is the last to go through. He turns to the man.

454
MS
NA
PU from man's f
PR

GEORGE: Sorry if we hurt your field, Mister.

INTERIOR, DRESSING ROOM

NORM and SHAKE enter the room. The BOYS' TAILOR is there waiting for the BOYS.

(NORM: Not here. Hello Dickie.)

SHAKE: Oh they've probably gone to the canteen, cup of tea, like.

NORM: That's too easy for Lennon.

He crosses to door leading to the fire escape.

NORM: (dramatically) He's out there somewhere, causing trouble just to upset me.

SHAKE: You're imagining it. You're letting things prey on your mind.

NORM: Oh no . . . this is a battle of nerves between John and me.

SHAKE: But John hasn't got any.

NORM: What?

SHAKE: Nerves.

NORM: I know, that's the trouble. (He puffs nervously at his cigarette.) Oh, I've toyed with the idea of a ball and chain but he'd only rattle them at me . . . and in public and all. Sometimes I think he enjoys seeing me suffer.

455
MS
LA
PL

456 MS LA PR

INTERIOR, CORRIDOR ON WAY TO DRESSING ROOM

JOHN is behind. JOHN, BOYS and MILLIE are walking towards each other.

MILLIE: (as all pass) Hello.

JOHN: (stopping . . . the boys carry on past, not noticing her) Hello.

MILLIE: Oh, wait a minute, don't tell me you're . . .

JOHN: No, not me.

MILLIE: (insistently) Oh you are, I know you are.

JOHN: No, I'm not.

MILLIE: You are.

JOHN: I'm not. No.

MILLIE: Well, you look like him.

JOHN: Oh do I? You're the first one who ever said that.

MILLIE: Oh you do, look.

JOHN looks at himself in the mirror. JOHN examines himself in the mirror carefully.

JOHN: My eyes are lighter.

MILLIE: (agreeing) Oh yes.

JOHN: And my nose . . .

MILLIE: Well, yes your nose is. Very.

JOHN: Is it?

MILLIE: I would have said so.

JOHN: Aye, but you know him well.

MILLIE: (indignantly) No I don't, he's only a casual acquaintance.

JOHN: (knowingly) That's what you say.

MILLIE: (suspiciously) What have you heard.

JOHN: (blandly) It's all over the place, everyone knows.

MILLIE: Is it, is it really.

JOHN: Mind you, I stood up for you, I mean I wouldn't have it.

MILLIE: I knew I could rely on you.

JOHN: (modestly) Thanks.

MILLIE touches his arm then walks away. After a moment she turns.

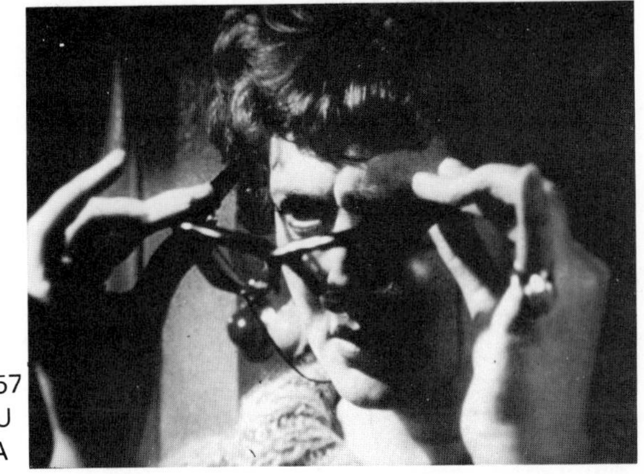

457 CU LA

MILLIE: You don't look like him at all.

[*JOHN winks at her and she winks back.*]

458A MCU LA PU to

458B
FS
LA

JOHN: She looks more like him than I do.

INTERIOR, T.V. THEATRE CORRIDOR

Announcement over P.A.: "There will be a full rehearsal in ten minutes time." GEORGE comes round the corner, [looking for RINGO,] then grins and walks past a sign saying "Canteen and Executive Office Opposite." [He comes to the exit door crosses to a modern building across from the theatre. He enters building.]

459A
MS
NA
PL, PU to . . .

459B
MS
LA

459
460
Dissolve to . . .

460
MS
NA

INTERIOR, OFFICE

It is the reception room that leads to an inner office. Behind a desk sits a smart young woman typing busily as GEORGE enters. He is surprised when he sees the girl; she looks up and speaks to him at once.

SECRETARY: Oh, there you are!

GEORGE: Oh, I'm sorry, I must have made a mistake.

461
FS
NA

SECRETARY: (tartly) You haven't, you're just late. (She rises and crossing over to him examines him critically.) Actually, I think he's going to be very pleased with you.

462
MS
NA
PD

GEORGE: Really?

SECRETARY: Yes, you're quite a feather in the cap. (She crosses to the desk and picks up the inter-office phone.) Hello, I've got one . . . oh, I think so . . . yes, he *can* talk . . . Well . . . I think you ought to see him. (She smiles.) Alright.

463
MS
NA

464
MS
NA

465A
MS
NA
PD to . . .

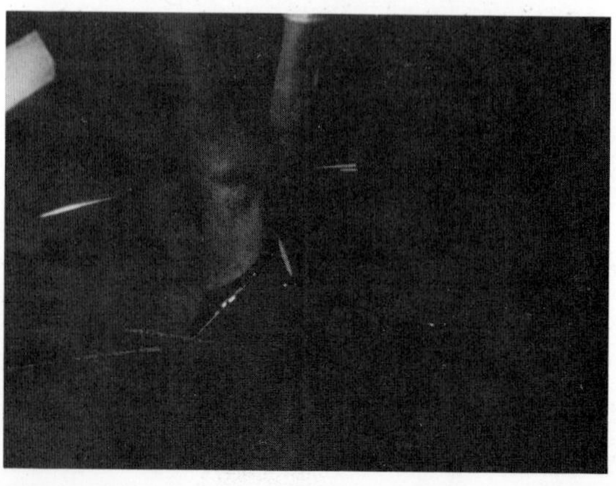

465B
MS
HA

466
MS
NA

467
MS
NA

468
MS
NA

469
MS
NA

She crosses to the inter office door. On the door is written SIMON MARSHAL . . . she opens it.

SECRETARY: Well . . . come on.

GEORGE: Sorry. You don't see many of these nowadays, do you?

470A
FS
NA
PL to . . .

SECRETARY: Come on.

He follows her quickly in.

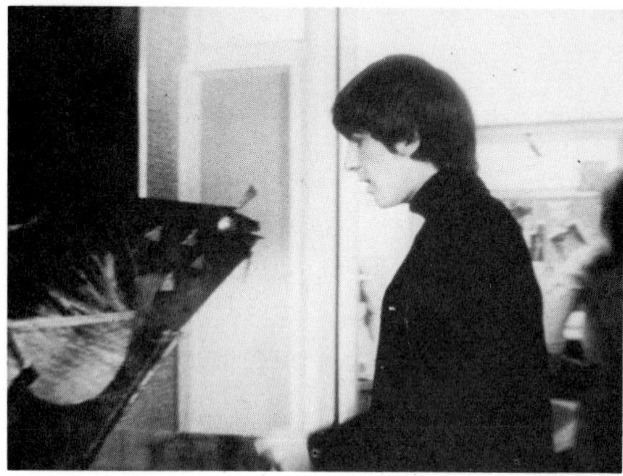

470B
MS
NA

INTERIOR, INNER OFFICE

A large room, part production office with models and sets, drawing board with ground plans, the other part of the room a mixture of Pop *and* Queens' *magazine decor.*

*Behind a large desk sits SIMON MARSHAL, a bland but slightly irritable young man of about thirty-five. He is wearing the ultimate in the current smart set fashion. He is attended by one underling (ADRIAN) and behind him on the wall is a poster of a girl. Across the poster is printed, "*Way Out*, your own T.V. Special with Susan Campey" Director, Simon Marshal.*

SECRETARY: (proudly) Will this do, Simon?

471
LS
LA

SIMON: (looking at George) Not bad, dolly, not really bad. (He motions to George.) Turn around, chicky baby.

GEORGE does so.

SIMON: Oh yes, a definite poss. He'll look good alongside Susan. (He indicates the girl on the poster.) Alright, Sonny Jim, this is all going to be quite painless. Don't breathe on me, Adrian.

472
MCU
NA

473
MCU
NA

ADRIAN has recognised GEORGE and is trying to stop SIMON.

GEORGE: Look, I'm terribly sorry

474
MCU
NA

but I'm afraid there's been some sort of a misunderstanding.

475
MCU
NA

SIMON: (sharply) Oh, you can come off it with us. You don't have to do the old adenoidal glottal stop and carry on for our benefit.

476
MCU
NA

GEORGE: I'm afraid I don't understand.

SIMON: Oh, my God, he's a natural.

SECRETARY: (anxiously) Well, I did tell them not to send us any more real ones.

SIMON: They ought to know by now the phonies are much easier to handle. Still he's a good type.

He now speaks to GEORGE in the loud voice that the English reserve for foreigners and village idiots.

SIMON: We want you to give us your opinion on some clothes for teenagers.

477
LS
LA

478A
MCU
LA
PL to . . .

478B
MCU
LA

GEORGE: Oh, by all means, I'd be quite prepared for that eventuality.

479
MCU
LA

480
MCU
LA

SIMON: Well, not your real opinion, naturally. It'll be written out and you'll learn it. (to secretary) Can he read?

GEORGE: Of course I can.

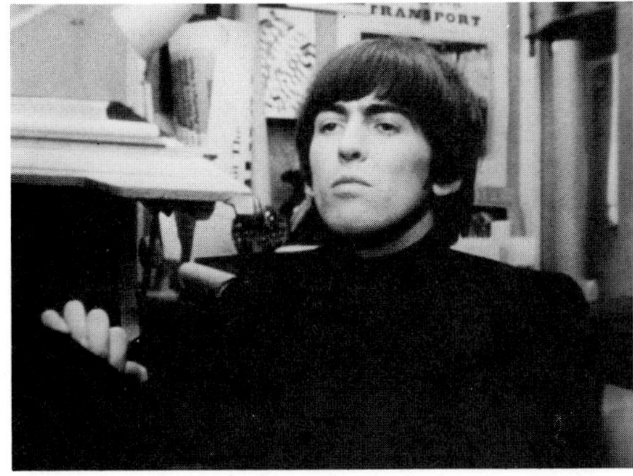

481
MCU
LA

SIMON: I mean lines, ducky, can you handle lines?

GEORGE: I'll have a bash.

SIMON: Good. Hart, get him whatever it is they drink, a cokearama?

GEORGE: Ta.

SIMON: Well, at least he's polite. Show him the shirts, Adrian.

A collection of shirts are produced and GEORGE looks at them. While he is doing this SIMON briefs him.

482
FS
LA

SIMON: Now, you'll like these. You really "dig" them. They're "fab" and all the other pimply hyperboles.

483
MS
LA

484
MCU
LA

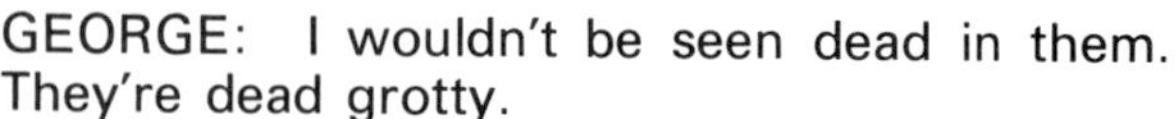

GEORGE: I wouldn't be seen dead in them. They're dead grotty.

485
FS
LA

SIMON: Grotty?

GEORGE: Yeah, grotesque.

486A
CU
LA
PU to . . .

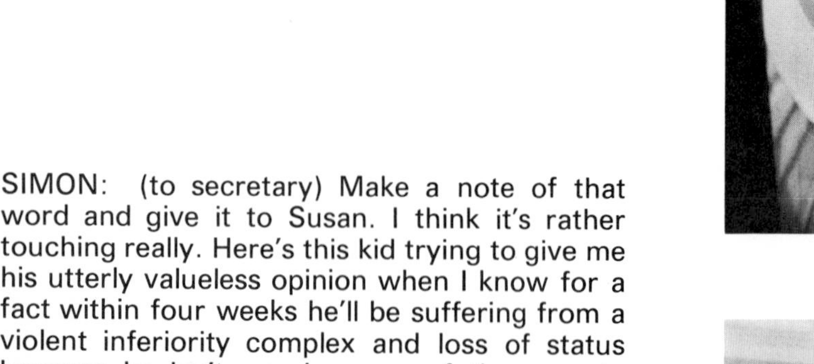

SIMON: (to secretary) Make a note of that word and give it to Susan. I think it's rather touching really. Here's this kid trying to give me his utterly valueless opinion when I know for a fact within four weeks he'll be suffering from a violent inferiority complex and loss of status because he isn't wearing one of these nasty things. Of course they're grotty, you wretched nit, that's why they were designed, but that's what you'll want.

486B
MCU
LA
PR

487
LS
LA

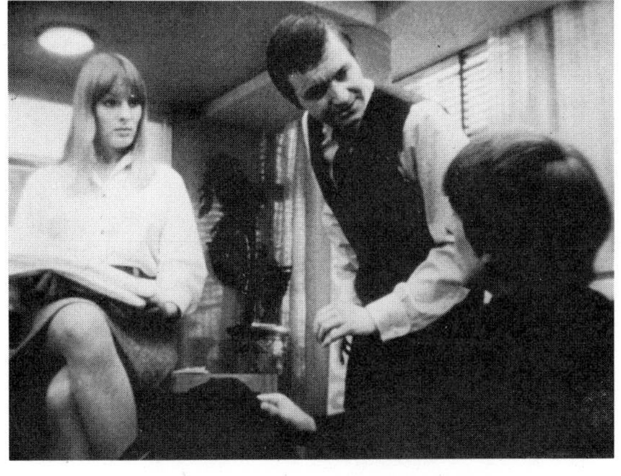

488
MS
LA

GEORGE: I won't.

SIMON: You can be replaced you know, chicky baby.

GEORGE: I don't care.

489
MCU
LA
PR

SIMON: And that pose is out too, Sunny Jim. The new thing is to care passionately, and be right wing. Anyway, you won't meet Susan if you don't cooperate.

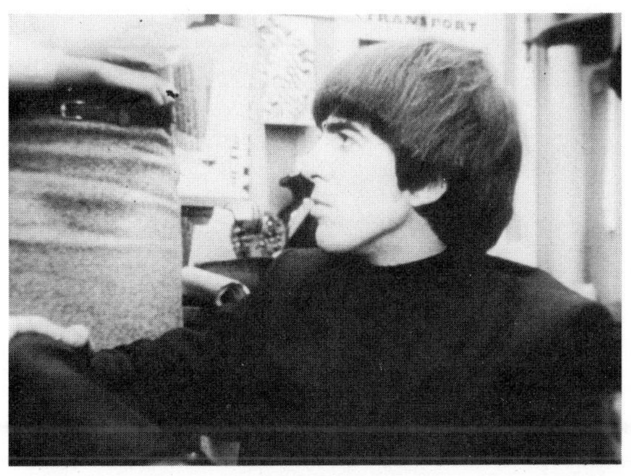

490
MCU
LA

GEORGE: And who's this Susan when she's at home?

SIMON: (playing his ace) Only Susan Campey, our resident teenager. You'll have to love her. She's your symbol.

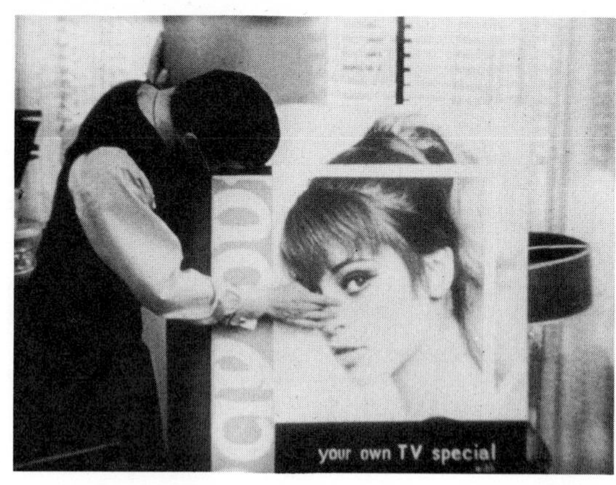

491
MS
NA

GEORGE: Oh, you mean that posh bird who gets everything wrong?

492
MCU
LA

SIMON: I beg your pardon?

GEORGE: Oh, yes, the lads frequently gather round the T.V. set to watch her for a giggle. Once we even all sat down and wrote these letters saying how gear she was and all that rubbish.

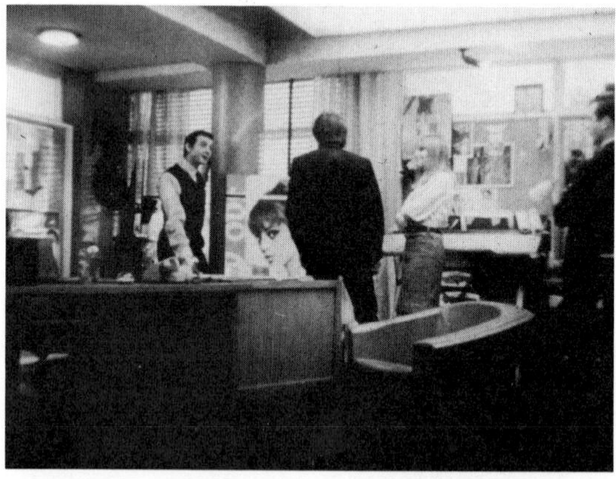

493
LS
LA

494
MS
NA

495
MCU
LA

SIMON: She's a trend setter. It's her profession!

496
MCU
HA

GEORGE: She's a drag. A well-known drag. We turn the sound down on her and say rude things.

497
MCU
LA
PL

SIMON: Get him out of here!!

GEORGE: (genuinely surprised) Have I said something amiss?

SIMON: Get him out of here. He's knocking the programme's image!!

498
FS
LA

The underlings hustle GEORGE to the door.

GEORGE: (smiling) Sorry about the shirts.

He is ejected through the door.

SIMON: Get him out. (He stops in mid shout.) You don't think he's a new phenomenon do you?

SECRETARY: You mean an early clue to the new direction?

499
MCU.
LA

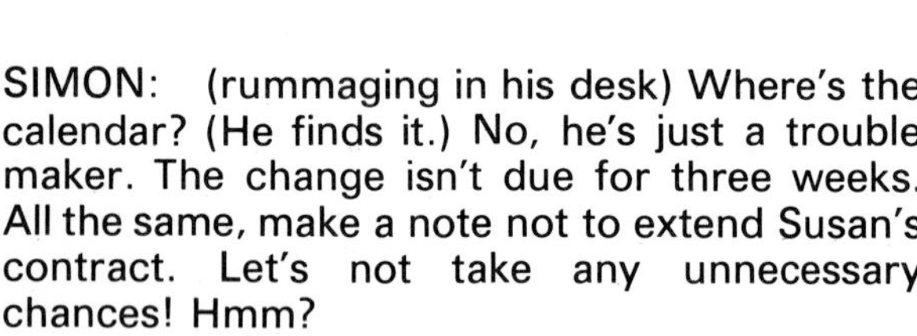

SIMON: (rummaging in his desk) Where's the calendar? (He finds it.) No, he's just a trouble maker. The change isn't due for three weeks. All the same, make a note not to extend Susan's contract. Let's not take any unnecessary chances! Hmm?

500A
MCU
LA
PL + PD to . . .

500B
MCU
HA
PR to . . .

500C
MCU
LA

501
XLS
NA

502
MCU
NA

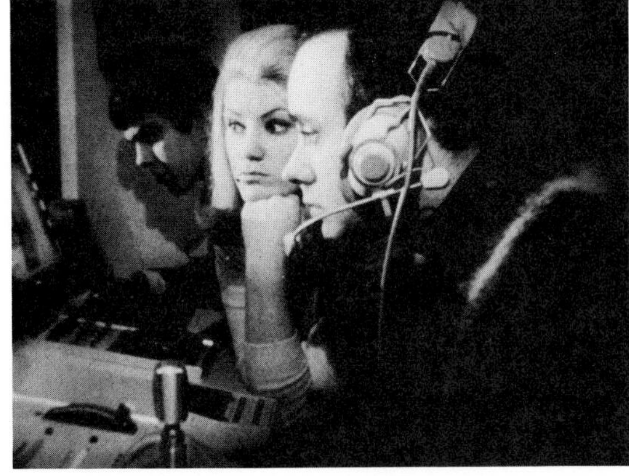

503A
MS
NA
PR to . . .

INTERIOR, BACKSTAGE CORRIDOR

GRANDFATHER is sneaking down the corridor, a pile of photos under his arm.

503B
MCU
NA
PD
(to feet going down stairs.)

(GIRL: . . . He's a very clean man . . .)

INTERIOR T.V. THEATRE UNDERNEATH THE STAGE

Under the stage the usual set of wooden columns that support the stage with lots of furniture and a single light is on; it is placed by the orchestra's entrance to the orchestra pit. GRANDFATHER comes down the stairs and winds his way through the columns until he finds himself a safe little cubby hole and settles himself under the light. He spreads the signed photo of the BOYS in front of him and, adjusting an old fashioned pair of glasses, ball-point pen in hand begins to copy the BOYS' signatures on to the fresh photos, tutting at his failures and chuckling at his successes. After a moment, there is a sound of someone coming down the stairs. GRANDFATHER darts into a dark patch out of sight. The menacing shadows appear on the stairway.

504A
XLS
NA
PL to . . .

504B
LS
LA

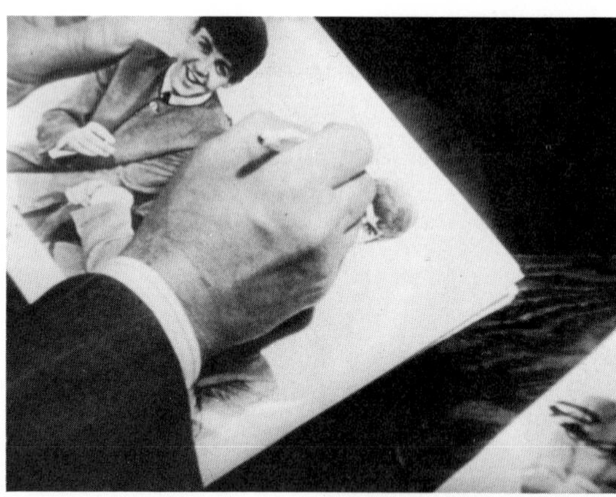

505
CU
HA
PL

506
FS
NA

507
XLS
NA

NORM: (voice off) There's no one here.

SHAKE: (voice off) Well, where have they gone?

508
LS
LA

We now see GRANDFATHER holding himself stiffly in; he is on some sort of raised platform and he fidgets and in doing so he knocks a lever of some sort. Slowly GRANDFATHER ascends OUT OF SHOT with a light that grows bigger above him.

509
FS
LA

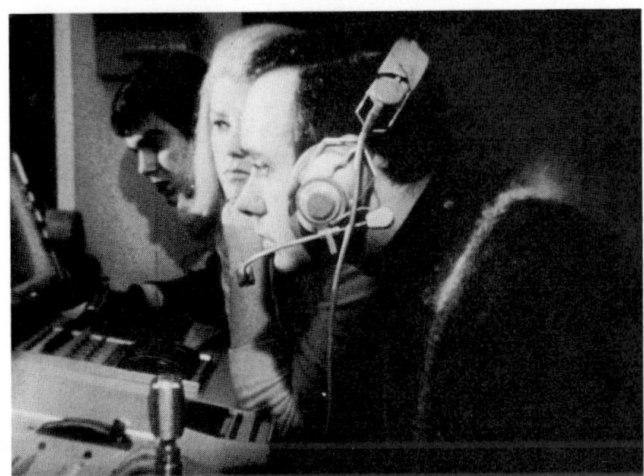

510
MCU
NA

INTERIOR, T.V. THEATRE STAGE

511
XLS
NA

A rehearsal of the toast scene from a Strauss Operetta. The entire stage is full of SINGERS. Glasses in hand they are singing away at each other but in true opera tradition they are addressing out to the audience. Slowly in between the leading man and leading woman, who are about to embrace, a stage trap opens and a blinking, surprised, GRANDFATHER appears. Here we INTERCUT to the T.V. control room for amazed REACTION SHOTS of the DIRECTOR and control room CREW.

Back now on the stage the toast song reaches its climax and the LEADING MAN and WOMAN rush into each other's arms, GRANDFATHER sandwiched between them.

512
MS
LA

(DIRECTOR: That's wrong, isn't it? Surely that's wrong.

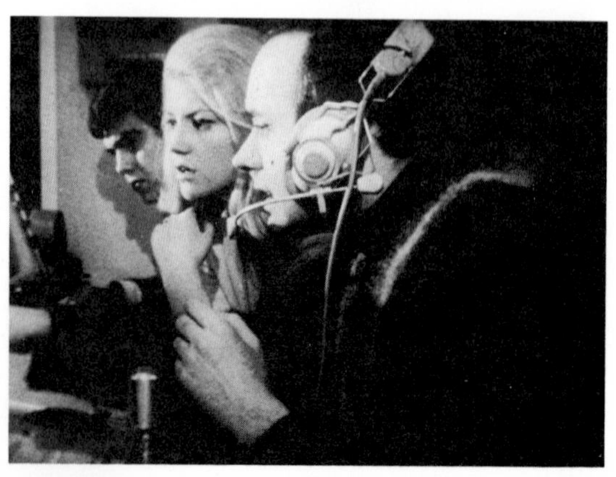

513
MCU
NA

514
MCU
NA

Get him out!)

515
FS
NA

516A
MS
LA
PR to . . .

INTERIOR, DRESSING ROOM

NORM: (He hears something.) Someone's coming. Quick, hide!

516B
LS
LA

The two men hide behind the door.

(NORM: Stop being taller than me.

SHAKE: It's not my fault.)

517A
FS
LA

The BOYS enter the room, as JOHN is last he shuts the door and faces SHAKE and NORM.

JOHN: What are you doing there?

SHAKE: Hiding.

JOHN: I think you're soft or something.

517B
FS
LA
PR to...

NORM: We weren't hiding. We were resting.

[TAILOR: Now?]

NORM: [Now. We were trying to catch you redhanded.] I thought I told you lot to stop here?

RINGO: Well . . .

517C
3/4 S
LA

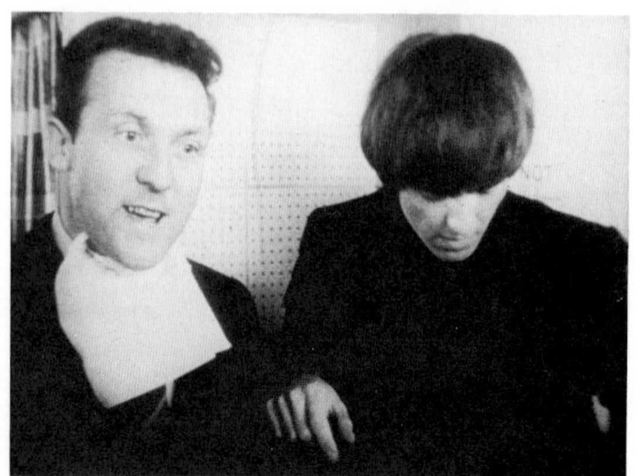

NORM: When I tell you to stay put, stay put.

518
MS
LA

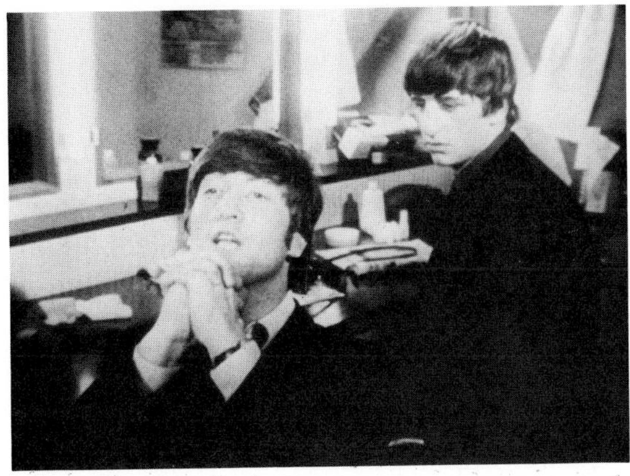

519
MS
HA
PD

JOHN: (down on his knees) Don't cane me, sir, I was led astray.

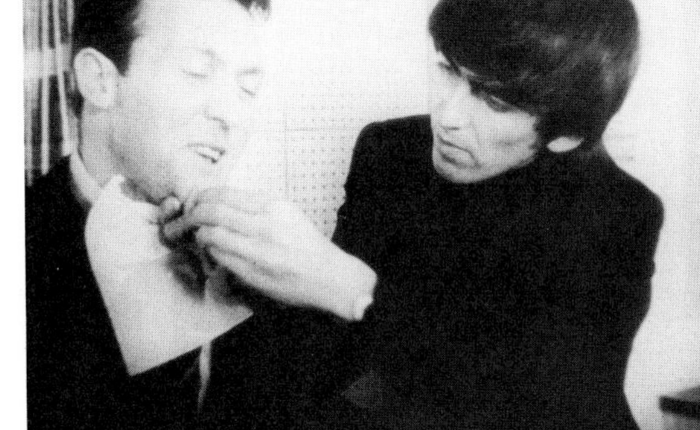

520
MS
LA

NORM: Oh shurrup and come on. They're waiting for you in the studio.

521
MS
LA
PU

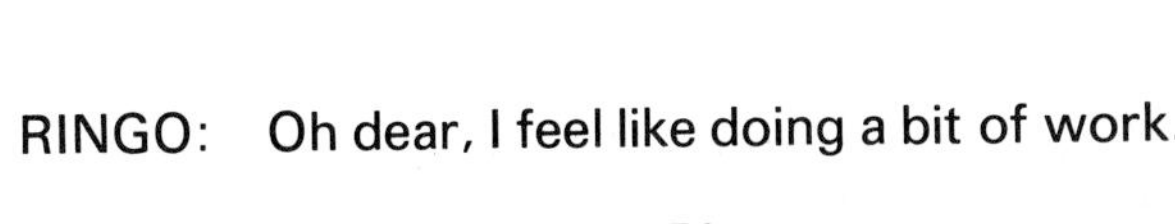

RINGO: Oh dear, I feel like doing a bit of work.

NORM: God bless you, Ringo.

522
MS-3/4 S
LA

PAUL: Oh, listen to teacher's pet.

GEORGE: You crawler.

523
MS
LA

JOHN: He's betrayed the class.

RINGO: Oh, leave off!

OHN: Temper! Temper!

INGO: Well . . .

524
MS
LA

CLOSE UP on NORM's long suffering face.

NORM: Will you all get a move on. They're waiting for you!

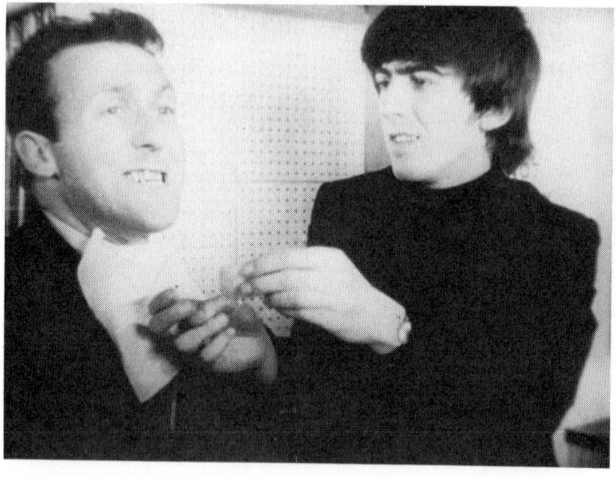

525
MS
LA

(PAUL: Sorry.)

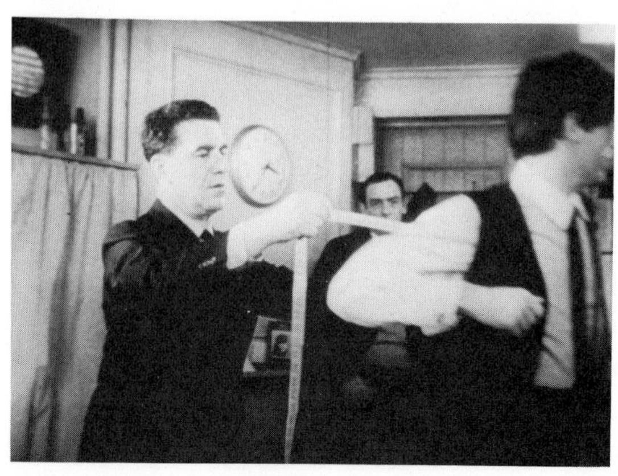

526
MS
LA

527
MS
LA

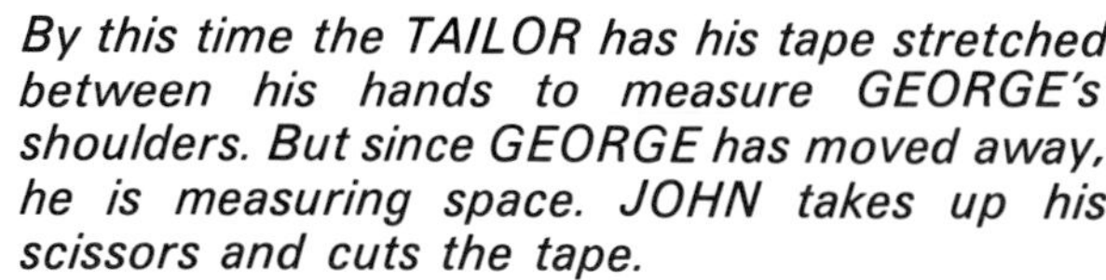

By this time the TAILOR has his tape stretched between his hands to measure GEORGE's shoulders. But since GEORGE has moved away, he is measuring space. JOHN takes up his scissors and cuts the tape.

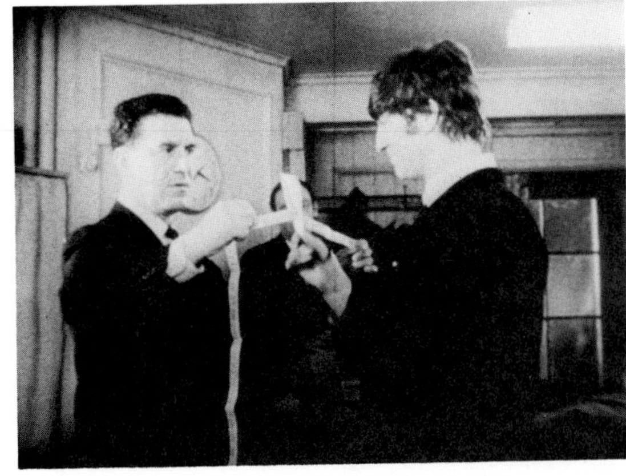

528
MS
LA

JOHN: I now declare this bridge open.

The BOYS run out the door.

[*INTERIOR, BACKSTAGE AREA*

Five beautiful MODELS are standing about in costume. One is knitting a loose wool sweater which is almost completed. There is the sound of a juggling act's music off and a few of the girls are looking off towards the centre stage. At the edge of frame is a collapsible table covered with green baize. On it are three spaced white plates.

From the door off stage above which is a sign "To Canteen and Production Offices," GRANDFATHER enters eating a plate of spaghetti on toast. The knitting GIRL sees him and, in mime, asks him to stand still so that she can measure the sweater against him. GRANDFATHER, eager to help, puts his plate of food on the green table between plates two and three. He goes to be measured with the sweater.

From the onstage area, a juggler's assistant (pretty girl) in costume backs up and with the usual theatrical flourishes picks up, without looking, plate number ONE and throws it off screen towards centre stage. There is a drum roll from orchestra. She then throws plate number TWO. We CUT on stage to the JUGGLER now balancing the two spinning plates on two poles, one in each hand. He has another pole in his mouth and nods to his assistant, asking for the THIRD plate.

We CUT BACK to the assistant who, still not looking, throws plate THREE which is GRANDFATHER's. There is the sound of an orchestra raggedly stopping and all the hangers-on in the scene look off interestedly.

We hear the DIRECTOR's voice.]

[DIRECTOR: (V.O.) All right, hold it, hold it . . . O.K. John, wipe him down and we'll carry on with the next act.

[*We CUT TO centre stage. The JUGGLER is as before but the spaghetti is covering his head, having slipped off the third plate.*

The FLOOR MANAGER is bustling around, trying to help.

We CUT BACK to backstage. GRANDFATHER has finished being measured and goes to the green table where he put his plate down. He picks up the only remaining plate, looks at it, wondering where his food has gone, shrugs and heads back towards the exit door as we hear the DIRECTOR's VOICE.]

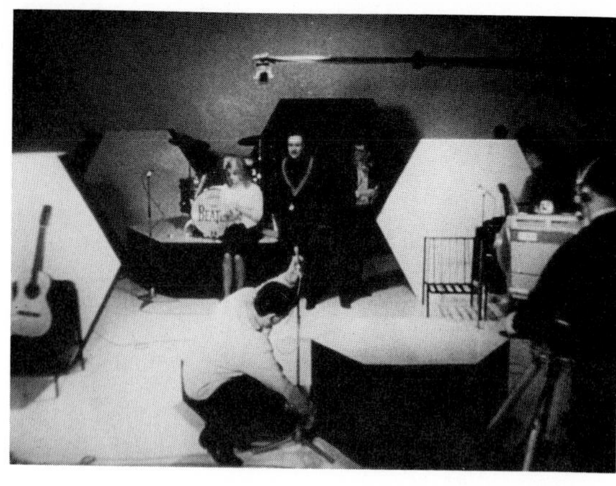

529
LS
HA

INTERIOR, T.V. STUDIO FLOOR

CLOSE UP on the distraught DIRECTOR.

DIRECTOR: Where are they? I said, where are they? Where are they?

530
3/4 S
NA

FLOOR MANAGER: (placating) They're coming, I promise you.

DIRECTOR: (fiercely) Now look, if they're not here on this floor in thirty seconds there's going to be trouble . . . understand me . . . trouble!!!

[*Two STAGE HANDS are walking disinterestedly past, they look at the DIRECTOR.*]

[1st STAGE HAND: What's he on about, Taff?

WELSH STAGE HAND: Well . . . he's being the director. Of course, he lives in a world of his own, mind.]

At this moment the BOYS, NORM, SHAKE and GRANDFATHER appear. The BOYS grab their instruments and prepare to play.

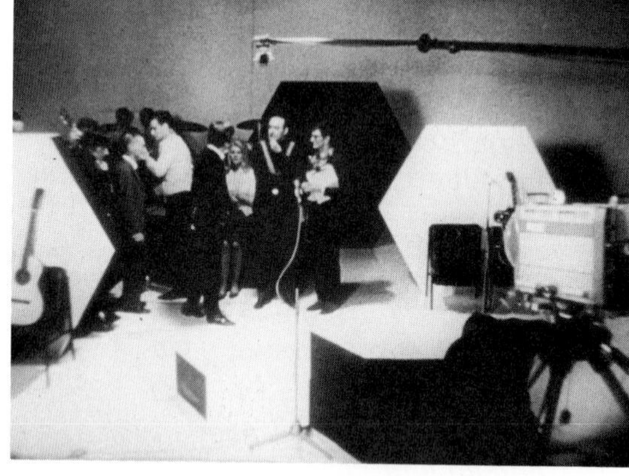

531
LS
HA

JOHN: (to the director) Standing about, eh?

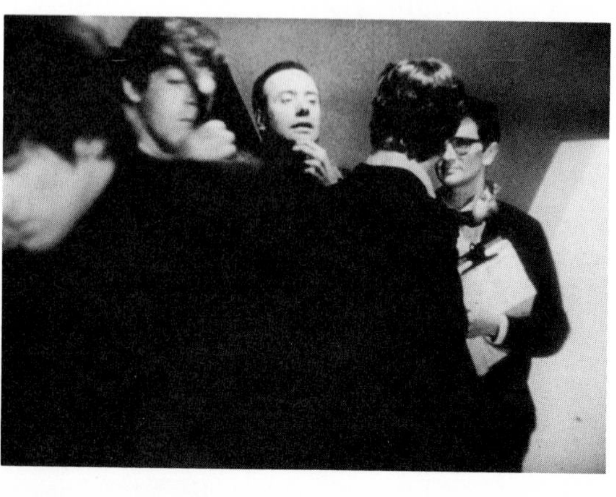

532
MS
LA

Some people have it dead easy, don't they?

The DIRECTOR is about to blow his top but manages to hold on and mutter to the heavens.

DIRECTOR: (to himself) Of course, once you're over thirty, you're finished. It's a young man's medium and I just can't take the pace.

RINGO: Are you as young as that, then?

(DIRECTOR: I was.)

533A
MS
NA
PL to . . .

[BOYS: Shurrup!

GRANDFATHER: Isn't it always the way? Picking on us little fellas.

PAUL: (to Shake) Shove the gentleman jockey in the make up room and keep your eye on him, will you?

SHAKE: I'm an electrician, not a wet nurse, y'know.

PAUL: (threateningly) I'll set John on you!

SHAKE: (hastily) Oh, anything you say, Paul]

[*He leads GRANDFATHER away.*]

533B
LS
NA

(GEORGE: Ah, there he goes. Look at him. I bet his wife doesn't know about her.

JOHN: I bet he hasn't even got a wife. Look at his sweater.

PAUL: You never know, she might have knitted it.

JOHN: She knitted him.)

534
LS
HA

The BOYS are placed in position, instruments ready. The boom moves in near them. There is a mike hovering just over JOHN's head. JOHN starts attacking it.

DIRECTOR'S VOICE: (over Tannoy) Alright, standby. Run through the number and try not to jiggle out of your positions.

535
MS
HA

Three, coming to you, three . . . three . . .

(VOICE: We're on three.

DIRECTOR: Oh yes.

Song: *"And I Love Her"*
The BOYS start the number, as the stage hands adjust their settings. When they've finished, they stand about spare. So we can watch every aspect of their work, and with so many monitors, it gives the impression that there are many more boys than just four. When the number ends we are back in the studio on the floor.

538
(CU
NA)

536
LS
HA

538
539
Dissolve to...

537
CU of T.V.
NA
(3/4 S
LA
image on
screen)

539
(CU
NA)

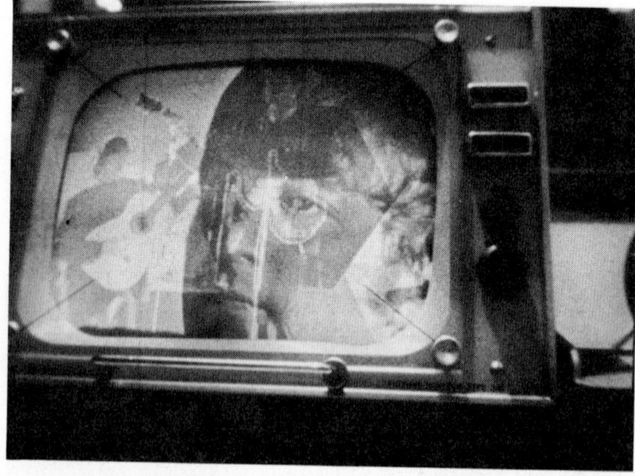

537
538
Dissolve
to...

539
540
T.V.
Wipe to...

540A
T.V. screen
CU
NA
ZO to . . .
(3/4 S
LA
image on
screen)

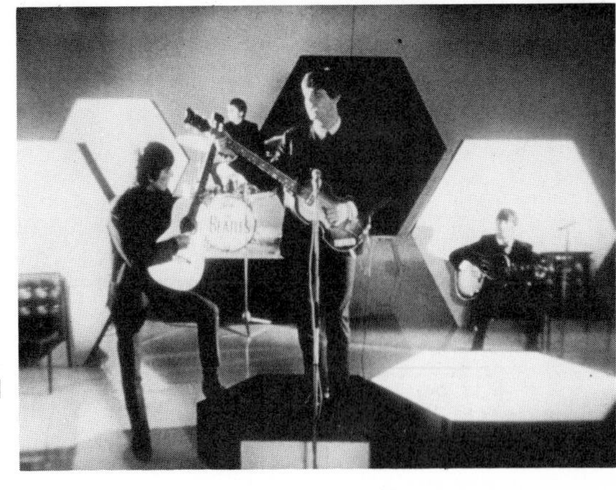

541
LS
HA

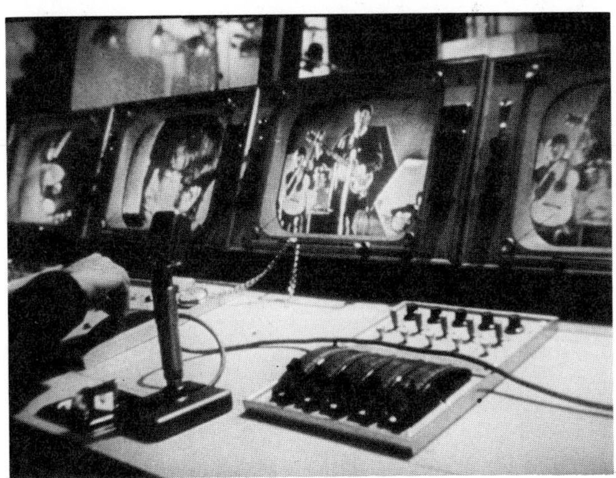

540B
MS
NA
TI & TU to . .

541
542
Dissolve to . . .

540C
LS
NA

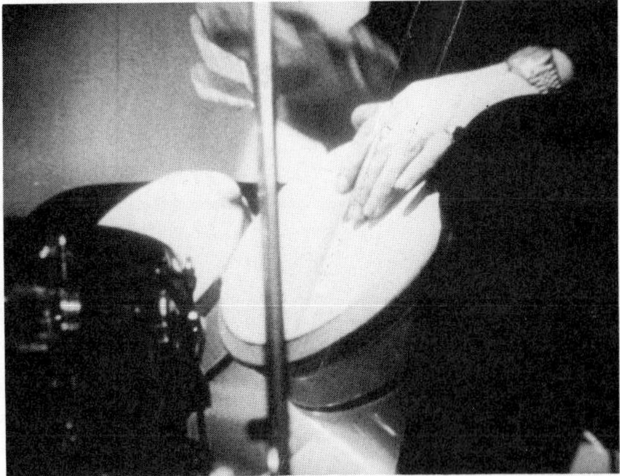

542
CU
HA

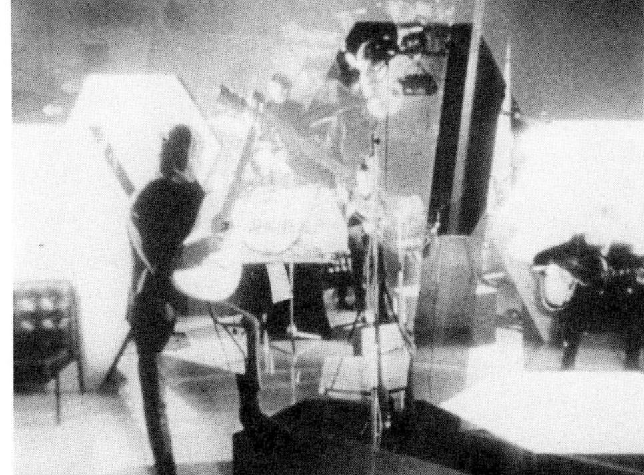

540
541
Dissolve to . . .

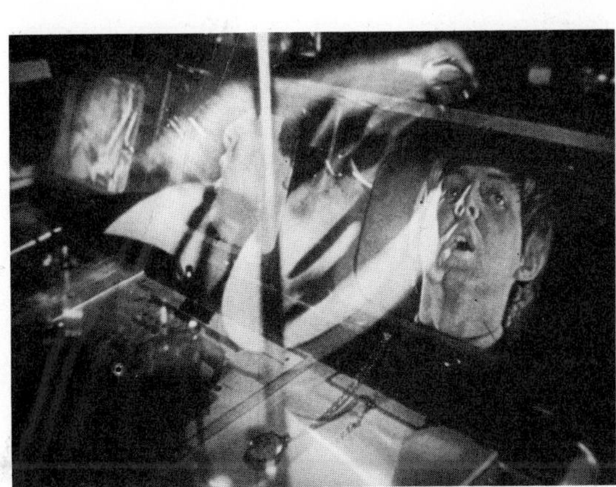

542
543
Dissolve to . .

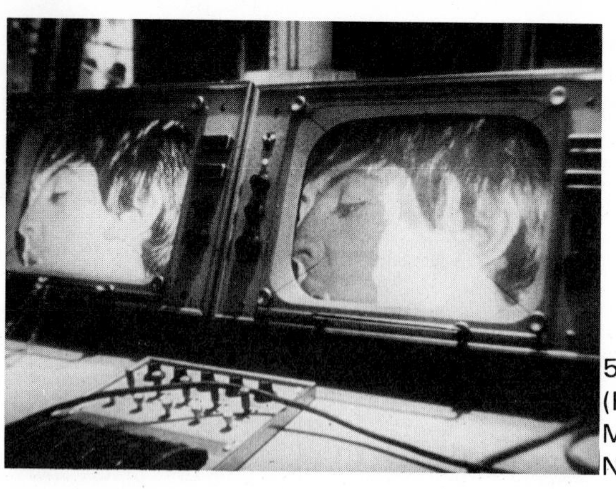
543
(PR)
MS
NA

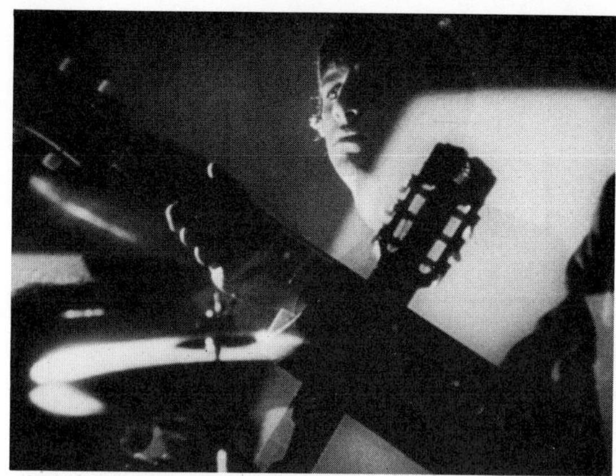
544
545
Dissolve to . . .

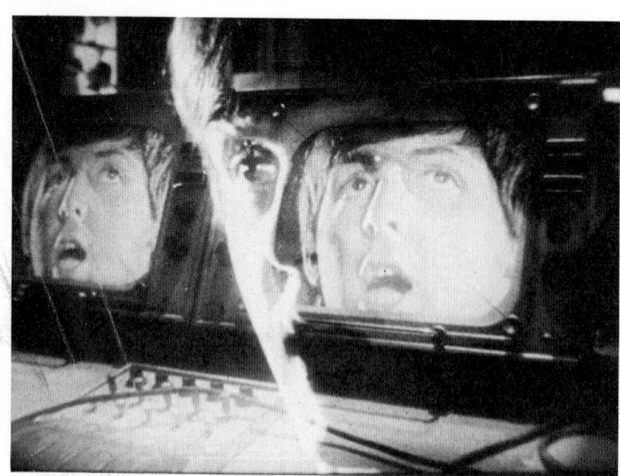
543
544
Dissolve to . .

545
MS
LA

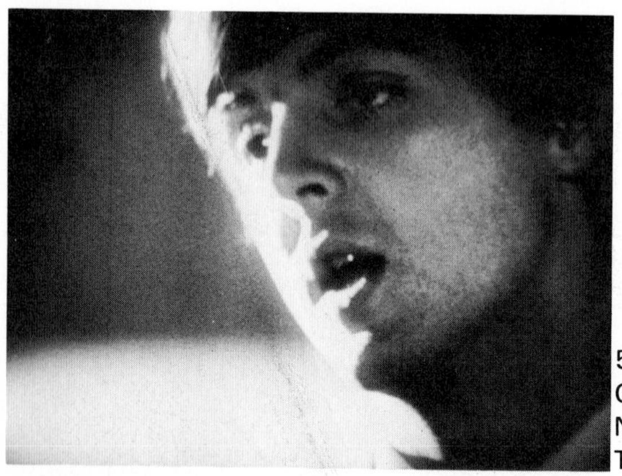
544A
CU
NA
TL&TO to . . .

545
546
Dissolve to . . .

544B
MS
NA

546
MS
LA

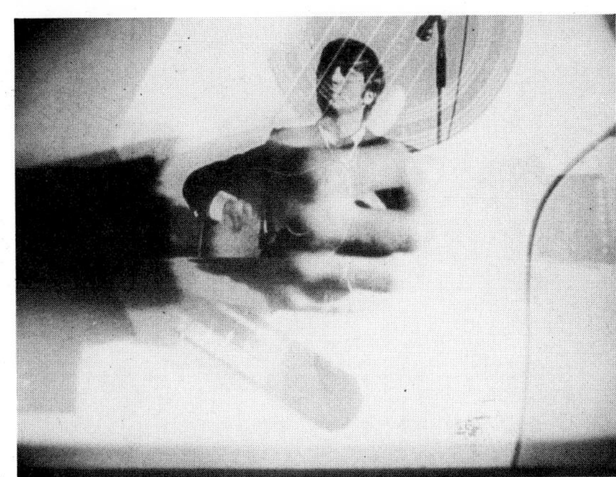

546
547A
Dissolve to . . .

547B
CU
NA

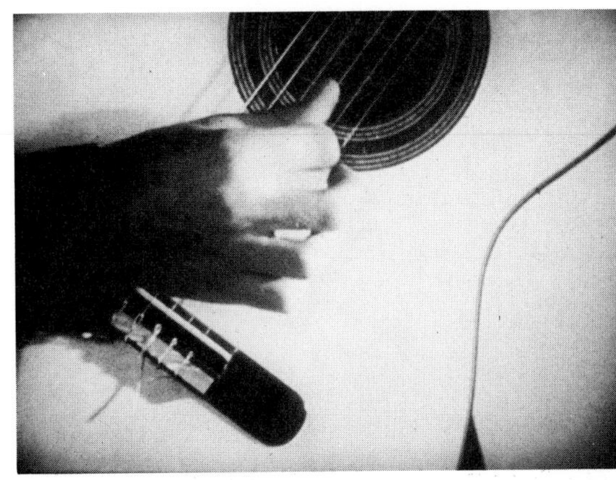

547A
CU
NA
TU to . . .

548A
CU
NA
T around
90° to . . .

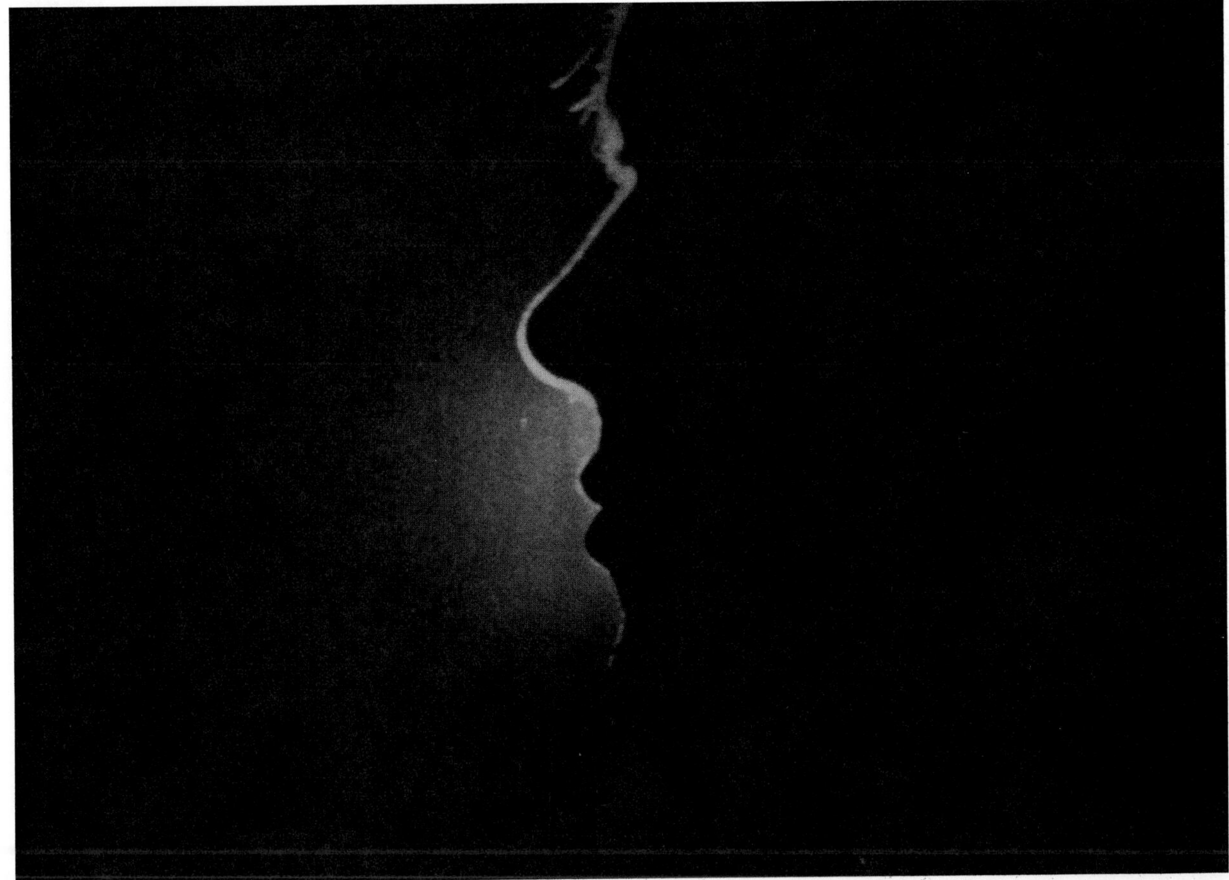

548B
CU
NA

549A
3/4 S
HA
ZO to . . .

549B
XLS
HA

DIRECTOR: Thank you, very nice.

INTERIOR, T.V. CONTROL ROOM

The room is crowded with the usual personnel, P.A., elecs, racks, etc., make-up supervisor and wardrobe mistress.

DIRECTOR: [That was more or less alright for me. I'll give them one more run through then leave them alone until the dress . . .] (to make-up woman) Make-up?

MAKE-UP WOMAN: Not really, they don't need it. We'll just powder them off for shine.

DIRECTOR: Good. Norm, get them along to make-up will you? *(Powder them up—the shine.)*

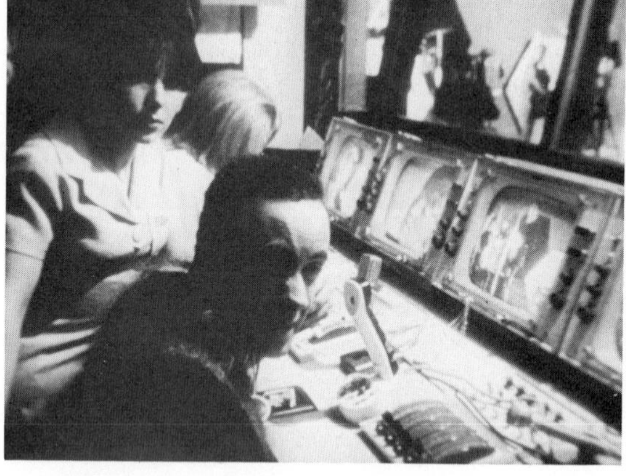

550
MS
HA

NORM: (rising) Sure.

[DIRECTOR: (looking into the monitor) And hurry, they're not looking too happy.]

From the DIRECTOR's P.O.V. we see into the monitor. The BOYS crowding around RINGO.

551
MCU
NA

552A
3/4 S
NA
TI to...

INTERIOR, MAKE-UP ROOM

A smallish room with a line of chairs facing a wall mirror and a long table. Each place is clearly marked and above each mirror is a girl's name: Betty, Angela, Deirdre, Jenny.

SHAKE and GRANDFATHER are sitting in splendid isolation. They are staring each other out.

SHAKE: You blinked!

[GRANDFATHER: I never did, you did.]

The BOYS enter.

552B
3/4 S
NA

SHAKE: Hello, your grandfather's not talking to me. He's having a sulk.

GEORGE: Well, it must be catching on. He's given it to Ringo here.

He indicates RINGO, he ignores him.

NORM: Stop picking on him.

RINGO: I don't need you to defend me, y'know, Norm.

JOHN: Leave him alone, he's got swine fever.

NORM: Sit down, the lot of you.

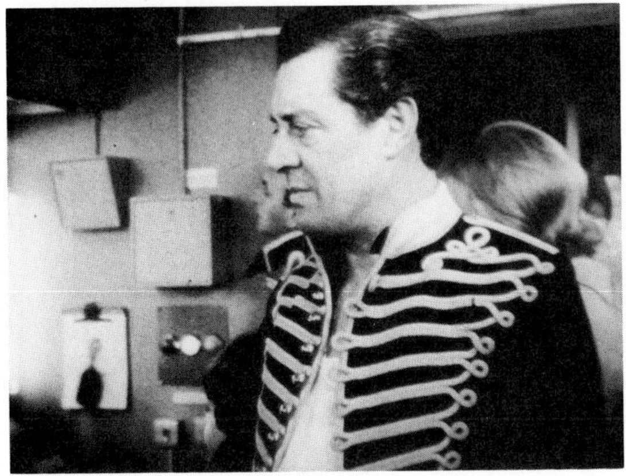

553A
MCU
NA
PL+PD to..

At this moment several ACTORS come into the room. They are all dressed in the uniform of officers in Wellington's army. Together with the BOYS they sit down, Beatles and soldiers all mixed up.

Now a group of several pretty make-up girls make an entrance and the BOYS herald their arrival with a chorus of "aye aye's" and wolf whistles. JOHN meanwhile has helped himself to a big beard and the other lads are generally messing about with assorted make-up things.

HEAD MAKE-UP GIRL: Oh, this is impossible! We'll never get you all done in time.

ACTOR: Well, you'll just have to do us first . . . it makes no difference to them whether they're made up or not . . . (sees John with beard) And by the way, what's that?

553B
MS
NA
(PR)

JOHN: (charmingly) My name's Betty . . . (pointing to the name on the mirror) Do you want a punch up your frogged tunic?

(ACTOR: No.)

NORM fights his way to JOHN.

NORM: Now listen, John, behave yourself or I'll murder you and, Shake, take that wig off, it suits you.

554
CU
NA

555
MCU
NA

SHAKE has a girl's long blonde wig on. With the assistance of the girls, NORM gets the BOYS seated into the chairs nearest the door. For some reason RINGO now has a guardsman's busby wedged down almost over his eyes and is sitting with it on under a hair drier, reading a copy of Queen *magazine.*

NORM: (to Ringo) What do you think you're up to?

556
MCU
NA

557
MS
NA

RINGO: [Someone put it on me.] *(Page five.)*

JOHN: [Excuses, that's all we get and you know you fancy yourself in the Coldstreams.] *(You always fancied yourself as a guardsman, didn't you.)*

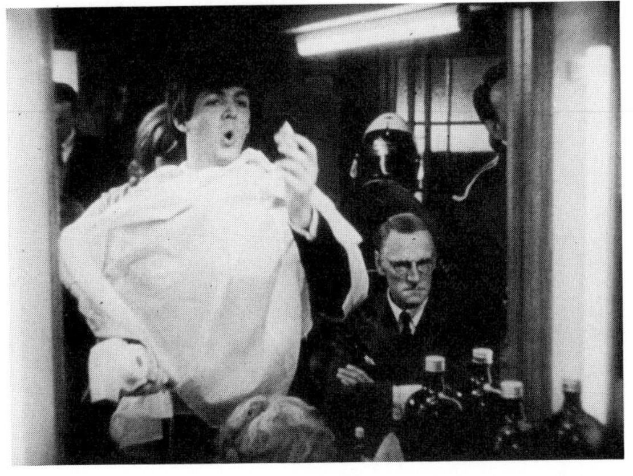

558A
3/4 S
NA
PR to . .

The girls now move in and put make-up bibs on the BOYS and start to powder them off.

(PAUL: Oh, that this too, too solid flesh would melt. Zap!)

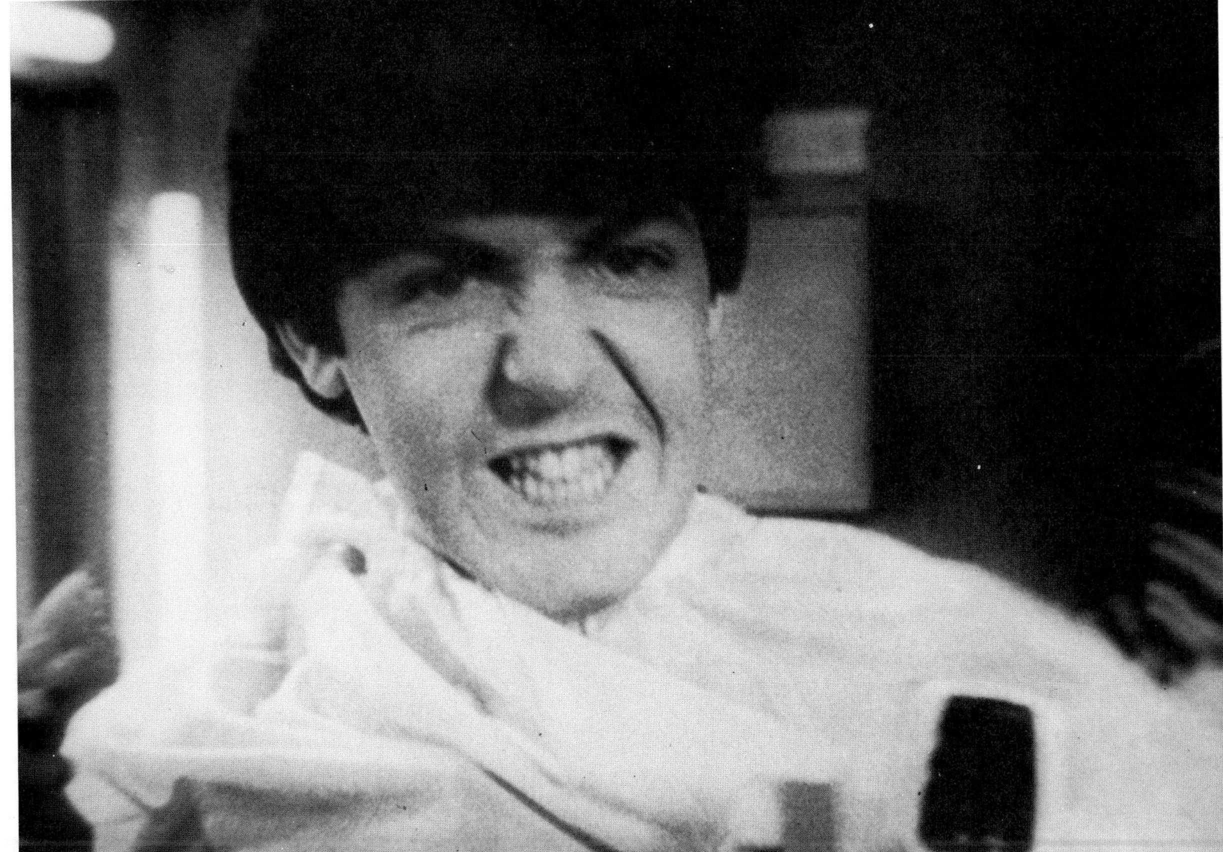

558B
MCU
NA

[JOHN] GEORGE: You won't interfere with the basic rugged concept of my personality, will you, madam?

[PAUL: Eh, don't take out me lines.

GEORGE: Yeah, they give him that "Je ne sais quoi" rakish air.]

[*The lads laugh with pleasure. RINGO decides to try a little joke.*]

[RINGO: (indicating the busby he is still wearing) Short back and sides, please.]

[*The others look at him with mock disgust.*]

[PAUL: Behave . . .

JOHN: Foreign devil . . .

GEORGE: Control yourself . . .]

559
MCU
NA

(JOHN: Say, he's reading the Queen. *That's an "in" joke, you know.*

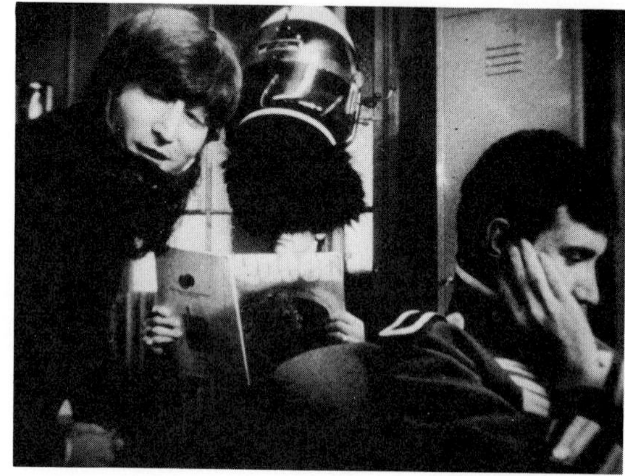

560
MS
NA

PAUL: Shazzam!)

561A
MCU
NA
PR to . .

[*GRANDFATHER has been watching the powdering process.*]

GRANDFATHER: In my considered opinion you're a bunch of sissies.

561B
MS
NA

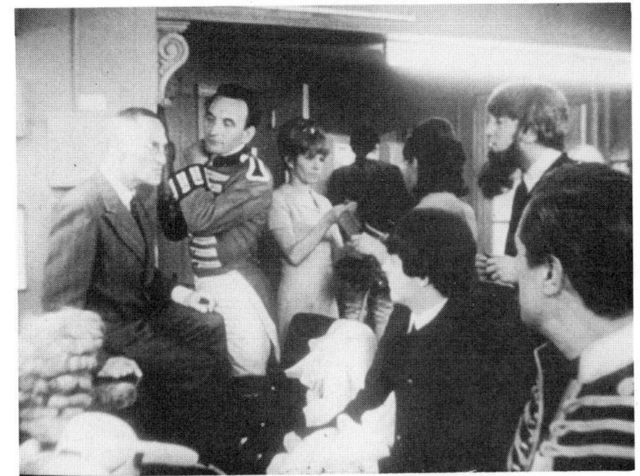

562
3/4 S
LA

[*JOHN grabs a powder puff from his girl.*]

[JOHN] PAUL: You know you're only jealous!

[*And dabs the old man liberally with the powder much to GRANDFATHER's annoyance.*]

NORM: Leave him alone, Lennon, or I'll tell

563
MCU
NA

them all the truth about you.

JOHN: You wouldn't!

NORM: I would though.

NORM goes out.

[PAUL: What's he know?

JOHN: Nothing, he's trying to brain wash me and give me personality doubts . . . oh, he's a swine but a clever swine, mind.]

GRANDFATHER: (impatiently) Lookit, I thought I was supposed to be getting a change of scenery and so far I've been in a train and a room, a car and a room and a room and a room. Well, that's maybe alright for a bunch of powdered gee-gaws like you lot but I'm feeling decidedly straight-jacketed. [This is no life for a free-booting agent of my stamp, I'm a frustrated man and that class of McCartney is a dangerous McCartney.]

564
3/4 S
LA

565
MCU
NA

GIRL: (admiringly) What a clean old man.

566
MCU
LA

GRANDFATHER: (touchily) [You're too young for a fella of my cosmopolitan tastes, so] don't press your luck.

JOHN: He's sex-obsessed.

567
MCU
NA

The older generation are leading this country to galloping ruin.

568
MCU
LA

569
MCU
NA

570
MCU
NA

(SHAKE: What's a pretty girl like you doing in a place like this?)

NORM returns leaving the door open; the BOYS hear the sound of music coming from the studio.

571
3/4 S
LA

NORM: They're nearly ready for you. They're just finishing the band call.

(JOHN: I say, did you go to Harrod's? I was there in '58, you know. I can get you on the stage.

GIRL: Oh, how?

JOHN: Turn right here at the corridor . . .)

[JOHN: (jumping up from his seat) Gear! Come on, girls, let's have a bit of a dance.

JOHN'S GIRL: I don't think it's allowed.

JOHN: Well . . . it wouldn't be any fun if it was!]

The BOYS drag the make-up girls out of the room and into the studio. The GIRLS are still trying to finish making the boys up.

572
MS
NA

(GEORGE: (to girl) . . . and I don't like yours.)

[*As the BOYS and MAKE-UP GIRLS dance past, we see one of the "Strauss" singers combing his long hair straight back. Two STAGE HANDS swing a windmachine past him and his hair is blown straight forward into a Beatle cut.*]

[JOHN: (passing him) Never.]

[*During dance, GEORGE takes off wig and places it on dummy, revealing identical hair underneath.*]

573
LS
HA

INTERIOR, T.V. STUDIO FLOOR

574
3/4 S-MS
NA
PR

575
3/4 S
NA

The work is still going on and the music is up full blast; the BOYS enter and with the girls they start a wild dance, hippy, shake, zulu, blue beat, the lot. LIONEL and DANCERS are doing their routine on one side of stage . . . it becomes a challenge dance between both groups. [JOHN swings his GIRL onto the motorised CAMERA, Western style and starts to track through the GROUP. GEORGE is on another CAMERA.]

576
LS
LA

INTERIOR, CONTROL ROOM

[The whole control room crew is watching the dance on all the monitors. The DIRECTOR is about to stop the BOYS but his GIRL P.A. glares at him, with a shrug he lets the dance go on.

We now CUT between the dancers on the monitors and the BOYS actual dancing down on the studio floor.] When the recorded music stops, they grab their instruments and go into a number.

577
FS
LA
PL

578A
MCU
NA
PL,
PR to . . .

578B
MS
LA

579
LS
LA

JOHN: Hey kids, I've got an idea. Why don't we do the show right here! One, two, three, four!

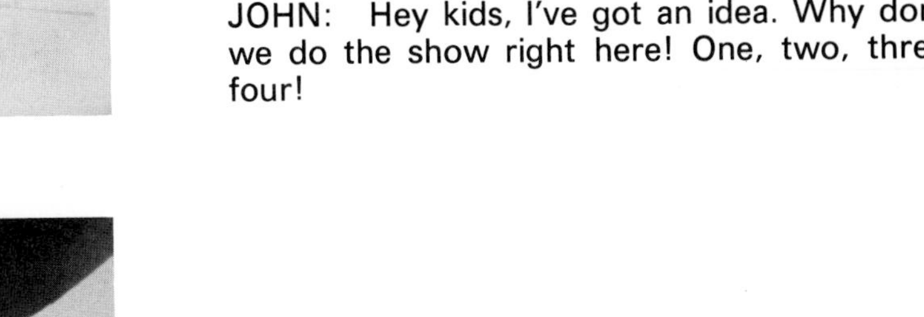

580
MS
LA

Song: *"I'm Happy Just to Dance With You"*

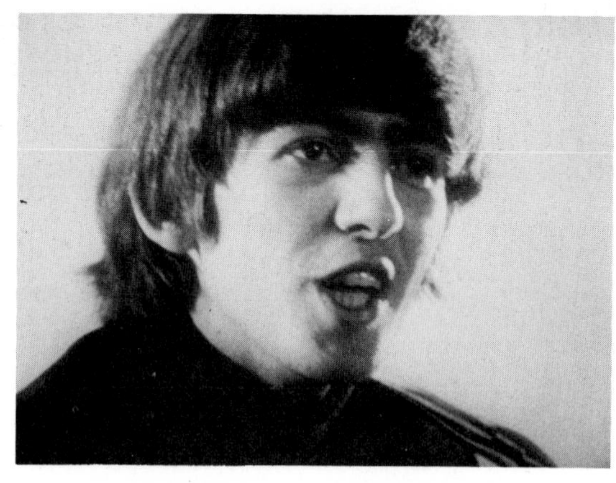

583B
CU
LA

581
MS
NA

584A
CU
NA
(Change Focus t

582
LS
HA

584B
MCU
NA

583A
MS
NA
ZI to . . .

585
MS
LA

586
FS
LA
(PRU)

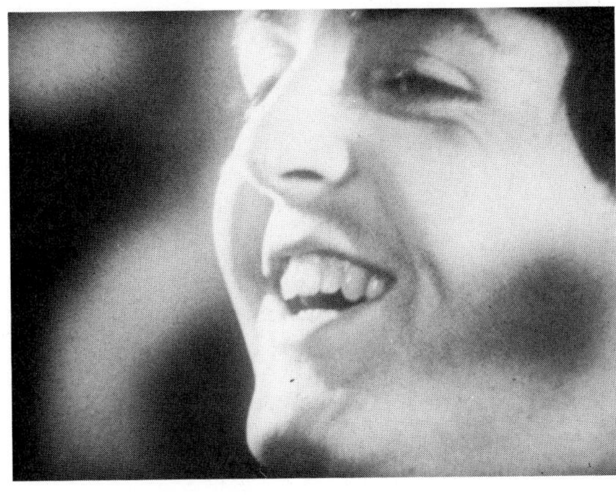

587
XCU
NA

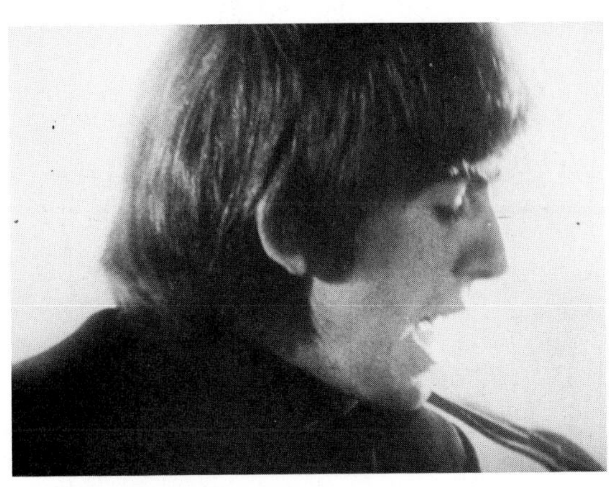

588
MCU
LA

589
FS
NA

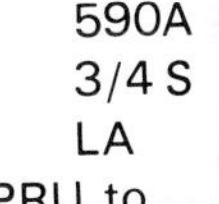

590A
3/4 S
LA
PRU to . .

590B
MS
LA

591
MCU
LA

592
LS
HA

593A
CU
NA
Change Focus to . . .

593B
MCU
NA

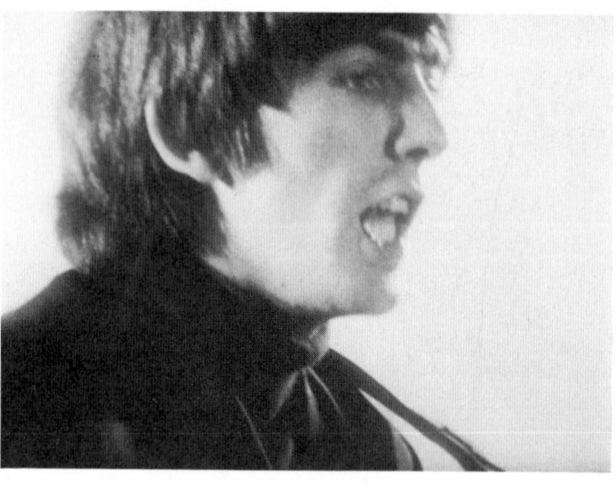

594B
MCU
LA

594A
CU
NA
PRU to . . .

595
MCU
LA

596
MCU
LA

597
3/4 S
LA

JOHN: Ah, very good, that George.

PAUL: We're trying.

598
MS
LA

INTERIOR, T.V. STUDIO FLOOR

[DIRECTOR'S VOICE OVER TANNOY: Thank you, gentlemen, you can break now while we push on with the show.]

[*The BOYS acknowledge this with a quaver of guitar chords and a drum roll. NORM is on them at once.*]

NORM: That was great, you've got about an hour but don't leave the theatre. Where are you going, John?

599
LS
HA
PR

JOHN grabs the arm of a sexy girl dancer.

JOHN: She's going to show me her stamp collection.

PAUL: (grabs a showgirl) So's mine.

NORM grabs JOHN's arm.

NORM: John, I was talking to you. The final run-through is important. Understand, important!

600
MS
NA

601
MCU
NA

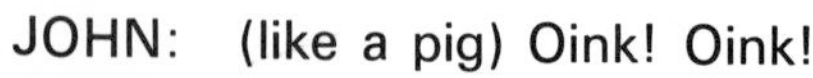
JOHN: (like a pig) Oink! Oink!

They dash off with the two beauties. GRANDFATHER is hovering in the background with SHAKE.

602
MS
NA

603
MS
LA
PD

GRANDFATHER: I want me a cup of tea.

604
LS
HA
PL

NORM: Shake.

SHAKE: I'm adjusting the decibels on the inbalance.

NORM: Clever. (He turns.) George!

605
MS
HA

But GEORGE is disappearing out of the door. NORM turns to RINGO.

606
MCU
NA

NORM: Ringo, look after him, will you?

607
(PU)
3/4 S
LA
PL

RINGO: But, Norm . . .

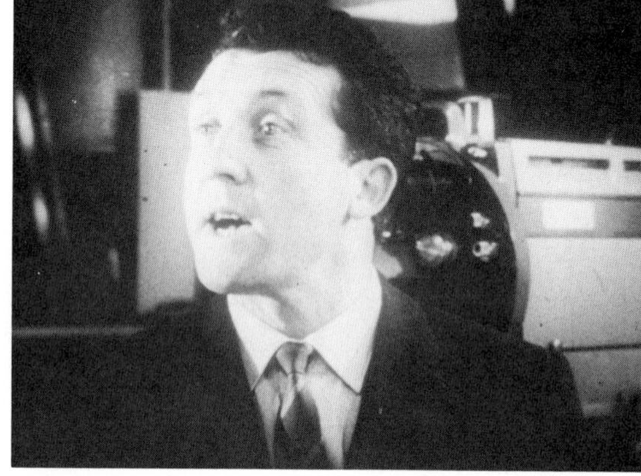
608
MCU
NA

NORM: Do I have to raise me voice?

609
MCU
LA

RINGO: (choked) Oh, alright. Come here, Grandad. *(I'm a drummer, not a wet nurse.)*

610
MS-MCU
NA

611
MCU
NA

612A
LS
LA
ZI to . . .

612B
MCU
LA

And the two of them walk off, RINGO leading.

[*INTERIOR, BACKSTAGE*

A man, whose act is playing tunes by hitting himself on the head, is swallowing a handful of aspirin tablets. He starts rehearsing his act, which consists of throwing his head back and slapping his cheeks. Next to him, a JUGGLER is practising with four table tennis balls.

GRANDFATHER passes him and bumps his arm slightly. Only 3 balls come down. There is the sound of coughing off.

We CUT TO THE HEAD-PLAYER being patted on the back. The ball drops out of his mouth and bounces slowly on the studio floor.]

INTERIOR, T.V. STUDIO CANTEEN

The canteen is about half full of actors many of which are dressed as Nazi soldiers, with mock blood bandages and arm bands. Also there are a sprinkling of T.V. people. At a table sits GRANDFATHER and RINGO. RINGO is deeply engrossed in a book and GRANDFATHER has a near empty cup of tea in front of him. The old man is bored and looks about him slyly.

613
MS
NA

He then looks at RINGO who is innocently occupied, a malicious gleam comes in to GRANDFATHER's eye. He decides to have a go at RINGO and sits staring at him. RINGO gradually becomes aware of the stare and shifts uncomfortably then tries to continue reading his book.

614A
MCU
LA
PR to . . .

GRANDFATHER: (disgustedly to no one in particular) Will you ever look at him, sitting there wid his hooter scraping away at that book!

614B
MCU
LA

RINGO: Well . . . what's the matter with that?

GRANDFATHER: (taking the book from him) Have you no natural resources of your own? Have they even robbed you of that?

RINGO: (snatching back his book) You can learn from books.

615A
MS
LA

615B
MS
LA

GRANDFATHER: Can you now? Aah . . . sheeps heads! You learn more by getting out there and living.

RINGO: Out where?

616A
MS
LA
ZI to . . .

GRANDFATHER: Any old where . . . but not our little Richard . . . oh no! When you're not thumping them pagan skins, you're tormenting your eyes wid that rubbish!

RINGO: (defiantly) Books are good!

616B
MC U
LA

GRANDFATHER: (countering) Parading's better!

617
MS
LA

RINGO: Parading?

GRANDFATHER: (marching up and down the canteen) Parading the streets . . . trailing your coat . . . bowling along . . . living!

618
MCU
LA
ZI

RINGO: Well, I am living, aren't I?

GRANDFATHER: You're living, are you? When was the last time you gave a girl a pink-edged daisy? When did you last embarass a sheila wid your cool appraising stare?

619A
MS
LA
ZI to . . .

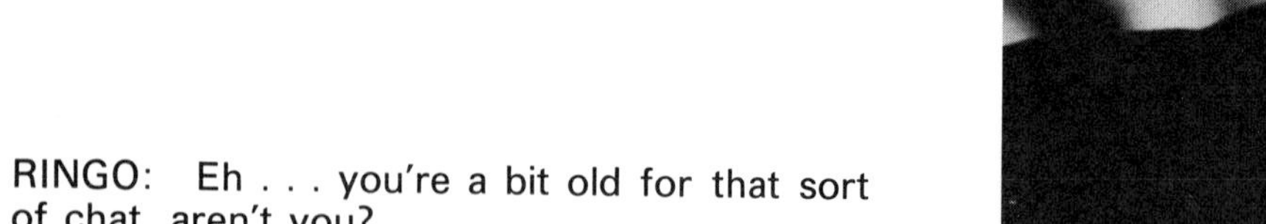

RINGO: Eh . . . you're a bit old for that sort of chat, aren't you?

619B
CU
LA

GRANDFATHER: At least I've a backlog of memories, but all you've got is that book!

620
CU
LA

621
CU
LA

RINGO: Aaah . . . stop picking on me . . . you're as bad as the rest of them.

622
LS
LA

GRANDFATHER: So you are a man after all.

RINGO: What's that mean?

GRANDFATHER: Do you think I haven't noticed . . . do you think I wasn't aware of the drift? Oh . . . you poor unfortunate scuff, they've driven you into books by their cruel, unnatural treatment, exploiting your good nature.

623
MCU
LA
TRO

624
(TL)
MCU
NA

RINGO: (not too sure) Oh . . . I dunno.

GRANDFATHER: (confidingly) And that lot's never happier than when they're jeering at you . . . and where would they be without the steady support of your drum beat, I'd like to know.

RINGO: Yeah . . . that's right.

GRANDFATHER: And what's it all come to in the end?

RINGO: (defensively) Yeah . . . what's in it for me?

GRANDFATHER: A book!

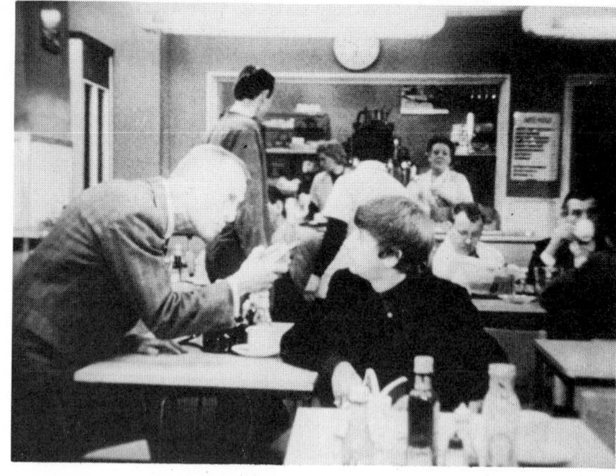

625
LS
LA

RINGO: Yeah . . . a bloomin' book!

He throws the book down.

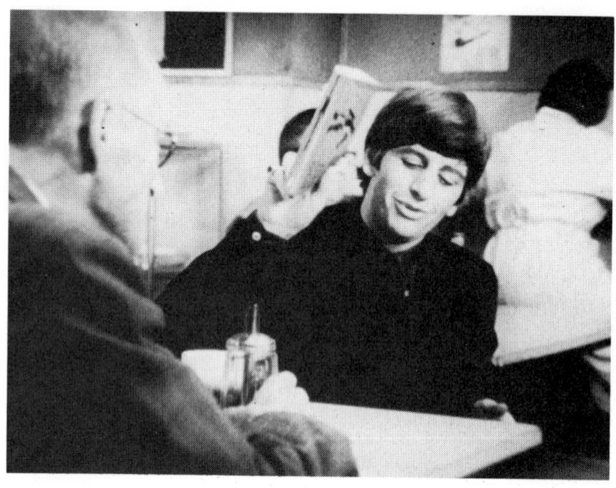

626
MS
LA

GRANDFATHER: When you could be out there betraying a rich American widow or sipping palm wine in Tahati before you're too old like me. [A fine neat and trim lad the class of you should be helping himself to life's goodies before the sands run out. Being an old age pensioner's a terrible drag on a man and every second you waste is bringing you nearer the Friday queue at the Post Office.]

627
MCU
LA

RINGO: Yeah . . . funny really, cos I'd never thought of it but being middle-aged and old takes up most of your time, doesn't it?

628
MCU
LA

629
MCU
LA

GRANDFATHER: (nodding) You're only right.

630
MS
LA

[RINGO: (nodding back) I'm not wrong.]

631A
MS
LA
ZI to . . .

There is a pause then RINGO rises and crosses to the door.

631B
MCU
LA

GRANDFATHER: Where are you going?

RINGO: I'm going parading before it's too late!

632
LS
LA

RINGO leaves and GRANDFATHER [*laughs at what he has done*] *then realizes its full meaning and looks worried.*

633
MCU
LA

INTERIOR, CORRIDOR AND STAIRWAY

RINGO comes along the corridor then down the narrow stairs. Half way down he comes face to face with GEORGE who is coming up the stairs.

634A
3/4 S-MS
NA
PR to . . .

GEORGE: Eh, Ringo, do you know what happened to me?

RINGO: (passing him) No. I don't.

As he goes round the corner RINGO turns on the surprised GEORGE.

RINGO: You want to stop being so scornful, it's twisting your face.

634B
3/4-LS
NA

634C
MS
NA

INTERIOR, T.V. THEATRE NEAR STAGE DOORMAN'S OFFICE

JOHN and PAUL are chatting up a couple of girls, when they see RINGO approaching they break off the conversation.

635
3/4 S
NA

JOHN: Here he is, the middle-aged boy wonder.

RINGO looks at JOHN hard.

[PAUL: Eh. I thought you were looking after the old man.

RINGO: (with simple dignity) Get knotted!]

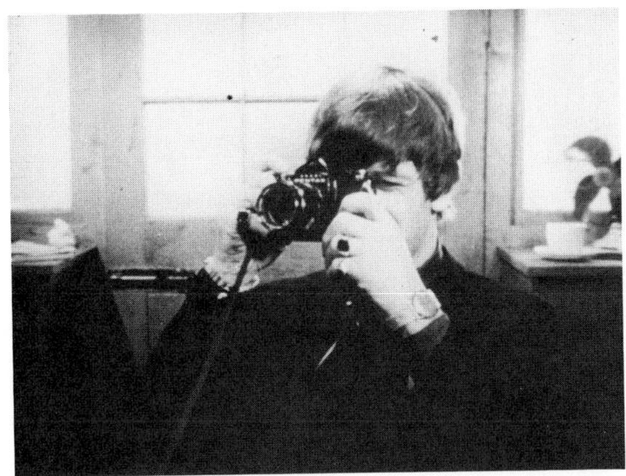

636A
MS
NA
PL to...

PAUL and JOHN gape at him. For good measure RINGO takes a quick photograph of them before he leaves them flabbergasted and walks off into the street.

636B
MCU
NA

PAUL: We've got only half an hour till the final run-through. He can't walk out on us.

JOHN: Can't he? He's done it, son!

637
MS
NA

GEORGE runs towards them.

GEORGE: Hey, you know what happened?

638A
LS
NA
PR to . . .

PAUL: We know.

GEORGE: Yes. Your grandfather's stirred him up.

PAUL: He hasn't.

GEORGE: Yes, he's filled his head with notions seemingly.

PAUL: The old mixer, come on we'll have to put him right.

The three of them go into the street.

638B
MS
NA
PL to . .

638C
FS
NA

639
LS
NA

EXTERIOR, T.V. THEATRE STAGE DOOR

The BOYS look up and down but RINGO has completely disappeared.

PAUL: Split up and look for him.

They now all start to go off in the same direction, they pause, there are three roads they can take but each time they begin to move they all go the same way.

640
MS
LA

JOHN: [It's happened at last,] we've become a limited company.

(GEORGE: I'll look in here again.)

641
LS
NA

PAUL gives him a push to the left and GEORGE to the right and going straight ahead himself they part and go their separate ways.

642
(TLU)
FS-MS
LA

EXTERIOR, STREET

643
LS-FS
NA

RINGO is walking along taking photographs with his camera when some girls recognise him and start to follow him. They quicken their pace and RINGO runs ahead of them. In the background a policeman watches him. He turns and comes into another street. He sees a second-hand clothes shop with a sign saying "We Buy Anything" and enters the shop just before the pursuing girls come round the corner. The girls stand about looking in all directions. After a moment RINGO comes out of the shop. He is wearing a long mackintosh and a natty cap pulled well down. He is ignored by the girls who don't recognise him. Realising this he goes back and ogles one of them. She glares at him.

644A
LS
NA
ZO,
PL to . . .

644B
FS
NA
(Stopped Action)

645A
FS
NA
PL to...

645B
LS
NA
Slight PL to...

GIRL: Get out of here, shorty.

[*Close up on RINGO's secret but happy smile as he walks briskly down the road.*]

645C
XLS
NA

646
XLS
HA
PL

EXTERIOR, TOW PATH CANAL

(RINGO attaches time mechanism onto camera, places it on log stump by river, steps back, presses injector. The camera falls backwards into river. Ringo hauls it out.)

647A
FS
NA
PR to . . .

647B
LS
NA

647C
LS
NA
Dissolve to . . .

648
LS
LA
Dissolve to . . .

649
CU
HA
TI
Dissolve to...

650
LS
LA

651A
FS
LA
PL to...

651B
LS
LA

RINGO kicks at a brick. He kicks stylishly but misses so tries again, misses again, but finally kicks the stone which doesn't budge. So he bends down and pulls it out of the ground; it is quite big, three quarters of it being below surface. Having got it he now decides to throw it away. As he does so the same POLICEMAN rides past on a bicycle.

POLICEMAN: Ain't you got no more bleeding sense than to go round chucking bricks about.

Before RINGO has time to answer the man has disappeared.

651C
LS
LA

RINGO: (shouting after him) Southerner!

652A
MCU
LA
ZO to . . .

He looks at the canal water moodily, and starts to photograph unimportant things. At this moment a large lorry tyre rolls down the incline and bashes him slap in the back, sprawling him on the path, the tyre on top of him. A small boy appears after the tyre and stands over the prostrate RINGO.

BOY: Here, mate, that's my hoop, stop playing with it.

652B
LS
LA

RINGO: Hoop, this isn't a hoop it's a lethal weapon. Have you got a licence for it?

652C
LS
LA

653
MCU
HA

BOY: Oh don't be so stroppy!

654
MCU
LA

655
MCU
HA

RINGO: (getting up) Well! A boy of your age bowling "hoop" at people. How old are you anyway?

BOY: (aggressively) [Nine] *(Eleven.)*

RINGO: Bet you're only [eight and a half] *(ten and a half.)*

BOY: (countering swiftly) [Eight and two thirds] *(ten and two thirds.)*

RINGO: Well, there you are and don't be rolling it at people.

656
MCU
LA

[BOY: Gerron out of it, you're only jealous 'cause you're old.

RINGO: Shurrup!

BOY: I bet you're (searching for an age)—sixteen!

RINGO: Fifteen and two thirds, actually.

BOY: Well.

RINGO: Alright take your hoop and bowl.]

He moves off and the BOY follows.

657
3/4 S
LA
TO

BOY: Oh you can have it, I'm packing it in—it depresses me.

RINGO: Y'what?

BOY: You heard, it gets on my wick.

RINGO: Well that's lovely talk, that is. And another thing, why aren't you at school.

BOY: I'm a deserter.

658
MCU
LA
TO

RINGO: [(smiling in spite of himself)] Are you now?

BOY: Yeah, I've blown school out.

RINGO: Just you?

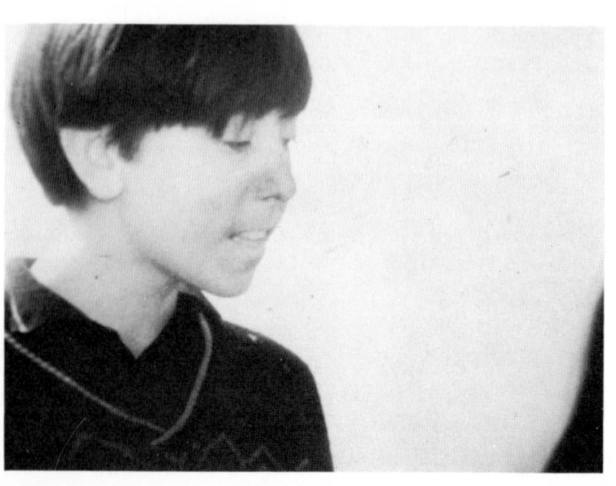
659
MCU
LA
TO

BOY: No, Ginger, Eddy Fallon and Ding Dong.

660
MCU
LA
TO

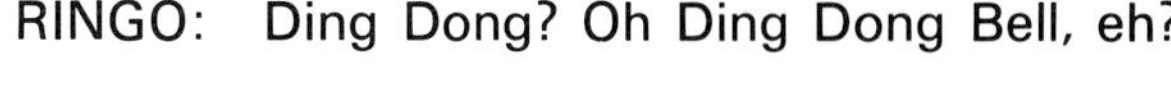

RINGO: Ding Dong? Oh Ding Dong Bell, eh?

BOY: Yeah, that's right, they was supposed to come with us but they chickened.

661
MCU
LA
TO

RINGO: Yeah? And they're your mates, are they?

BOY: (sighing) Yeah.

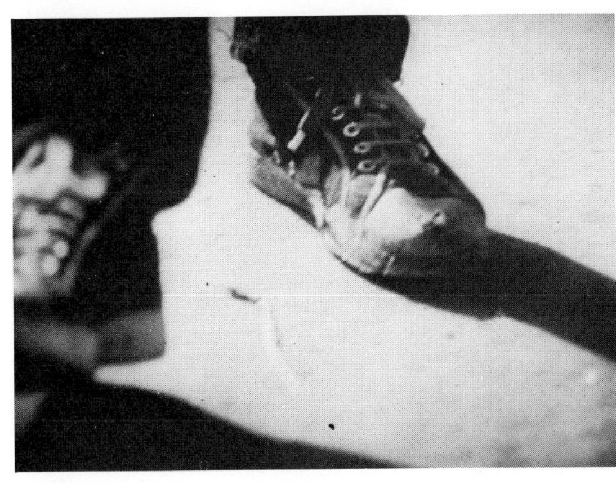

662
CU
HA
TO

RINGO: Not much cop without 'em, is it?

BOY: (defensively) Oh, it's alright.

[RINGO: (disbelievingly) Yeah?

BOY: Yeah.]

663
CU
HA
TI
Dissolve to . . .

RINGO: What're they like?

BOY is glad to have something to talk about.

BOY: (enthusiastically) Ginger's mad, he says things all the time and Eddy's good at punching and spitting.

RINGO: How about Ding Dong?

BOY: He's a big head and he fancies himself with it but it's alright cos he's one of the gang.

664
LS
NA
Dissolve to . . .

665
FS
LA
Dissolve to . . .

RINGO nods his understandingly and they mooch on together.

BOY: Why aren't you at work?

666A
MS
LA
TO to . . .

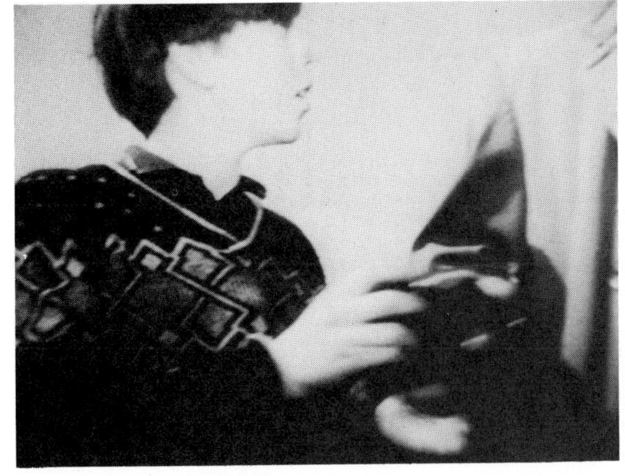

666B
MS
LA

RINGO: I'm a deserter, too.

BOY: Oh.

667A
(PRD)
XLS
HA
PU to...

At this moment a child's voice shouts out "Charley" and from RINGO's P.O.V. we see three kids. RINGO turns to the BOY and looks at them enquiringly.

BOY: (to Ringo) See you.

667B
LS
HA

The BOY runs off to join his mates. As he joins them they punch and scuffle together. They are obviously a gang. RINGO is left alone.

668
MCU
LA
TO

(VOICE: Come in, number 7 your time's up.)

669
XLS
HA

INTERIOR T.V. CONTROL ROOM

The atmosphere is tense. GRANDFATHER is standing miserable in front of the director, the criminal confronted by the judge. SHAKE and NORM are flanking him grimly.

GRANDFATHER: I'm sorry lads, I didn't mean it, honest.

670A
MS
LA
PR to...

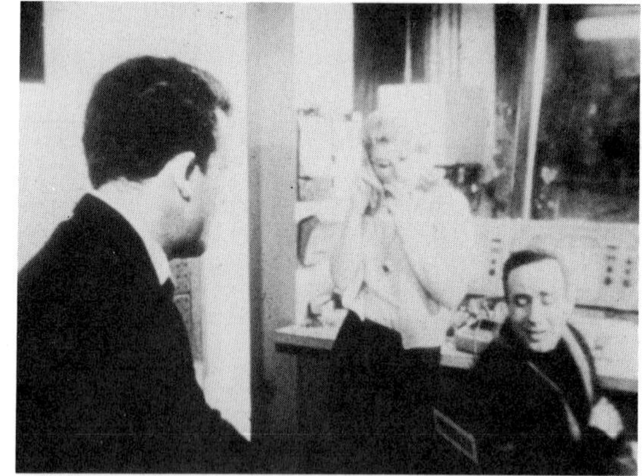

DIRECTOR: If he says that again, I'll strike him.

SHAKE: (unconvincingly) They'll be back, they're good lads, they'll be back.

DIRECTOR: Yes? Well we've got only twenty minutes to the final run through.

670B
MS
HA
PL to . . .

GRANDFATHER: I meant no harm. I was only trying to encourage little Ringo to enjoy himself.

NORM: (grimly, C.U.) God knows what you've unleashed on the unsuspecting South. It'll be wine, women and song all the way with Ringo once he's got the taste for it.

670C
MS
LA

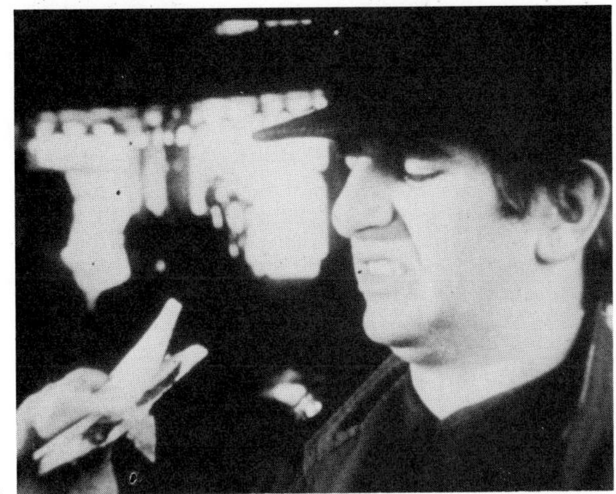

671A
CU
NA
PL to...

[EXTERIOR STREET PUB ON THE CORNER

The sign on the pub is Liverpool Arms. RINGO is standing looking up at it. He decides to go in and does so.]

INTERIOR PUB PUBLIC BAR

CLOSE UP on RINGO. He is eating a bone dry sandwich that curls up at the end. He puts it down with disgust. He has a lager glass in his hand.

671B
MCU
NA

BARMAID: (accusingly) That was fresh this morning.

We now see the pub is full of enormous cockney workmen downing pints. RINGO is very much alone he moves away from the bar towards a group that is standing together. They've an average height of over six feet. There is a group at a dart board. Another group is playing bar skittles and a third group is around a pinball table. Near the bar is a shove-halfpenny board with two players. There is a caged parrot nearby.

BARMAID: (to Ringo) That'll be two and nine . . .

672
CU
HA

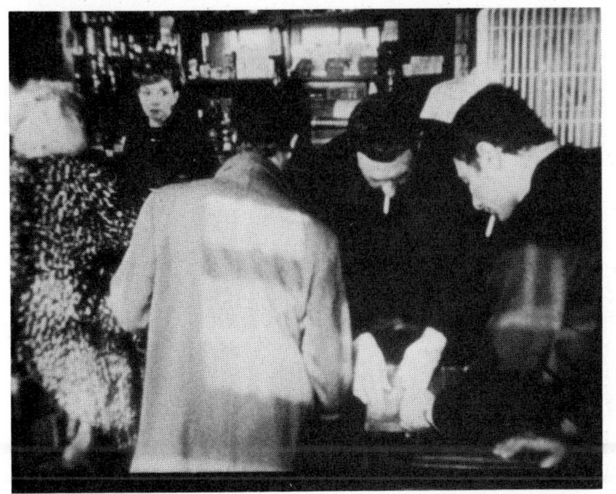

673
3/4 S
NA

RINGO fumbles some change out of his pocket.

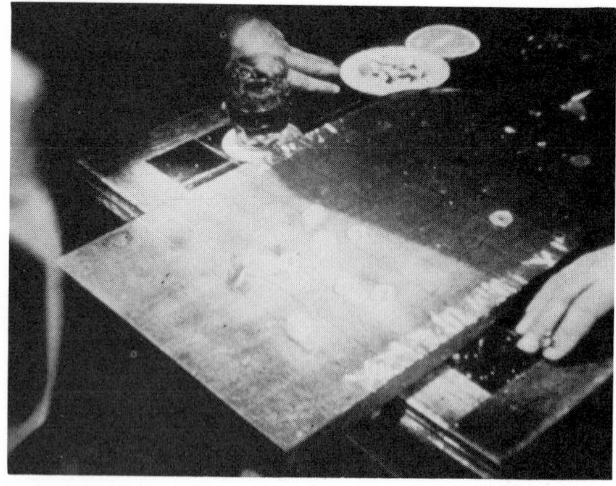

674
CU
HA

A few coppers fall from his hand on to the shove-halfpenny board just as the crucial point has been made. The men glare at him. Embarrassed, he moves away and without looking, places his glass on the skittles table just as a player swings the string, which hits Ringo's glass. [More embarrassed, RINGO backs away, unfortunately into the pin table, just as a winning score is about to be reached. He bumps it very slightly, but enough to cause it to TILT.]

675
3/4 S
NA

676
CU
HA

He then moves to the dart board. By this time, most of the pub is staring at him. With great style, he takes the darts. The first throw goes into a cheese sandwich which a man is pointing in demonstration. The second we see arrive into a pint of bitter and then we see RINGO shoot the third dart and hear the sound of the parrot shouting angrily off. The BARMAID has had enough.

677
LS
NA

678
MCU
NA

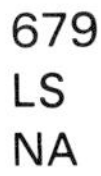

679
LS
NA

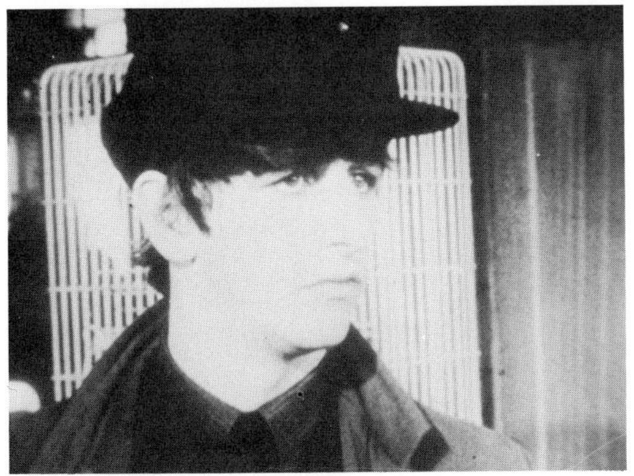

680
MCU
NA

681
(TR)
FS
NA

682
MCU
NA

683
LS
NA

684
MCU
NA

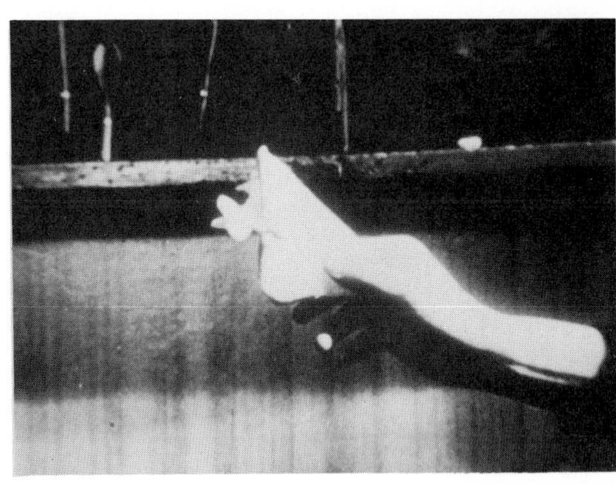

685
CU
NA

686
LS
NA

687A
MCU
NA

687B
MCU
NA

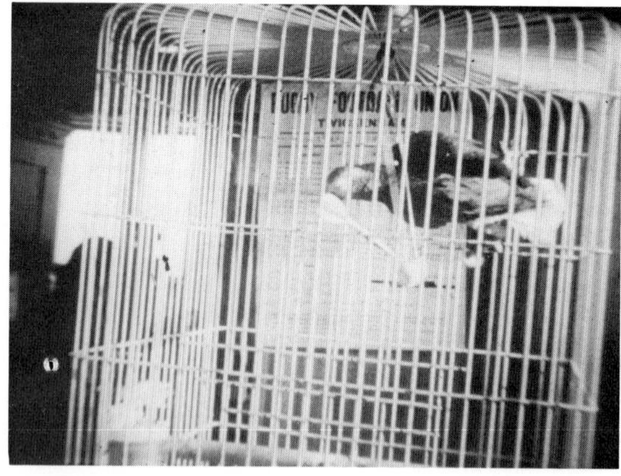

688A
CU
NA
TO to . . .

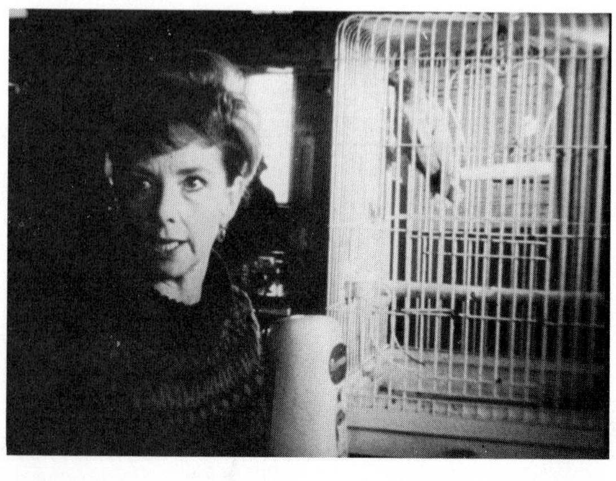

688B
MCU
NA

BARMAID: Right . . . on your way!

689
MCU
NA
PL

RINGO: Y'what?

BARMAID: You heard, on your way, trouble-maker!

690
MCU
NA

Now the centre of attention, RINGO backs out of the pub, followed by every eye in the place, the BARMAID and a few players following him to the door . . .

691A
LS
NA
ZI to...

EXTERIOR, STREET OUTSIDE PUB

RINGO comes out and crosses road, watched by the POLICEMAN who is now quite suspicious.

(POLICEMAN: Hey, watch it.)

691B
MS
NA

[*EXTERIOR, STREET*

PAUL comes down the street looking about him for RINGO. In the street is an old building, the sort of place that is highly favoured for TV rehearsals. There is a sign on the door, "TV Rehearsal Room." As PAUL draws near, a load of actors and extras, etc., are leaving. They are in costume; they are the ones who earlier had been going to a word rehearsal. When PAUL gets near the entrance he decides to go inside.

INTERIOR, HALL

PAUL enters and wanders about. He reaches a door, pushes it open and looks in. He sees a girl clad in period costume. She is moving around the room and obviously acting. PAUL watches her for a moment and then decides to go in.

INTERIOR, REHEARSAL ROOM

PAUL goes into the room. The girl is in mid flight. She is very young and lovely and completely engrossed in what she is doing. The room is absolutely empty except for PAUL and herself. She is acting in the manner of an eighteenth century coquette, or, to be precise, the voice English actresses use when they think they are being true to the costume period. Her youth however makes it all very charming.]

[GIRL: If I believed you, sir, I might do those things and walk those ways only to find myself on Problems Path. But I cannot believe you and all those urgings, serve only as a proof that you will lie and lie again to gain your purpose with me.]

[*She dances lightly away from an imaginary lover and as she turns she sees PAUL who is as engrossed in the scene as she was.*]

[GIRL: (surprised) Oh!

PAUL: (enthusiastically) Well . . . go 'head, do the next bit.

GIRL: Go away! You've spoilt it.

PAUL: Oh, sorry I spoke.]

[*He makes no attempt to go. He simply continues to look steadily at the girl; then he smiles at her. She is undecided what to do next.*]

[GIRL: Are you supposed to be here?

PAUL: I've got you worried, haven't I?

GIRL: I'm warning you, they'll be back in a minute.

PAUL: D'you know something, "They" don't worry me at all. Any road, I only fancy listening to you . . . that's all but if it worries you . . . well . . .

GIRL: You're from Liverpool, aren't you?

PAUL: (ironically) How'd you guess?

GIRL: (seriously) Oh, it's the way you talk.

PAUL: (innocently) Is it . . . is it, really?

GIRL: (suspiciously) Are you pulling my leg?

PAUL: (looking her straight in the eye) Something like that.

GIRL: (unsure) I see. (airily) Do you like the play?

PAUL: Yeah . . . I mean, sure, well, I took it at school but I only ever heard boys and masters saying those lines, like, sounds different on a girl. (smiles to himself) Yeah, it's gear on a girl.

GIRL: Gear?

PAUL: Aye, the big hammer, smashing!

GIRL: Thank you.

PAUL: Don't mench . . . well, why don't you give us a few more lines, like?

[*GIRL pouts.*]

[PAUL: You don't half slam the door in people's faces, don't you? I mean, what about when you're playing the part, like, hundreds of people'll see you and . . .

GIRL: (cutting in) I'm not . . .

PAUL: Oh, you're the understudy, sort of thing?

GIRL: No. (aggressively) I'm a walk-on in a fancy dress scene. I just felt like doing those lines.

PAUL: Oh, I see. You are an actress though, aren't you?

GIRL: Yes.

PAUL: Aye, I knew you were.

GIRL: What's that mean?

PAUL: Well, the way you were spouting, like . . . (he imitates her) "I don't believe you, sir . . ." and all that. Yeah it was gear.

GIRL: (dryly) The big hammer?

PAUL: (smiling) Oh aye, a sledge.

GIRL: But the way you did it then sounded so phony.

PAUL: No . . . I wouldn't say that . . . just like an actress . . . you know. (He moves and stands about like an actress.)

GIRL: But that's not like a real person at all.

PAUL: Aye well, actresses aren't like real people, are they?

GIRL: They ought to be.

PAUL: Oh, I don't know, anyroad up, they never are, are they?

GIRL: (teasingly) What are you?

PAUL: I'm a group; I mean . . . I'm in a group . . . well . . . there are four of us, we play and sing.

GIRL: I bet you don't sound like real people.

PAUL: We do, you know. We sound like us having a ball. It's fab.

GIRL: Is it really fab or are you just saying that to convince yourself?

PAUL: What of? Look, I wouldn't do it unless I was. I'm dead lucky 'cos I get paid for doing something I love doing. (He laughs and with a gesture takes in the whole studio.) . . . all this and a jam butty too!!

GIRL: I only enjoy acting for myself. I hate it when other people are let in.

PAUL: Why? I mean, which are you, scared or selfish?

GIRL: Why selfish?

PAUL: Well, you've got to have people to taste your treacle toffee.]

[*She looks at him in surprise.*]

[PAUL: No, hang on, I've not gone daft. You see when I was little me mother let me make some treacle toffee one time in our back scullery. When I'd done she said to me, "Go and give some to the other kids." So, I said I would but I thought to meself, "She must think I'm soft." Anyroad, I was eating away there but I wanted somebody else to know how good it was so in the end I wound up giving it all away . . . but I didn't mind cos *I'd* made the stuff in the first place. Well . . . that's why you need other people . . . an audience . . . to taste your treacle toffee, like. Eh . . . does that sound as thickheaded to you as it does to me?

GIRL: Not really but I'm probably not a toffee maker. How would you do those lines of mine?

PAUL: Well, look at it this way, I mean, when you come right down to it, that girl, she's a bit of a scrubber, isn't she?

GIRL: Is she?]

(Lester substituted the following sixteen exchanges of dialogue between Paul and the girl for the previous eight exchanges of dialogue.)

[GIRL: I only enjoy acting for myself. I hate it when other people are let in.

PAUL: Why? I mean, which are you, scared or selfish?

GIRL: Why selfish?

PAUL: Well, doing it for yourself. Aw come off it, you know you're doing it for them.]

[*He indicates people in the street.*]

[GIRL: Them?

PAUL: Yeah, look when I was a kid in Speke there was this fella—Joe or something—I can't remember his . . . he was a dustman, collected bins and that . . . well he was always giving kids bikes.

GIRL: Bikes?

PAUL: Yeah—I know it sounds daft but he did—gave the kids bikes, scruffy thing he was, but he'd buy these old bikes do 'em up and give them away; all the kids were mad about him. Never gave me one but that was alright. He was always giving spare kids a bike. Well you could be like that. Eh, look at that fella (he points to street) down there. If you share out your acting with him you could make his day.

GIRL: Could I?

PAUL: Of course you could, stands to reason.

GIRL: Oh, I don't know.

PAUL: Nobody does till they try.

GIRL: Alright, how would you do those lines of mine.

PAUL: Well, look at it this way, I mean, when you come right down to it, that girl, she's a bit of a scrubber, isn't she?

GIRL: Is she?

PAUL: Of course . . . Look, if she was a Liverpool scrubber . . . (PAUL starts acting a Liverpool girl; he minces about then turns, extending his leg.) Eh, fella, you want to try pulling the other one, it's got a full set of bells hanging off it. Y'what? . . . I know your sort, two cokes and a packet of cheese and onion crisps and suddenly it's love and we're stopping in an empty shop doorway. You're just after me body and y'can't have it . . . so there!

GIRL: (shattered) And you honestly think that's what she meant?

PAUL: Oh, definitely, it sticks out a mile, she's trying to get him to marry her but he doesn't want . . . well . . . I don't reckon any fella's ever wanted to get married. But girls are like that, clever and cunning. You've got to laugh. (He laughs.)

GIRL: Well, it's nice to know you think we're clever.

PAUL: (grinning) And cunning.

GIRL: And what do you do about it?

PAUL: Me? Oh, I don't have the time, I'm always running about with the lads . . . no, we don't have the time.

GIRL: Pity.

PAUL: (not noticing the invitation) Aye, it is but as long as you get by, it's alright, you know . . . bash on, happy valley's when they let you stop. Anyroad, I'd better get back.

GIRL: Yes.

PAUL: (going) See you.

GIRL: Of course.]

[*PAUL stands at the doorway, shrugs then goes out.*]

INTERIOR, T.V. THEATRE NEAR STAGE DOOR

The DIRECTOR is pacing up and down the corridor. NORM is also walking up and down, SHAKE is leaning against the wall quite unconcerned. NORM gives SHAKE a push.

NORM: Worry, will you!

SHAKE adjusts his features to a worrying expression.

692A
MS
NA
PR, PL to . . .
DK

692B
MS
NA
PR to . . .

DIRECTOR: (bitterly) Well, that's it, two minutes to the final run through . . . They're bound to miss it . . .

NORM: I'll murder that Lennon.

DIRECTOR: But I suppose we can survive a missed runthrough as long . . .

SHAKE: . . . as they head up for the show. Oh yes, well I mean it'ud be a pity to miss the show, wouldn't it like.

NORM: Shurrup, cheerful.

The horrible prospect hits the DIRECTOR.

DIRECTOR: You don't think . . .

NORM: (reassuring him) Don't worry.

DIRECTOR: Oh now, they can't do that to me. (turning on Norm) It's all your fault. (over-riding Norm) Oh yes it is and if they don't turn up I wouldn't be in your shoes for all the . . .

SHAKE: (helping out) . . . tea in China. Oh you're right, neither would I.

He steps away from NORM and stands near the DIRECTOR.

NORM: You dirty traitor!

SHAKE nods his agreement to this assessment of his character.

SHAKE: Of course.

(DIRECTOR: Yes, of course.)

At this moment JOHN, GEORGE and PAUL enter from the stage door. They are completely unconcerned and walk past the DIRECTOR, SHAKE and NORM.

JOHN: (as he passes by) Hi Norm!

NORM: (preoccupied) Hi, John.

The BOYS walk on when after a moment NORM snaps to.

692C
MCU
NA
(PL, PR)

NORM: John!

GEORGE: (mildly) Did you want something.

NORM: (beaming with delight) I could eat the lot of you.

JOHN: You'd look great with an apple in your gob.

DIRECTOR: (accusingly) Do you realise you could have missed the final run through?

GEORGE: Sorry about that.

SHAKE: Norm, there's only three of them.

693
MS
LA

PAUL: Aye, we were looking for Ringo. But we realised he must have come back.

DIRECTOR: Do you realise we are on the air, live, in front of an audience, in forty-five minutes and you're one short.

694
MCU
NA

695
MCU
NA

696
MCU
NA

JOHN: Control yourself or you'll spurt. He's bound to be somewhere.

697
MCU
NA

NORM: Aye let's try the dressing room.

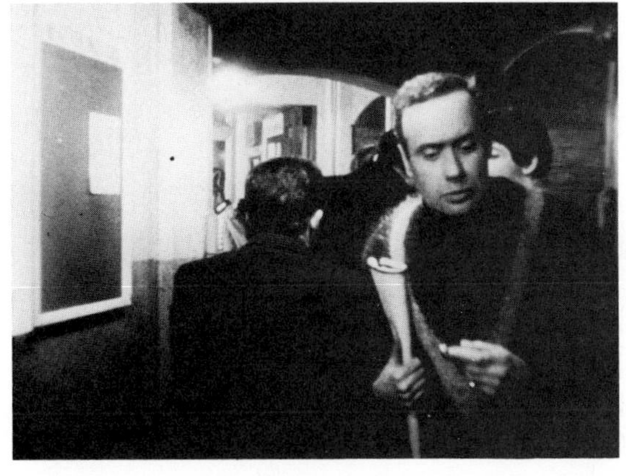

698
MS
LA

Everyone starts along the passage. NORM and PAUL last.

699
3/4 S
LA

PAUL: Eh, where's my grandfather?

NORM: Don't worry about him. He can look after himself.

PAUL: Aye, I suppose so.

They run after the others.

EXTERIOR, T.V. THEATRE

CLOSE UP

GRANDFATHER: Personally signed and handwritten by your own sweet boys. The chance of a lifetime. Be the envy of your less fortunate sisters!

The CAMERA PULLS back and we see GRANDFATHER is surrounded by girls who have broken from the queue and are doing a brisk trade with the old man. He has a large sign on which is written: "Get your genuine autographed Beatles photographs." On the edge of the crowd two POLICEMEN are trying to force the girls back into the queue. Finally they wade through the girls and confront GRANDFATHER. They look at the old man quizzically; he stares back coldly. They indicate he should hop it and quick but GRANDFATHER defiantly glares back at them. So with a sigh, they grab an arm each and escort the old man off.

700
(PL)
MS
NA

701
FS
HA

702
3/4 S
NA

703
MS
HA

704
3/4 S
NA
PL

EXTERIOR, STREET

In the street, workmen are collecting shovels, drinking tea and doing all the things people do around building sites. RINGO mooches around. In the road is a hole with a diameter of about three feet, and at least six feet deep. RINGO looks down and a man is busily working at the bottom of the hole. He glares at RINGO. After a moment RINGO turns away. We now see a very elegant young lady coming towards RINGO. She is daintily avoiding a series of puddles. RINGO has an idea and does a Sir Walter Raleigh with his large Mac spreading it over one of the puddles.

705
LS
NA

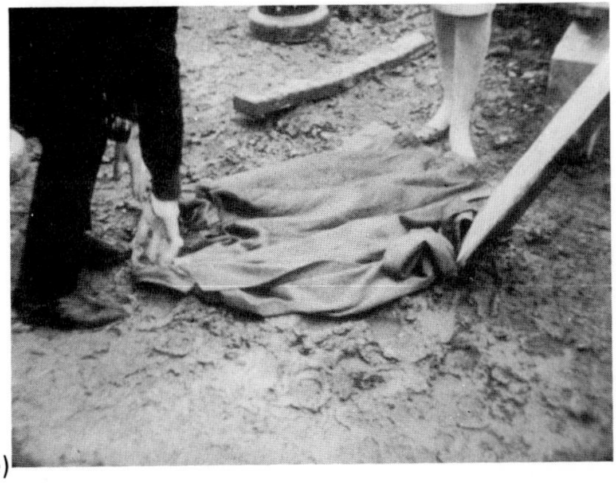

706
CU
HA
(PU to
girls face)

(GIRL: Thank you.)

707A
LS
NA

The girl walks across it smiling graciously. RINGO proceeds with the coat to the next puddle and to the next backing gradually towards the hole. At last he spreads the coat, without noticing what he is doing, over the hole. The girl steps onto the coat and disappears sharply. RINGO looks down the hole where the girl is held in the workman's arms. The WORKMAN rises out of the manhole until he is waist height. [At this point an elegantly dressed gentleman appears (the girl's husband) he looks at his wife in the WORKMAN's arms and hits the WORKMAN.] RINGO backs away through the puddles, and is nicked by the POLICEMAN.

707B
LS
NA

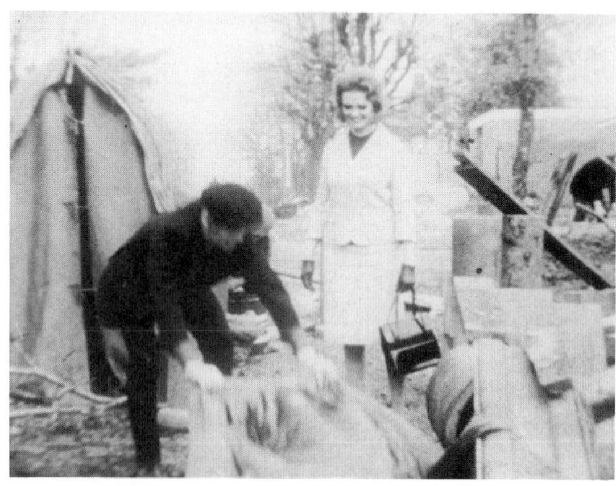

707C
FS
NA

708
LS
NA

709
MS
LA

710
LS
NA

(POLICEMAN: Got you, you nasty little person, you.)

711
MS
HA

712
(LS
TO to . . .
MS
LA

INTERIOR, POLICE STATION

It is the reception desk and behind it is the DESK SERGEANT. After a moment RINGO is dragged in by the POLICEMAN we saw him with before.

RINGO: Look, I'm Ringo Starr . . . I've got a show to do in a few minutes you've got to let me go . . . I'm Ringo . . .

POLICEMAN: Sure, they all say that these days. . . Anyway . . . I don't care who you are . . . you can save that for the stipendary. Here you are Sarge.

SERGEANT: What is he?

POLICEMAN: (reeling off the list) I've got a little list here. Wandering abroad. Malicious intent. Acting in a suspicious manner. Conduct liable to cause a breach of the peace. You name it, he's done it.

713
MCU
LA

SERGEANT: Oh, a little savage, is he?

POLICEMAN: A proper little Aborigine.

RINGO: (on his dignity) I demand to see me solicitor.

714
MCU
NA

SERGEANT: What's his name?

715
MCU
LA

RINGO: Oh, well if you're going to get technical.

716
MCU
NA

At that moment there is a loud series of noises off camera, furious shouting and dull crashes of wood.

SERGEANT: Hello, it's going to be one of those nights, is it. (to policeman) Sit Charley Peace down over there.

The POLICEMAN takes RINGO to a bench and sits him down as GRANDFATHER and the two POLICEMEN who were with him enter. The sign is tattered and is being lugged after them.

717
MS
NA

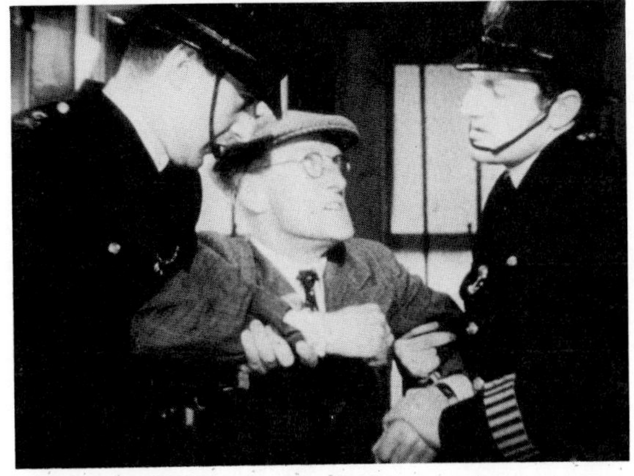

718
MS
LA

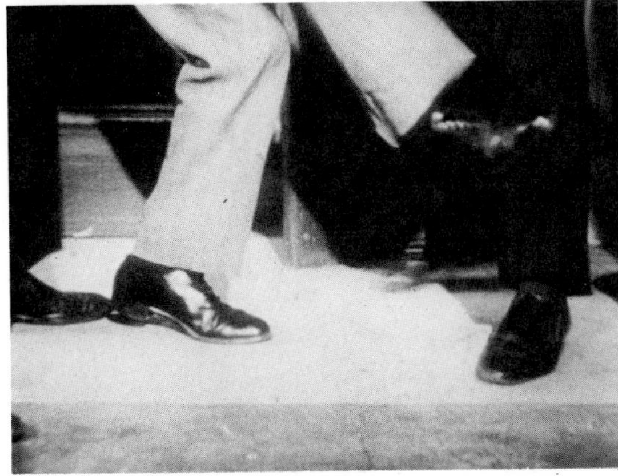

719
CU
NA

720A
CU
LA
PLD to...

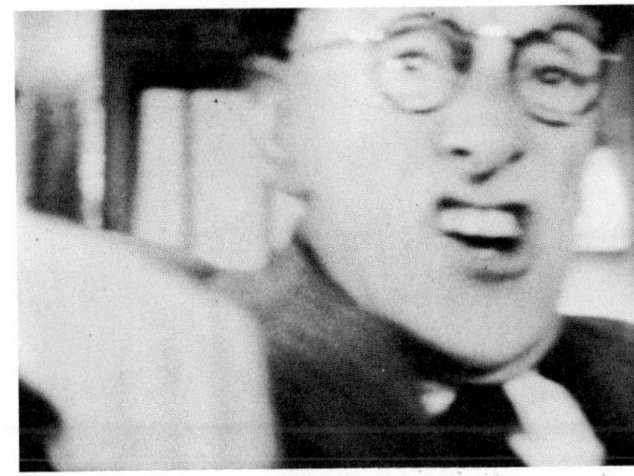

720B
CU
NA

GRANDFATHER: Well, you got me here so do your worst but I'll take one of you with me. (kicks the nearest policeman) Oh, I know your game, get me in the tiled room and out come the rubber hoses [but I'll defy you still.]

721
LS-MS
NA

SERGEANT: Is there a fire, then?

GRANDFATHER leans across the desk and hisses at the SERGEANT.

GRANDFATHER: You ugly, grey brute you, you have sadism stamped all over your bloated British kisser.

SERGEANT: Eh?

GRANDFATHER: I'll go on a hunger strike. I know your caper.

722
MCU
HA

723
MCU
LA

724
MCU
NA

725
MCU
HA

The kidney punch and the rabbit clout. The third degree and the size twelve boot ankle-tap.

726
MCU
LA

SERGEANT: What's he on about?

GRANDFATHER: (squaring up) I'm soldier of the republic, you'll need the mahogany truncheon for this boyo. A nation once again. A nation once again.

727
FS
NA

728
MCU
HA

729
MS
NA

SERGEANT: (to policemen) Get Lloyd George over there with that mechanic in the cloth cap while I sort this lot out.

(POLICEMAN: Sit down over here.)

The POLICEMEN hurtle GRANDFATHER firmly but gently over to the bench on which RINGO is sitting and then return to the desk for a whispered conference with the SERGEANT. Meanwhile in full conspiratorial fashion GRANDFATHER talks to RINGO out of the side of his mouth.

730
MS
NA

GRANDFATHER: Ringo, me old scout, they grabbed yer leg for the iron too, did they?

RINGO: Well I'm not exactly a voluntary patient.

GRANDFATHER: Shush! Have they roughed you up yet?

RINGO: What?

GRANDFATHER: (whispering) [Keep your voice down, this lot'll paste you, just for the exercise.] Oh they're a desperate crew of drippings and they've fists like matured hams for pounding defenceless lads like you.

731
3/4 S
LA

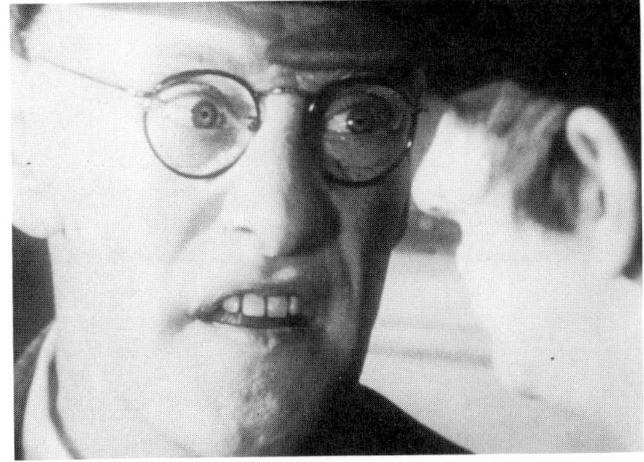

732
CU
NA

733
3/4 S
LA

(SERGEANT: So that's it, eh?)

[RINGO: (disturbed) Have they?]

GRANDFATHER: [That sergeant's a body-blow veteran if ever I measured one.] One of us has got to escape. I'll get the boys. Hold on son, I'll be back for you.

RINGO: (horrified) Me!

GRANDFATHER: And if they get you on the floor watch out for your brisket.

RINGO: (hopefully) Oh, they seem alright to me.

734
CU
NA

GRANDFATHER: That's what they want you to think. All coppers are villains.

SERGEANT: (calling) Would you two like a cup of tea?

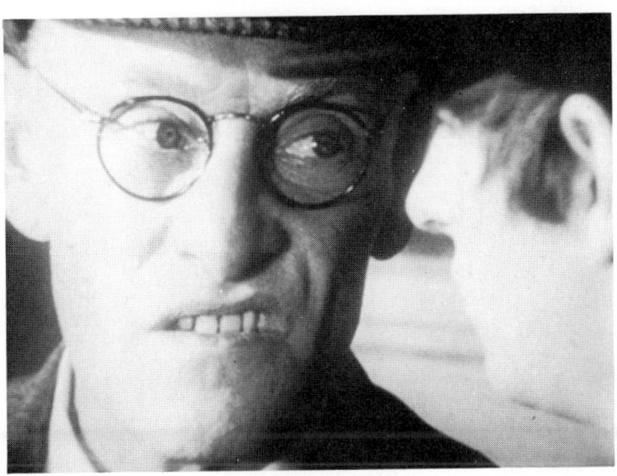

735
CU
NA

736
MCU
LA

GRANDFATHER: You see, sly villains.

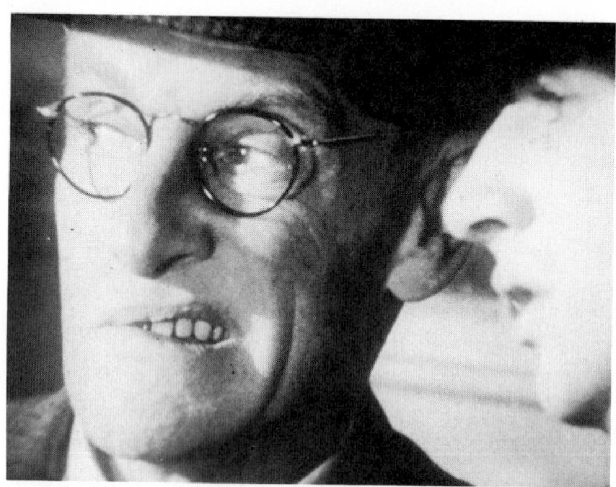

737
CU
NA

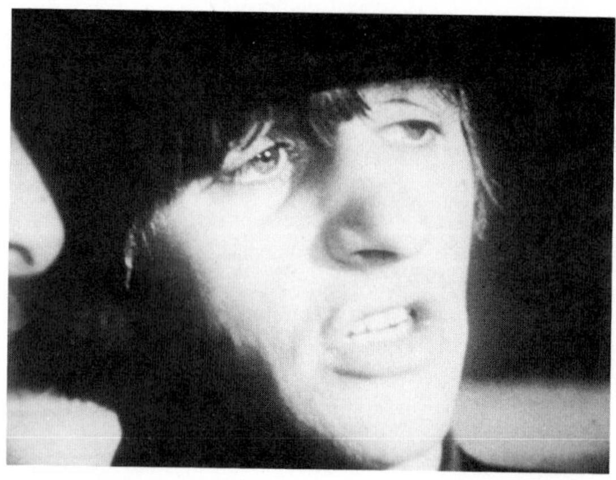

738
CU
NA

RINGO: (miserable) No thanks, Mr. Sergeant, sir.

We now have a CLOSE SHOT of POLICEMEN 'round the sergeant's desk.

SERGEANT: So you just brought the old chap out of the crowd for his own good.

POLICEMAN: [Yeah, but he insisted on us bringing him to the station.] *(Well, he was getting a bit nasty, you see, so we had to bring him.)*

SERGEANT: Well, he can't stop here. *(This is the stuff he's been hawking 'round is it?)*

739
MCU
LA

[Shot of GRANDFATHER watching POLICEMEN intently and muttering words as he does.]

(POLICEMAN: Yes Sergeant, photographs.)

SERGEANT: . . . Photographs . . .)

[RINGO: What are you doing?

GRANDFATHER: Lip reading.

RINGO: What are they saying?

GRANDFATHER: Nothing good.]

The POLICEMEN make a move towards GRANDFATHER and RINGO.

740
CU
NA

GRANDFATHER: Well son, it's now or never.

He jumps to his feet and scurries towards the door.

GRANDFATHER: Alright, you paid assassins. Johnny McCartney'll give you a run for your threepence ha'penny.

741A
(PU)
MS
NA
PL to . . .

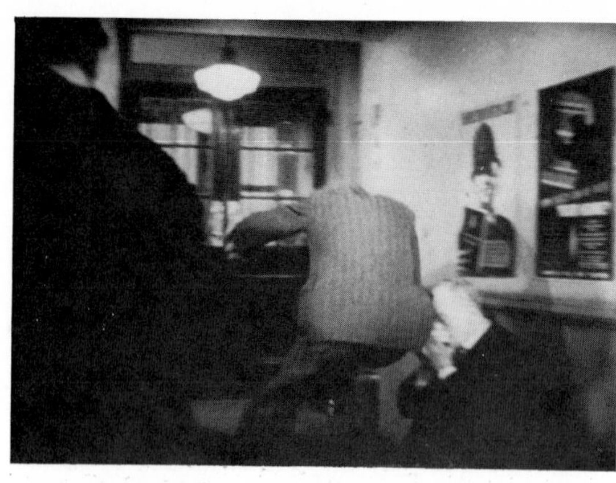

741B
LS
NA

He dashes out of the door followed by the POLICEMAN who has his pile of photos.

(POLICEMAN: Hey, you forgot your photographs.*)*

[SERGEANT: Now, what's he up to?

RINGO: He's allergic to bobbies, especially English bobbies.]

[*The POLICEMAN with the photos returns.*]

742
MS
NA

[POLICEMAN: (Irish accent) Your man disappeared like a leveret over a hill.

RINGO: Turncoat!]

[*The POLICEMEN turn on RINGO and walk towards him. CLOSE UP RINGO*]

[RINGO: Mother!]

EXTERIOR, STREET

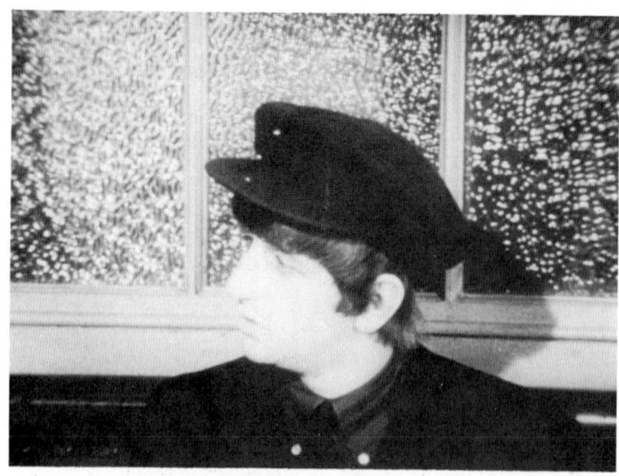

743
MCU
NA

GRANDFATHER is running at top speed down the street. He is breathing heavily and runs as if pursued by the hounds of hell. The street however is entirely empty and no one is even in sight. As he reaches the top of the street he pauses and turning, looks around him. From his P.O.V. we see just how empty the street is and heaving a sigh of relief GRANDFATHER cackles to himself. His triumph is short lived. At this precise moment down the street comes a parade of police vehicles, a Black Maria, an escorting police motor bike patrol and an ordinary squad car. The procession draws up and the street is full of policemen getting out of the Black Maria and squad car and off motor bikes. CLOSE UP GRANDFATHER's horrified face.]

GRANDFATHER: Be God, they've called up reinforcements, the dragnet's out!

[*He dashes off wildly in the general direction of the theatre. He has been completely unnoticed by the policemen who are lining up for a last minute inspection by the inspector in charge. The inspector is like a commander in chief of a spear-head attack force.*

They smartly march off in the direction taken by GRANDFATHER.]

744
LS
NA

745
MS
NA
PR

INTERIOR, T.V. THEATRE CONTROL ROOM

DIRECTOR: (watching the clock) Only half an hour and you're on!

GEORGE: Can I say something?

The director clutches at any straw.

DIRECTOR: (hopefully) Yes, anything.

GEORGE: (earnestly) It's highly unlikely we'll be on . . . I mean the law of averages are against you and it seems that, etc., etc. . . . *(I think if we could get the juggler on with a couple more clubs, that would fill in for a bit of time.)*

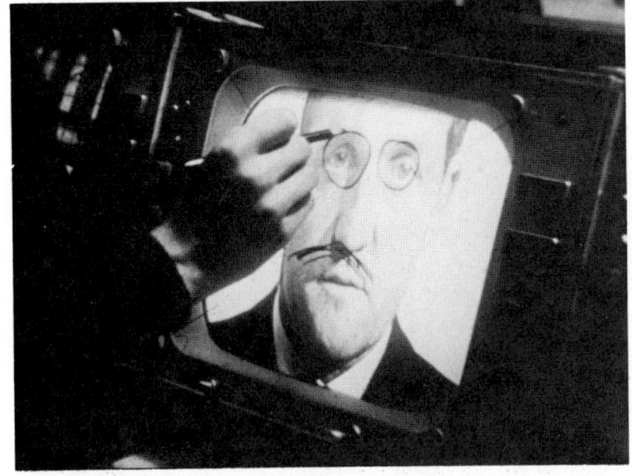

746
CU
NA

But his speech is drowned by the pitiful moans of the Director.

747
(PR)
LS
NA
PR

EXTERIOR, T.V. THEATRE STAGE DOOR

The [four little boys from the canal] (three little boys) are being driven away by the security guard.

748A
LS
LA

GUARD: (going back into theatre) I'll have the hides off of you lot.

748B
LS
LA
(PR)

749
MCU
HA

750
MCU
LA

751
(PL)
LS
LA

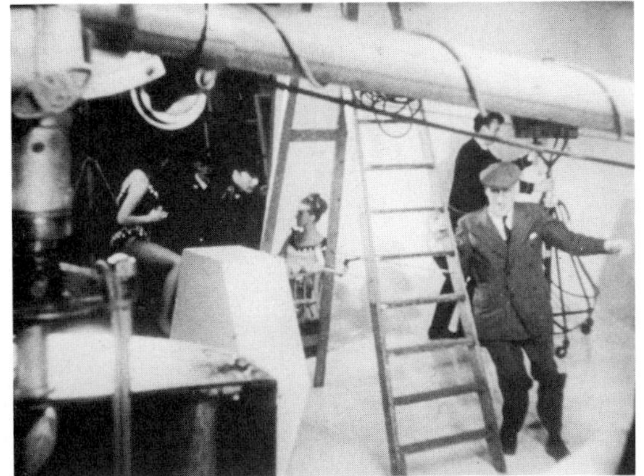

752
LS
NA

753
M-MCU
NA

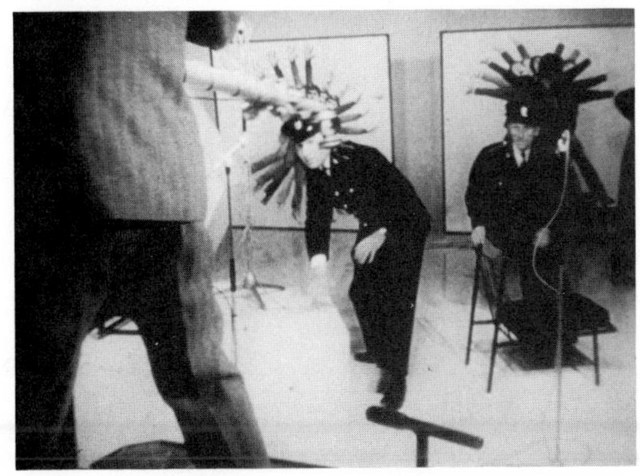

754
(TO
PU)
3/4 S
LA
PR

755
(PR)
CU
HA

756
(ZI, ZO to . . .)
LS
NA

757
LS
NA

758
(MS
ZO)
3/4 S
NA

759
(PL)
LS
NA
(PR)

760
LS
NA

761
LS
NA

762A
(ZO)
3/4 S
NA
ZI, ZO to . . .

762B
LS
NA
(PR)

763
LS
NA

764
MS
NA

765
LS
NA

766
MS
NA
ZI

767
LS
NA
(PR)

(NORM: Lads, lads, you're back. Thank goodness! Where's Ringo?

PAUL: There he is. We've got him.

NORM: Great!)

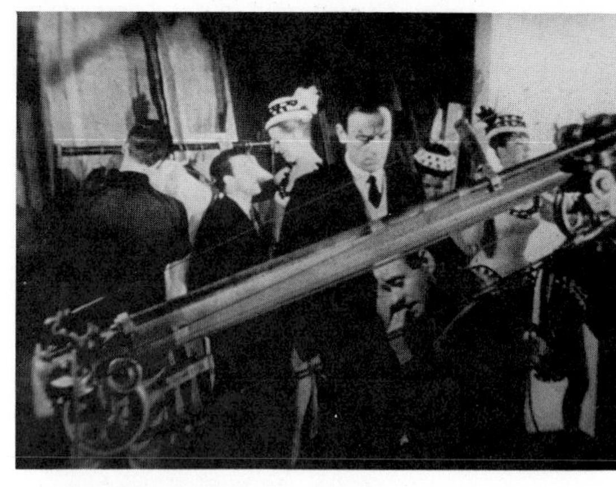

768
FS
NA

DIRECTOR: Boys, you don't know what this means to me. If you hadn't come back it would have been the epilogue or the news in Welsh for life.

769
MCU
NA

NORM: Aren't you supposed to be in that box?

(DIRECTOR: Yes.)

[*The Director gives NORM a final glare and dashes off.*]

PAUL: And another thing where's that old mixer?

770
FS
NA

GRANDFATHER: Here Pauly.

And sitting on a box sadly chastened sits GRANDFATHER.

PAUL: Well, I got a few things to say to you two-faced John McCartney.

771
MCU
NA

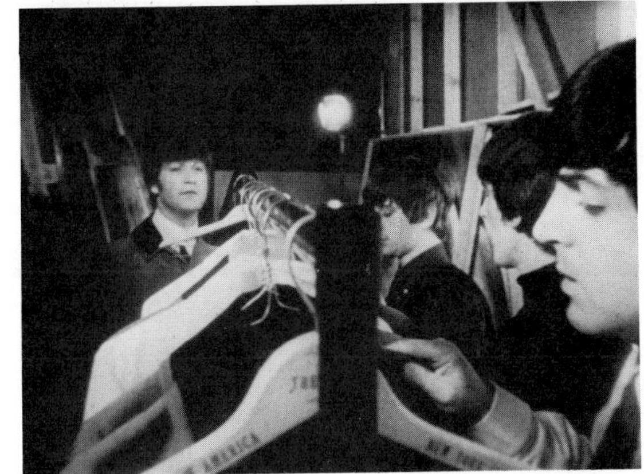

772
MCU
NA

JOHN: Aw leave him alone Paul, he's back, isn't he? And it's not his fault he's old.

PAUL: (hotly) What's old got to do with it? *(He's a troublemaker and a mixer and that's good enough for me.)*

[JOHN: You needn't bother.

PAUL: Y'what?

JOHN: Practising to be thick-headed, you're there already.

PAUL: Look he's a mixer and a trouble maker!]

773
MS
NA

JOHN: That's right, but he's only asking us to pay attention to him, aren't you?

From JOHN's P.O.V. we see GRANDFATHER. He looks what he is, a tired old man.

JOHN: You see. (to Grandad) You know your trouble—you should have gone west to America. You'd have wound up a senior citizen of Boston. As it is you took the wrong turning and what happened—you're a lonely old man from Liverpool.

774
MCU
LA

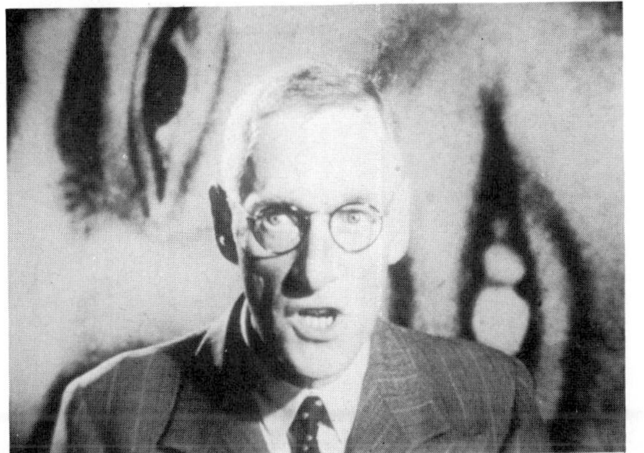

775
MCU
HA

GRANDFATHER: (fighting back) But I'm clean.

(JOHN: Are you?)

[The BOYS giggle and slap him on the back.]

776
MCU
LA

(SHAKE: Hey, Norm.

NORM: What?

SHAKE: I've been thinking . . . it's not my fault.

NORM: What isn't?

777
FS
NA

SHAKE: I'm not taller than you are, you're smaller than I am.

NORM: (raps on Shake's head) Any one at home?

GEORGE: Hey Shake, where's me boot? And will you get us some tea while you're there?

SHAKE: Okay, George.

GEORGE: Ta.

778
MS-MCU
LA

NORM: Now, come on, let's get changed.)

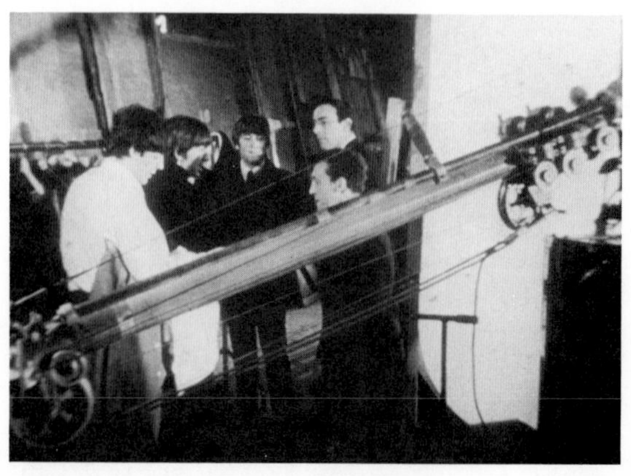

779
FS
NA

INTERIOR T.V. THEATRE AUDITORIUM

Songs: *"Tell Me Why," "If I Fell" (reprise),*

Songs: *"Tell My Why," "If I Fell" (reprise), "I Should Have Known Better" (reprise), "She Loves you."*

[We see the audience of girls steaming in and settling down in their places for the show. There is the usual business of getting the show ready and we see SHOTS of the girls faces, then JOHN, PAUL, RINGO and GEORGE looking at them.] At last on cue from the floor manager the BOYS start their act to the audience's screams. During the number we constantly CUT away to the audience with various SHOTS of the ecstatic girls. In the middle of these shots we see NORM standing at the side of the audience his face glowing with satisfaction. We follow his gaze and from NORM'S P.O.V. we see GRANDFATHER handcuffed to SHAKE, but in spite of this, the old man is enjoying himself. The BOYS now perform a medley of numbers i.e. a little of all the songs we have heard during the story. While they are doing so they look again in the general direction of SHAKE and GRANDFATHER and from their P.O.V., we see SHAKE is beating time to the music but from his wrist dangles an empty set of handcuffs. GRANDFATHER has gone again. As the BOYS are reacting to GRANDFATHER's disappearance once again, the trap door on the stage opens and GRANDFATHER appears in the centre of the group as they finish their act and take their final bows.

780A
MS
LA
ZO to . . .

780B
XLS
LA
DK

781
XLS
NA
DK

782
CU
NA

783
CU
NA

787A
NA
MS
DK
ZI to . . .

784
CU
NA

787B
CU
NA
DK

785
CU
NA

788
CU
NA
DK

786
LS
HA
DK
(ZO)

789
MS
LA
DK

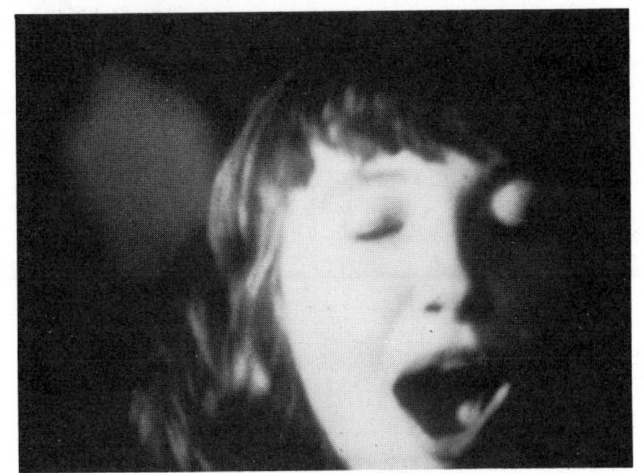

790
CU
NA
DK

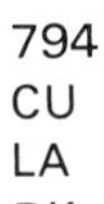

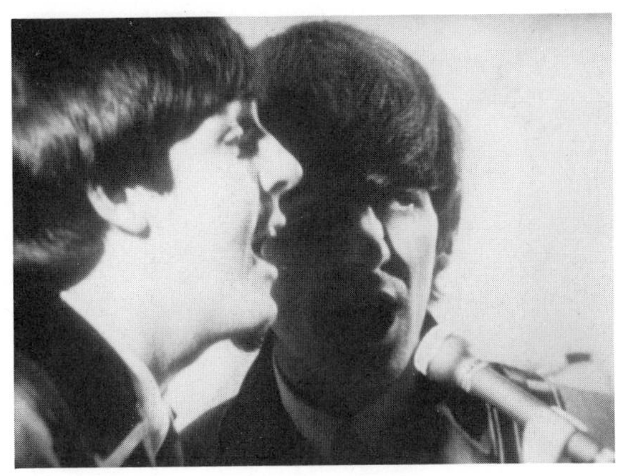

791
CU
NA
HK

792
CU
NA
HK

793
MCU
LA
DK

794
CU
LA
DK

795
MCU-MS
LA
HK

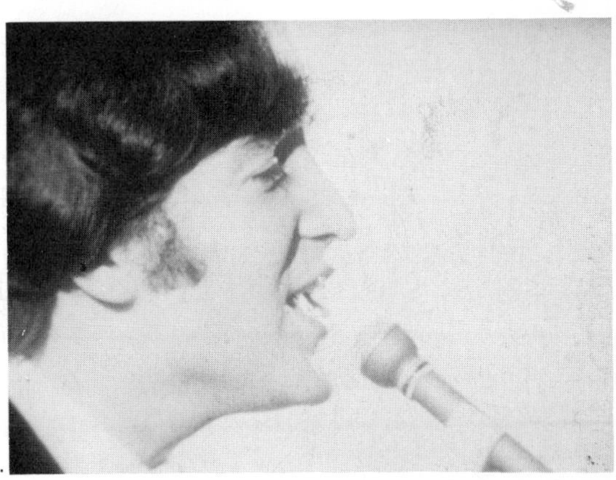

796A
CU
NA
HK
PD to . . .

796B
CU
NA

797
CU
LA
DK

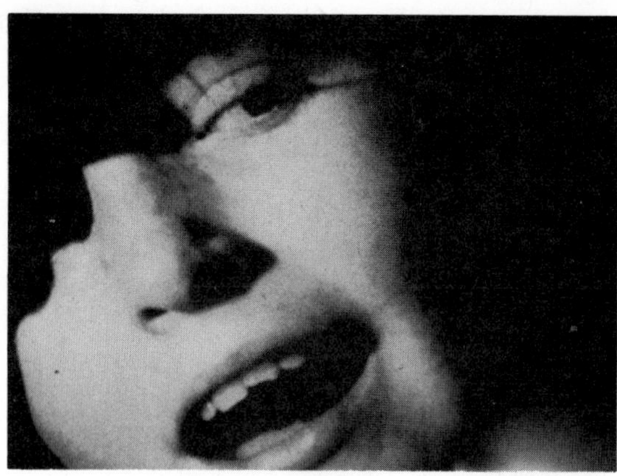

799B
CU
HA
DK

798
MS
NA

799A
MS
HA
DK
ZI to . . .

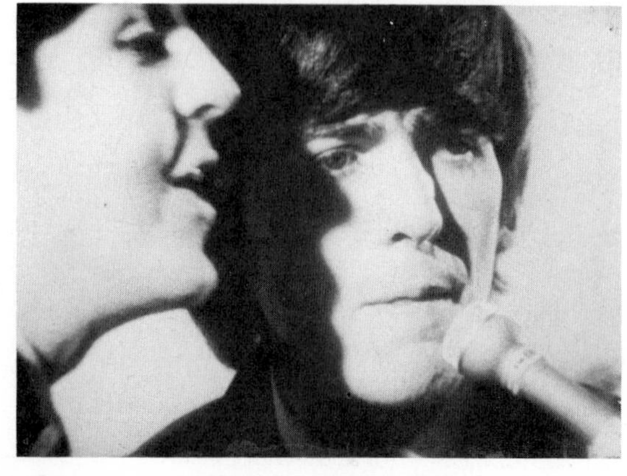

800
CU
NA
HK

801
CU
LA
HK

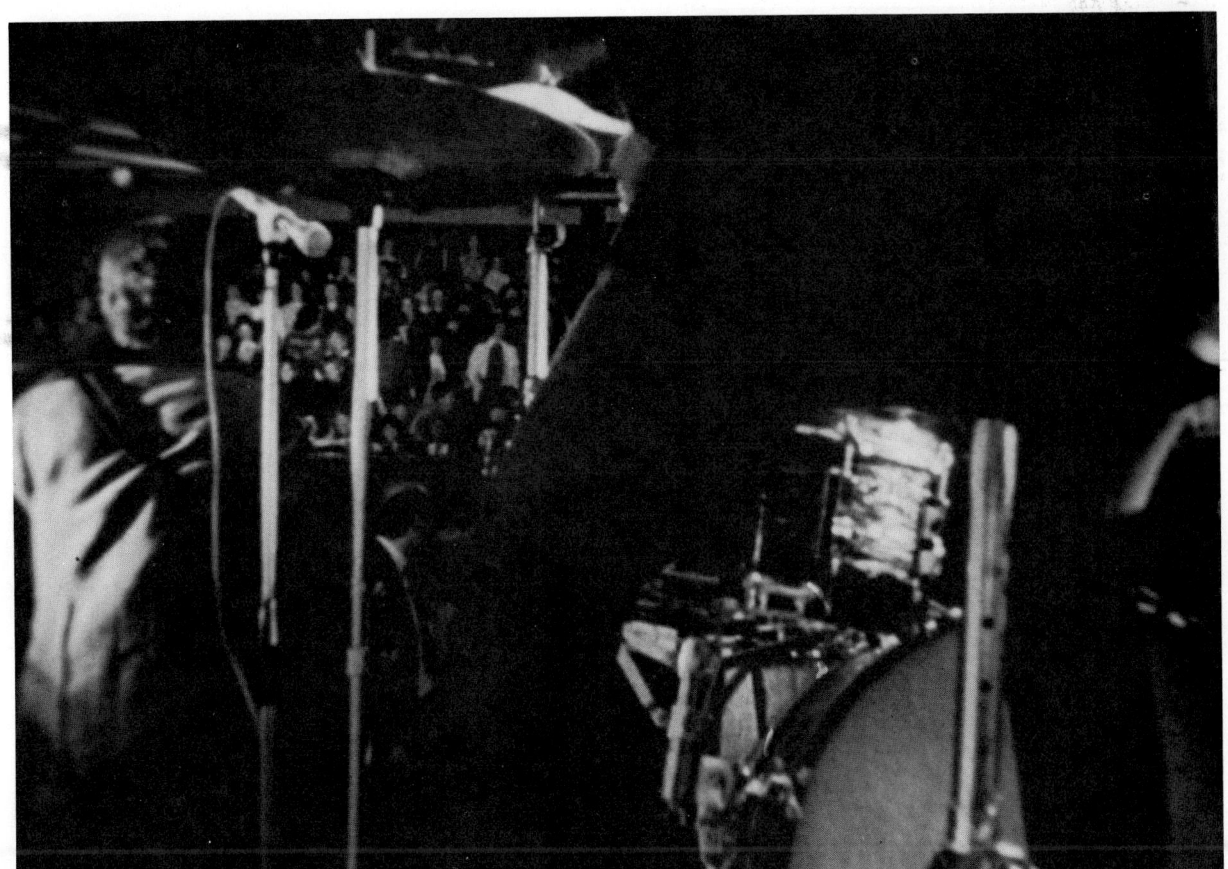

802
LS-XLS
LA
DK
(TR)
Dissolve to . . .

806
MS
HA
(TI)

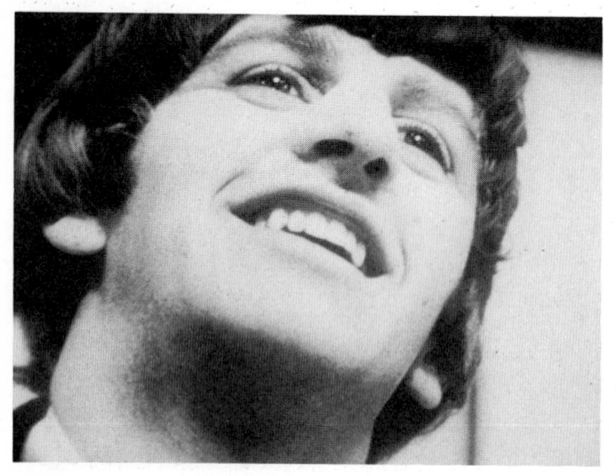

803
CU
LA
HK

807
MS
LA

804
CU
NA

808A
MCU
NA
ZI & PD to .

805
MS
LA

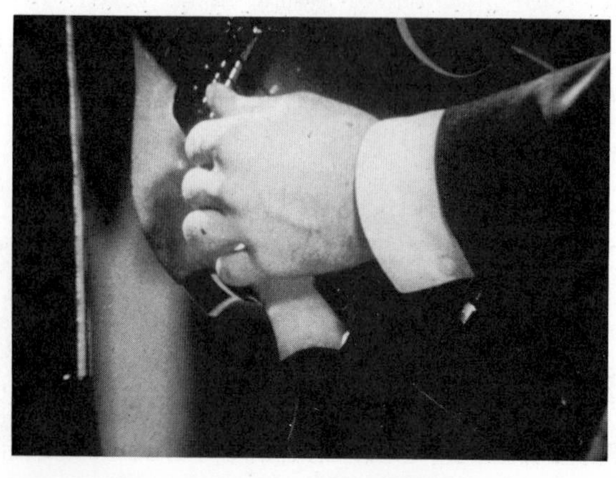

808B
CU
NA

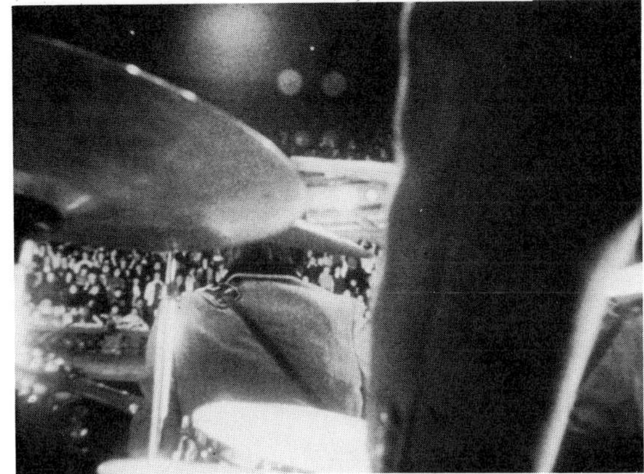

809
CU
LA

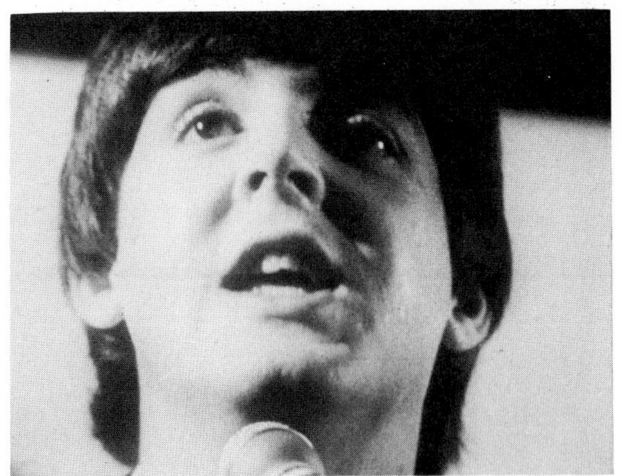

811
CU
LA
HK

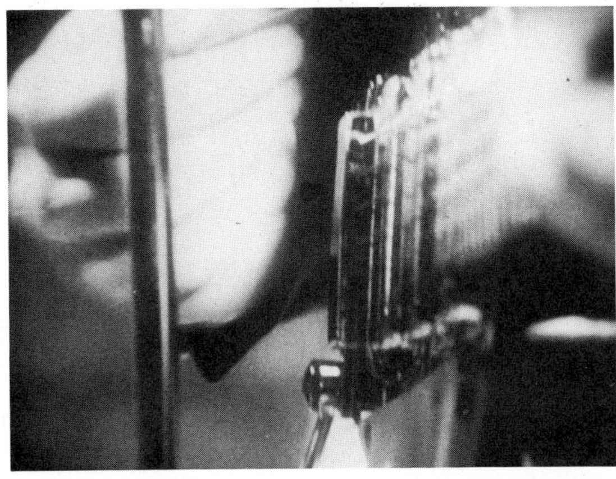

810A
CU
LA
TU to . . .

812
MS-XLS
LA

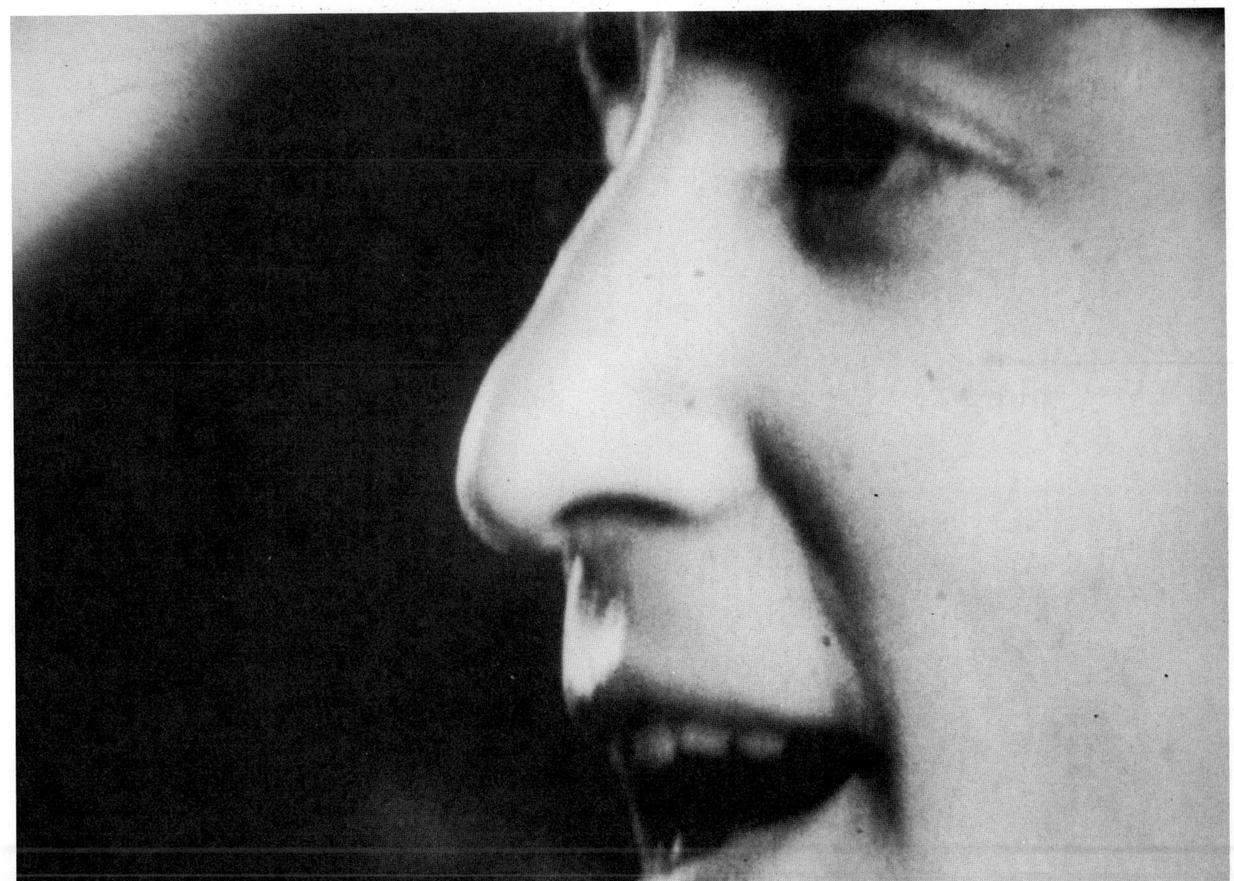

810B
XCU
NA

813
XLS
HA
DK

814
LS
HA
HK

815
LS
LA

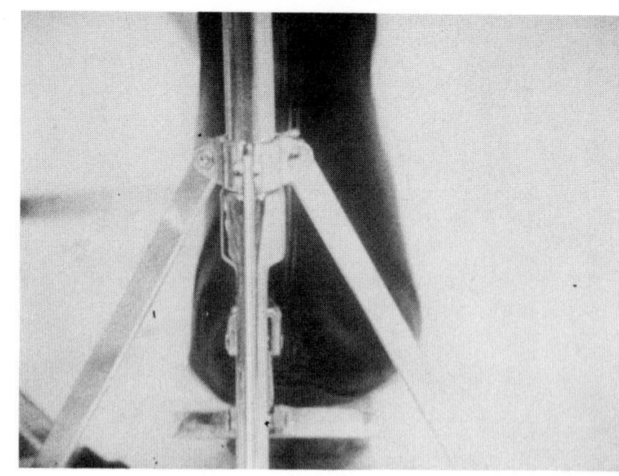
816A
CU
LA
HK
TU to . . .

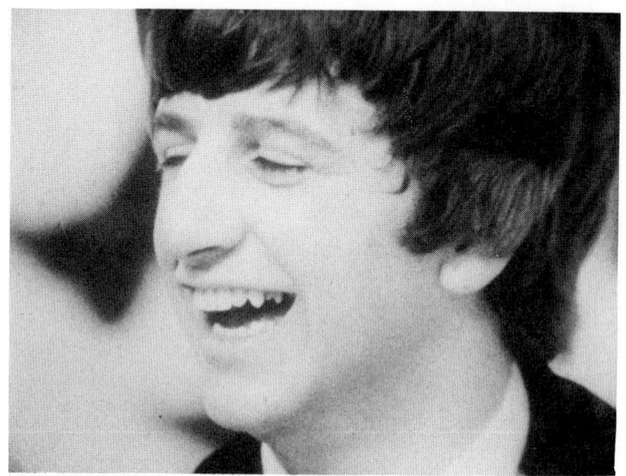
816B
CU
NA
HK

817
CU
NA

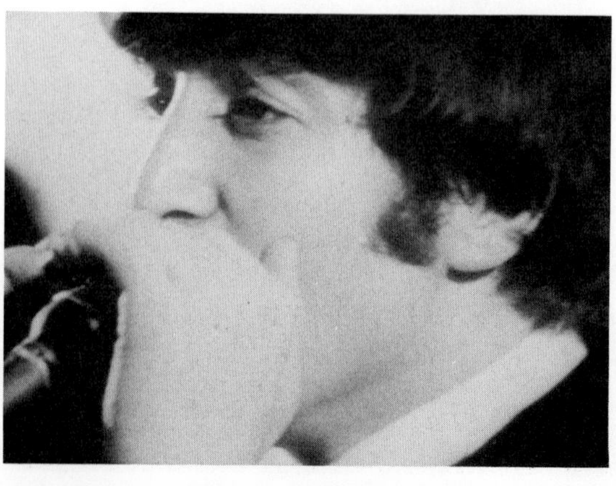
818
CU
NA
HK

819
LS
HA
HK

820
MCU-XLS
LA
TR

821
(ZI)
CU
LA
HK
(PD)

822
LS
HA
HK

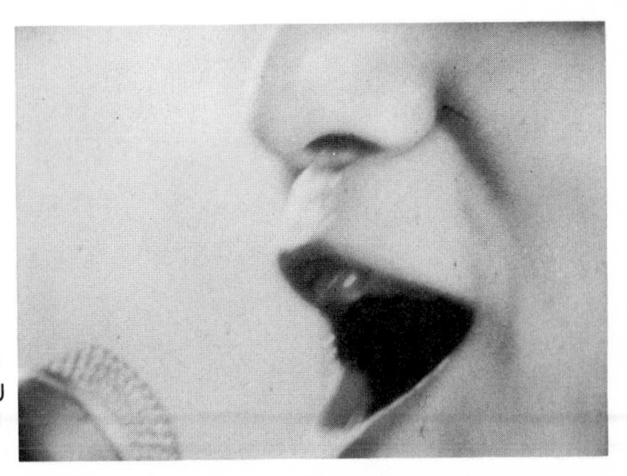

823
XCU
NA
HK

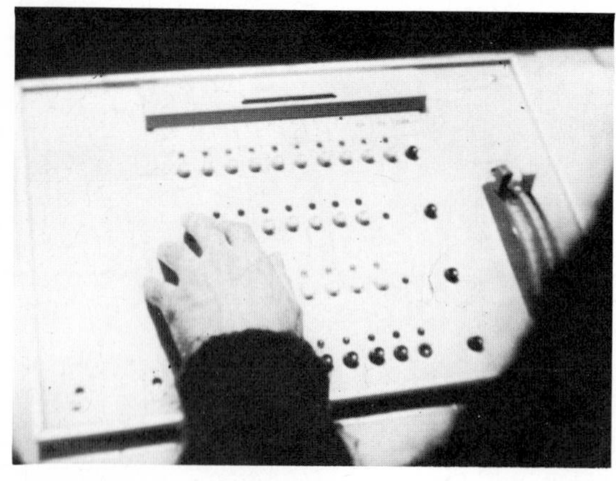

824A
CU
NA
PU to . . .

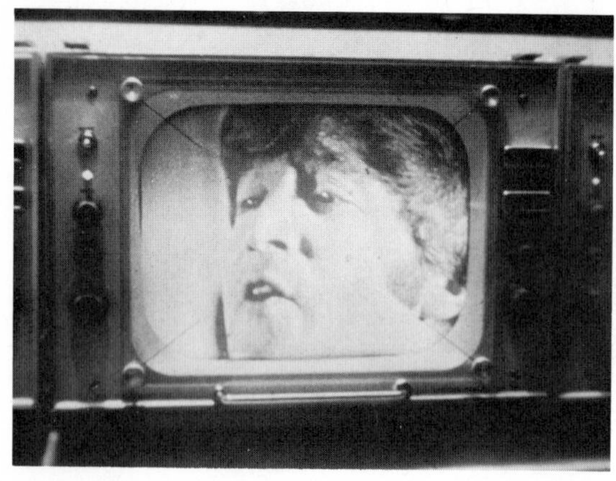

824B
CU
NA
PU to . . .

824C
XLS
NA
DK

825
LS
HA

826
LS
LA
DK

827
LS
LA
DK

828
LS
HA
DK

829
MS-LS
LA
DK

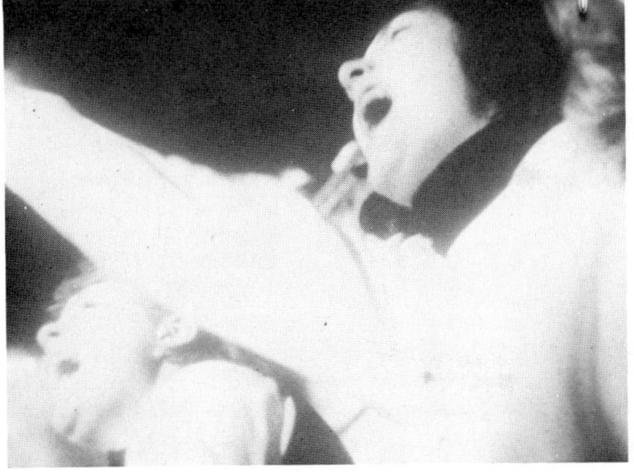

830
MS
LA

832
(PL)
MCU
NA

831
LS
HA

833
PR
(Blurred
Swish) to . . .

834
CU
LA
DK

835
PR
(Blurred
Swish) to . . .

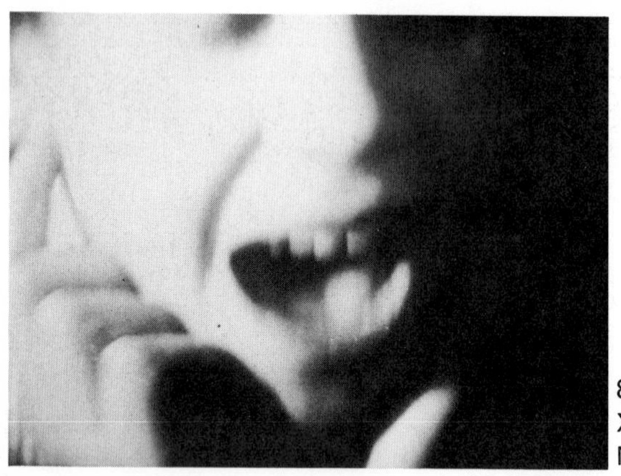

836
XCU
NA

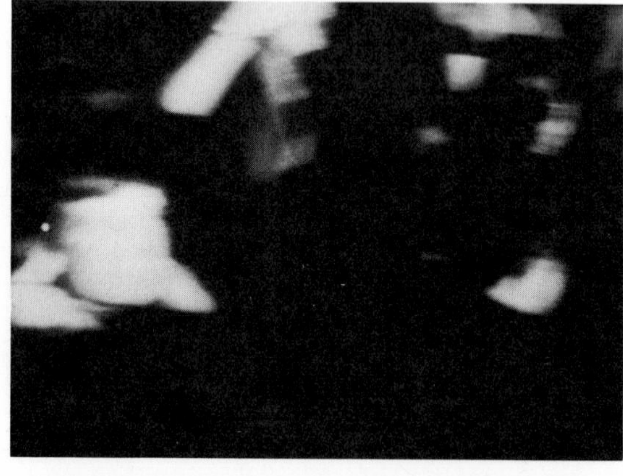

837
PL
(Blurred
Swish) to . . .

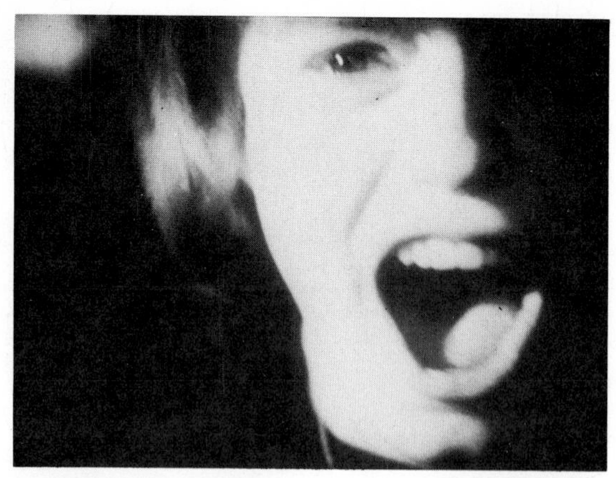

838
XCU
NA

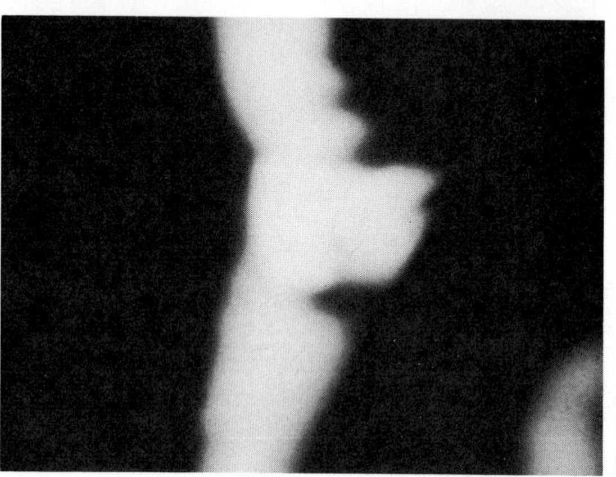

839
PL
(Blurred Swish) to . . .

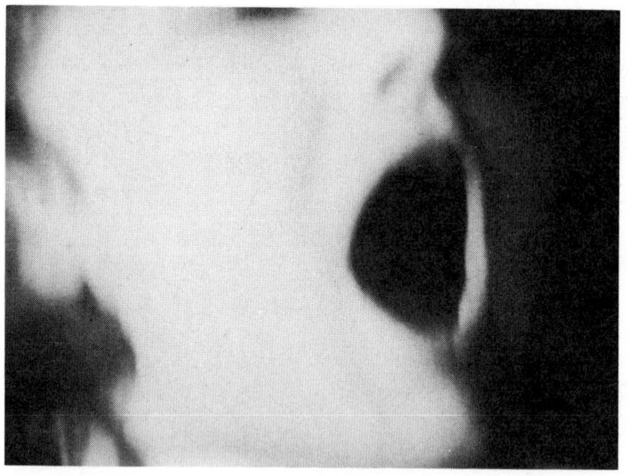

840
XCU
NA

841
PL
(Blurred Swish) to . . .

842A
CU
LA
TO to . . .

842B
MS
LA

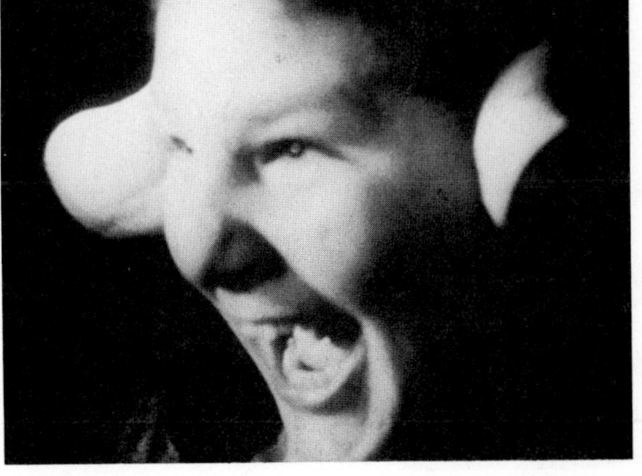

843B
CU
NA
DK

843A
MS
NA
DK
ZI to . . .

844
LS
NA
HK

845A
LS
HA
DK
ZI to . . .

846
XCU
NA

847A
LS
HA
DK
ZI to . . .

845B
MCU
HA

847B
CU
HA

848
(PD)
CU
NA
(PL)

850A
LS
NA
HK
ZI to . . .

850B
MS
NA
HK

849
MCU
NA

851
MCU-LS
LA
DK

852A
MCU
NA
DK
PR to . . .

852B
LS
LA
DK

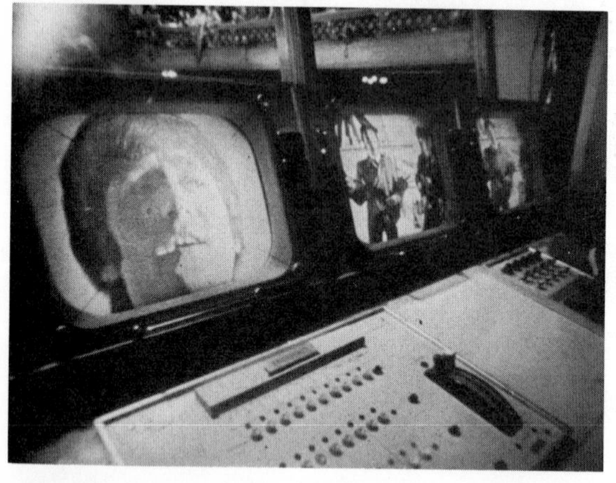

853
(TI)
MS
NA

854A
LS
LA
DK
PR to . . .

854B
LS
LA
DK

855
LS
NA
HK

856
MCU
NA
DK

857A
LS
LA
DK
PRU to . . .

857B
MS
LA
DK

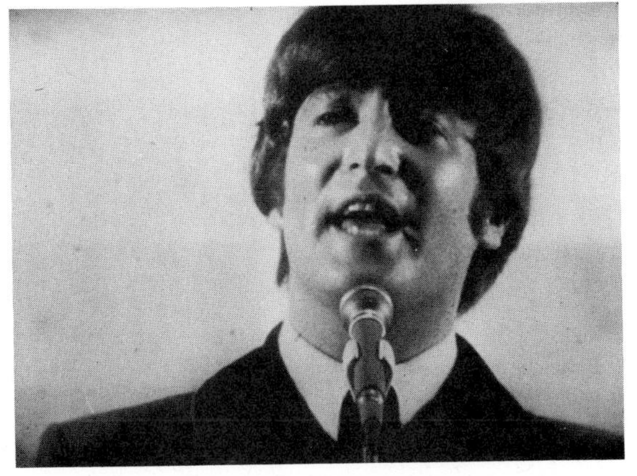

858
MCU
LA
HK

860
MS
LA
DK

859
LS
LA
DK
PRU to . . .

861
MS
LA
DK

862A
PL
(Blurred
Swish) to . . .

862B
MS
HA
DK

863
MCU
LA
HK

864
LS
NA
HK

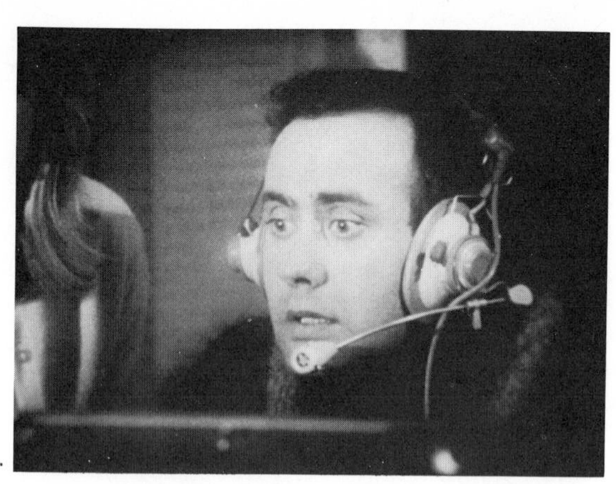

865
(ZI)
MCU
NA

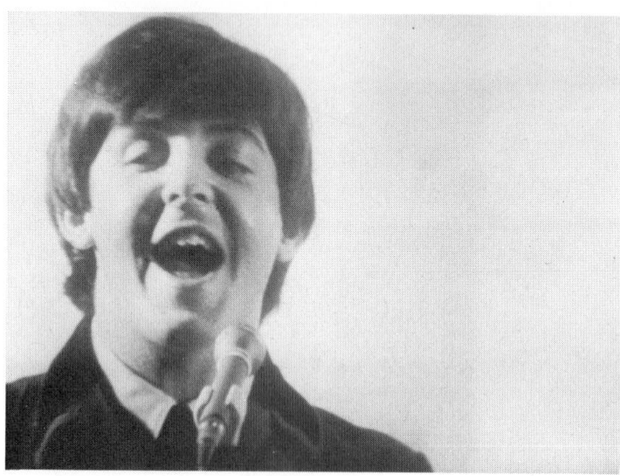

866
MCU
LA
HK

867
MCU
NA
DK

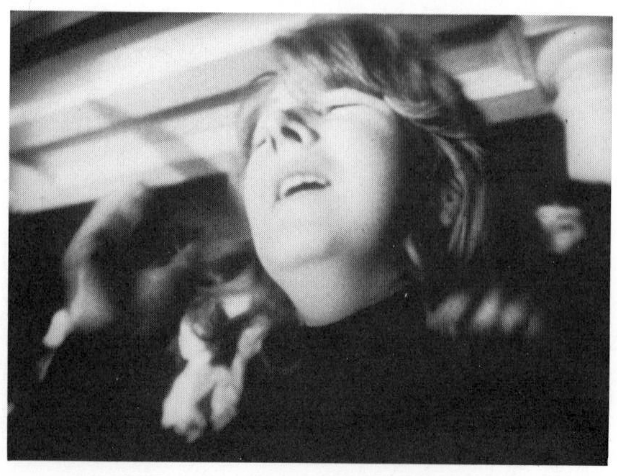

868
MCU
LA
DK

869
CU
LA
DK

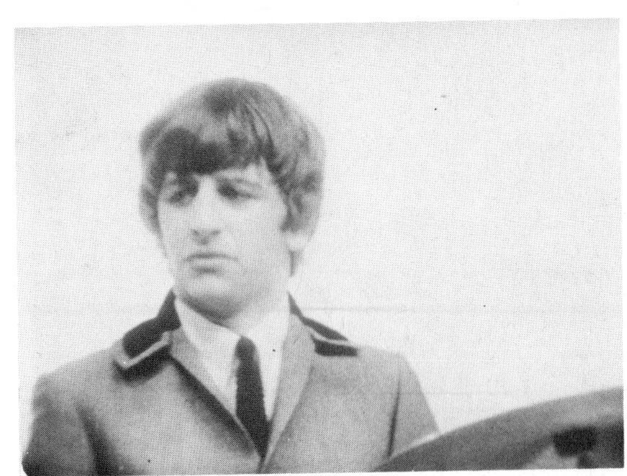

873
MCU
LA
HK

870
MCU
NA
DK

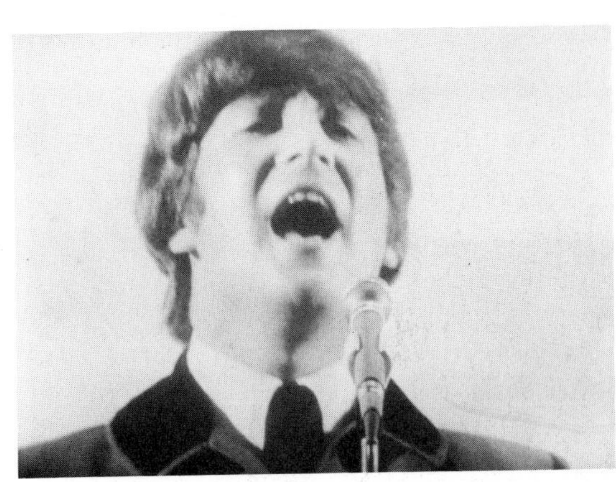

874
MCU
LA
HK

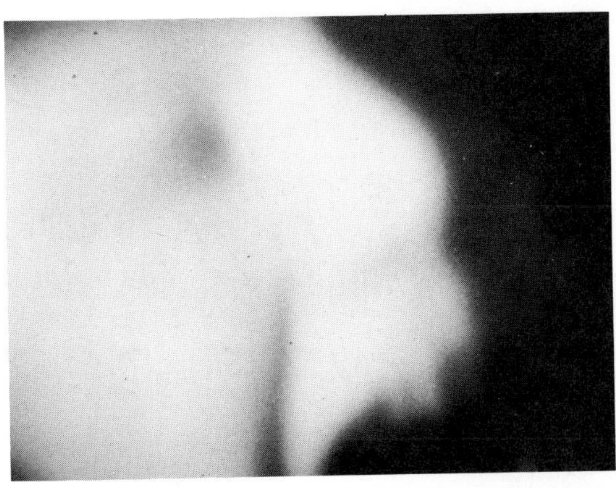

871
MCU
(Blurred)
LA

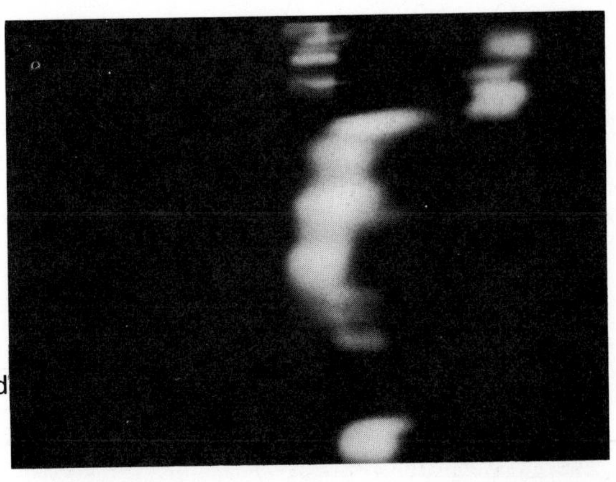

875
PR
(Blurred
Swish)
to . . .

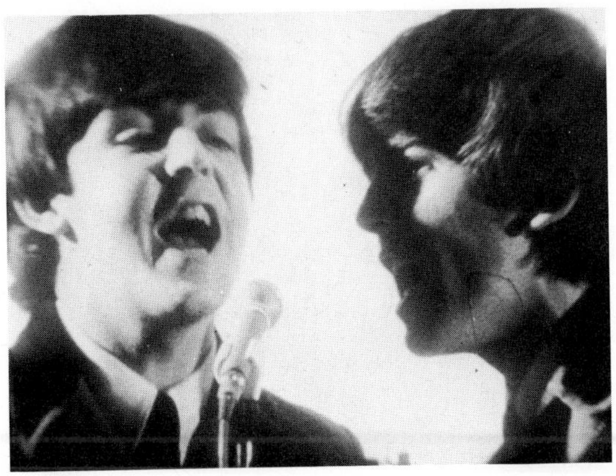

872
MCU
LA
HK

876
LS
LA
DK
(PR)

877
MS
LA
DK

881
CU
NA
DK

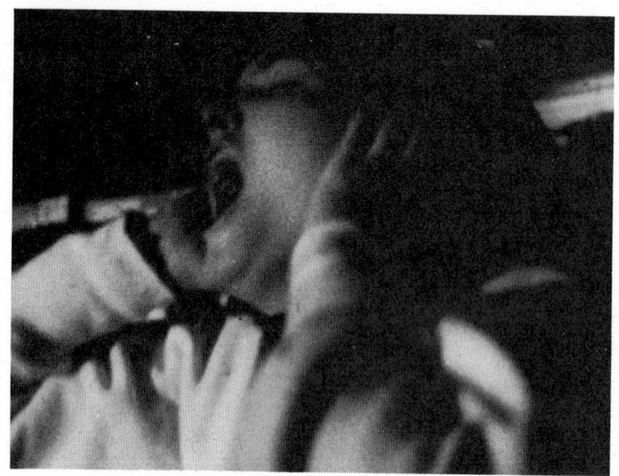

878
MCU
LA
DK

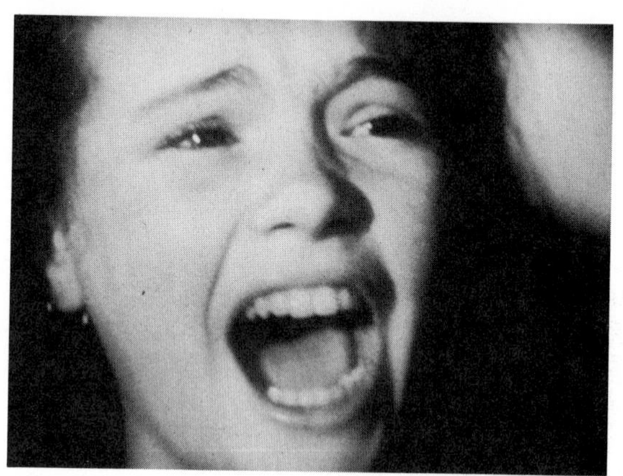

882
CU
NA
DK

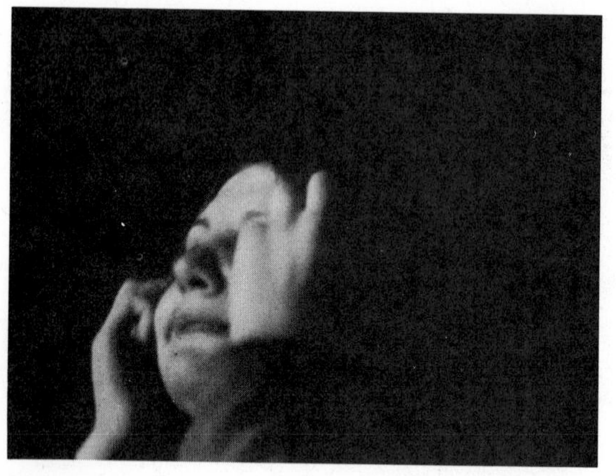

879
CU
NA
DK

883
(ZI)
CU
NA
DK

880
XCU
NA
DK

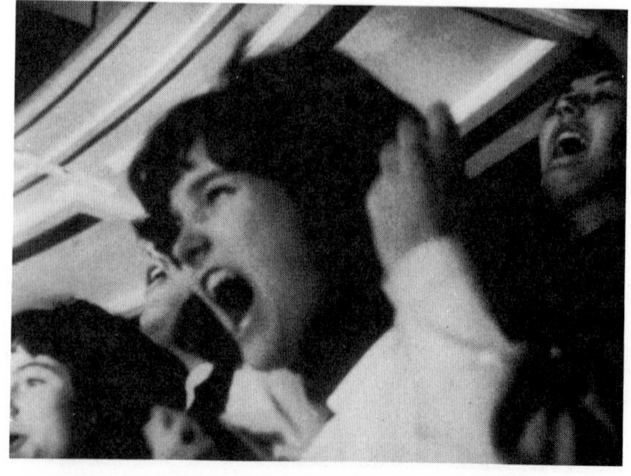

884
MCU
LA
(PL + PR)

885A
LS
NA
HK

885B
LS
NA
HK

886
CU
NA
DK
(PR)

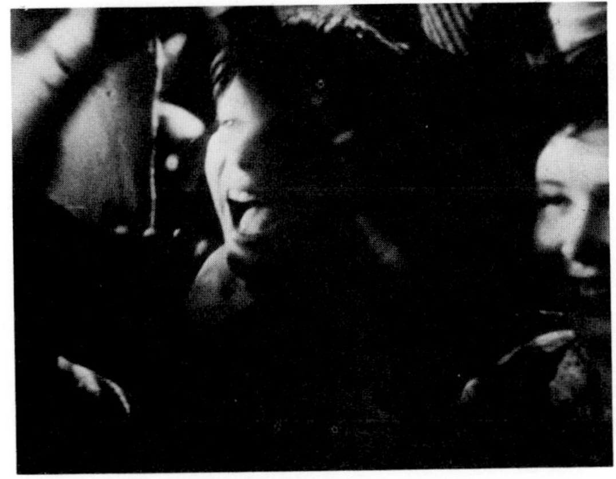

887
LS
NA
HK

888
MCU
NA
DK

889
MS
LA
DK

890
XLS
HA
DK

891
LS
NA
HK

891
LS
NA
HK

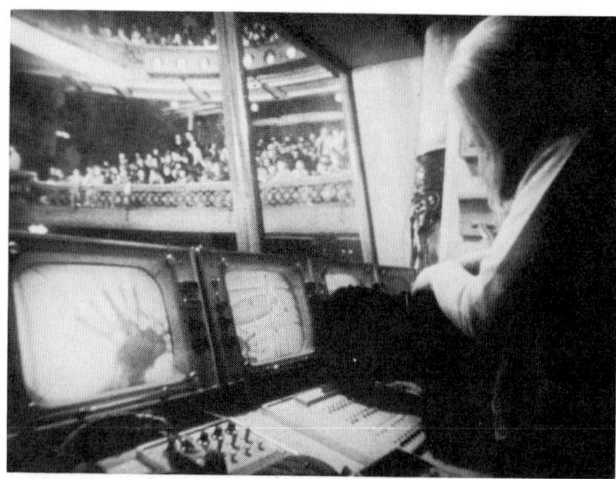

892
MS
NA

893
(TO)
MS
LA
(PL)

INTERIOR STUDIO CORRIDOR

NORM is waiting for the boys. With him are two studio attendants carrying the boys' luggage. As the BOYS excitedly appear he speaks them.

NORM: I've got the stuff. Come here.

PAUL: Aren't we . . .

NORM: No, we're not!

He hurries them along.

894
LS
HA

NORM: The office was on the phone, they think it'd be better if we pushed straight to Wolverhampton.

JOHN: Tonight? We can't make it . . .

NORM: You've got a midnight matinee.

JOHN: Now look here Norm.

NORM: No, you look here John. I've only one thing to say to you, John Lennon.

JOHN: What?

NORM: You're a swine. [So hurry up . . . we're travelling!]

NORM turns down a side exit where the door is open to the field. In it is an eight-passenger helicopter.

895A
XLS
HA
ZI to . . .

895B
FS
HA

896A
LS
LA
ZO to . . .

EXTERIOR STAGE DOOR T.V. THEATRE

Song: *"A Hard Day's Night"*
The boys and NORM come out of the building and start to run towards the helicopter.

896B
XLS
LA

[PAUL: (looking behind him) Where's my grandfather?

NORM: (arriving at helicopter door) Don't start. Look.]

897
(TI)
FS
NA

The boys look in the passenger bay and there is GRANDFATHER. He is still handcuffed to SHAKE but clutching his pile of photos.

[GRANDFATHER: (beckoning them in with his free hand which holds the photos) Come on, you're hanging up the parade.]

[*The boys shout "Get rid of those things," etc.*]

898
FS
NA

899
MCU
NA

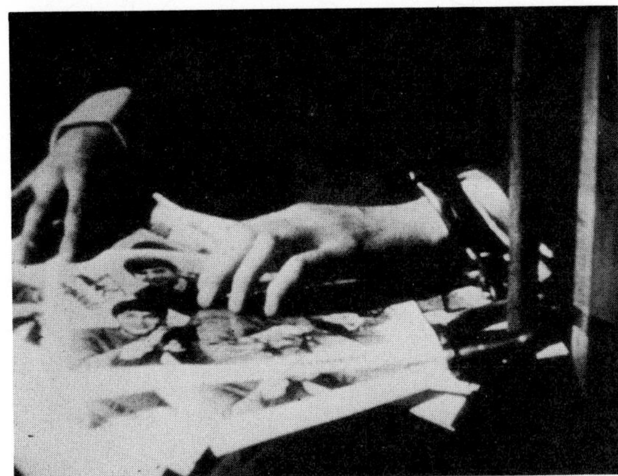

900
MCU
NA

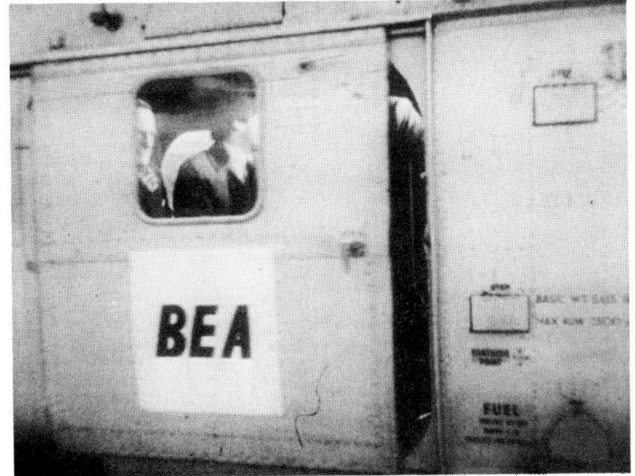

901
FS
NA

EXTERIOR FIELD

The final shot is of the helicopter rising up (SHOT FROM BELOW). As it disappears, a shower of photos come from its window.

[*We cut to a close-up of one signed photo as it hits the ground and super the closing credits over it.*]

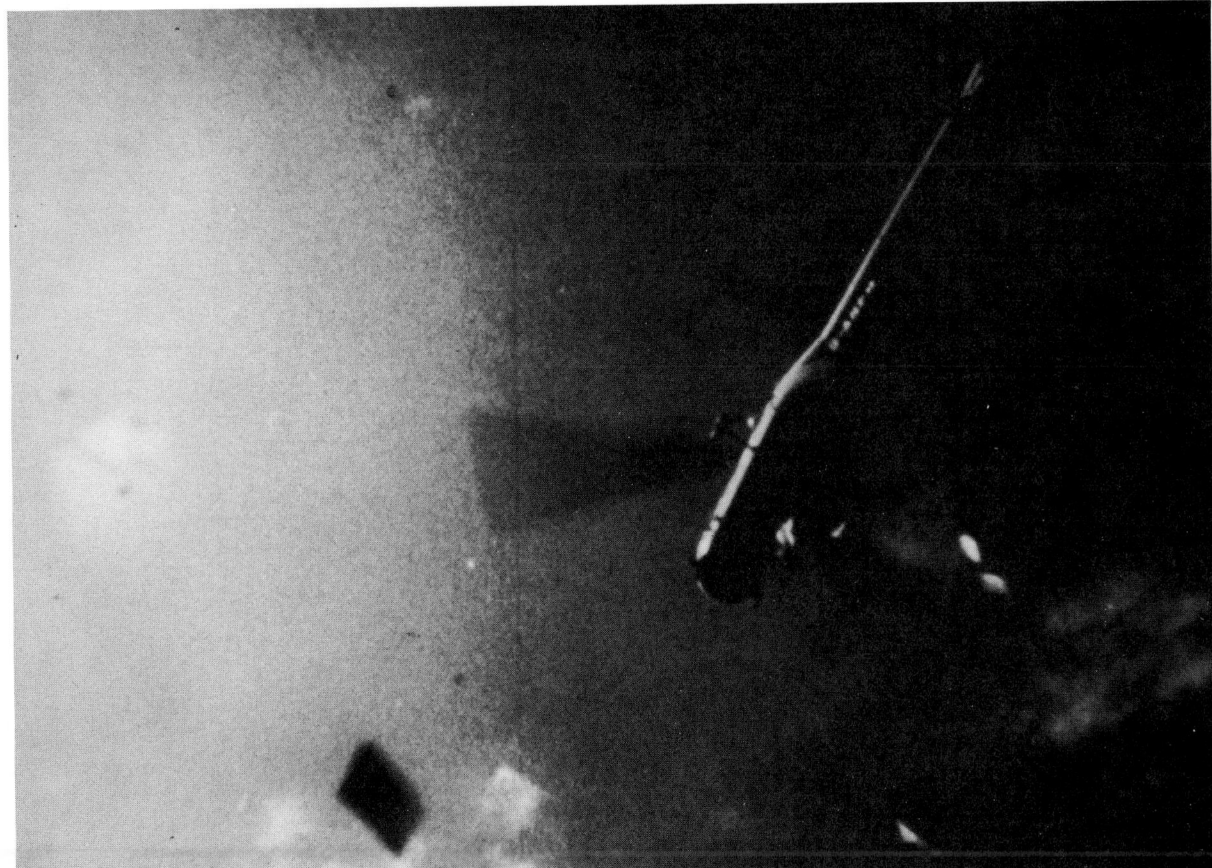

902
XLS
LA

THE CAST

John	**John Lennon**
Paul	**Paul McCartney**
George	**George Harrison**
Ringo	**Ringo Starr**
Grandfather	**Wilfred Brambell**
Norm	**Norman Rossington**
T.V. Director	**Victor Spinetti**
Shake	**John Junkin**
Millie	**Anna Quayle**
Simon	**Kenneth Haigh**
Man on Train	**Richard Vernon**
Hotel Waiter	**Eddie Malin**

CREDITS

Producer	**Walter Shenson**
Director	**Richard Lester**
Screenplay	**Alun Owen**
Production Manager	**Denis O'Dell**
Asst. Director	**John D. Merriman**
Lighting	**Gilbert Taylor**
Sound Mixer	**H.L. Bird**
Sound Camera	**M. Silverlock**
Art Director	**Ray Simm**
Set Dresser	**Ken Bridgeman**
Dress Designer	**Julie Harris**
Wardrobe Master	**Ernest Farrer**
Make-up	**John O'Gorman**
Hairdresser	**Netty Glasow**
Stillsman	**Bert Cann**
Musical Director	**George Martin**
Editor	**John Jympson**
Casting Director	**Irene Lamb**